India, China and ASEAN
Understanding Strategic Convergence and Divergence

INDIA, CHINA AND ASEAN
Understanding Strategic Convergence and Divergence

Col. (Retd.) S.C. Narang

PRASHANT PUBLISHING HOUSE
DELHI-110094

Published by :
Prashant Publishing House
C-34, 28 Foota Road, Gali-3,
West Karwal Nagar, Delhi-110094
Phone : 011-22963970, Mob. : 9810396373
e-mail.: prashantpublishinghouse@gmail.com

India, China and ASEAN: Understanding Strategic Convergence and Divergence

First Published 2016

ISBN 978-93-80565-71-2

PRINTED IN INDIA
Published by Mr. R.K. Jha M/s Prashant Publishing House and Published at H.S. Offset House Press, Delhi.

Contents

Preface

The past decade has witnessed rapid development in ASEAN-China relations. Both sides now have more in common than before, though differences still exist. ASEAN and China have established a promising strategic partnership ensuring peace, stability, co-operation as well as prosperity for the region. The three decades of the ASEAN experiment in regional cooperation has brought in a new model of conflict management, regional stability and integration quite distinct from other regional organisations.

The past decade has witnessed rapid development in ASEAN-China relations. Both sides now have more in common than before, though differences still exist. ASEAN and China have established a promising strategic partnership ensuring peace, stability, co-operation as well as prosperity for the region. New challenges will, however, continue to emerge to test the resolve of the partnership. This book examines some of the areas of convergence and divergence and the possible trajectories of the development of ASEAN-China relations.

The present research volume on India and the ASEAN has been produced by leading experts in the field of Asian economic studies. It presents a multifaceted analysis of the growing interaction of the Indian economy with the economies of the ASEAN countries while both are going through a process of economic liberalization and the formation of a regional free trade area like the Asean Free Trade Area (AFTA).

India's engagement with Southeast Asia accelerated after the announcement of the Look East Policy (LEP) in the early 1990s. This is visible from the increase in bilateral trade, cross-border capital flows and people-to-people contact. India and ASEAN have upgraded their ties to a strategic partnership. India has also embedded deeper in the Southeast Asian regional architecture through trade and investment agreements with the ASEAN and individual Southeast Asian countries like Singapore and Malaysia. The Regional Comprehensive Economic Partnership (RCEP) being negotiated by the ASEAN, Australia, China, India, Japan, New Zealand and South Korea would integrate India deeper with the region.

Getting the India-ASEAN services and investment agreement off the ground and improving the utilisation of existing free trade agreements (FTAs) will augment economic momentum. The Modi government must also work with Southeast Asian countries for facilitating transport transit and border trade for greater integration of the Indian industries in regional value chains. In the long term, a purposive 'Act East' strategy would require making the Indian diplomacy in the region more business-focused. The large Indian diaspora in the region should be utilised for the purpose.

This book explores various facets of ASEAN and its style of functioning to find an answer to these questions. It examines the ASEAN experience in establishing a regional community as well as its relevance for South Asia.

—Editor

1

Convergence in India China Relations Politics

In the ASEAN summit 2010 in Hanoi, capital of Vietnam, Indian Prime Minister Dr. Manmohan Singh stressed the need for both India and China to show sensitivity to each other's core issues while meeting his Chinese counterpart Mr. Wen JiabaoWen Jiabao. Although the core issues were not defined in detail, it is clear that the border dispute and policy shift of China on Kashmir are crucial for India .However, the interesting point to note is that both leaders agreed to work together to demolish the great wall of differences between the two giant Asian neighbors. The meeting is seen as very significant in the world politics. Mr. Wen Jiabao will visit India in December 2010 in order to strengthen the bilateral relations between the two nations. The unfolding of these political events involving the national leaders of both countries signifies the growing realization among both the nations regarding the geo-strategic veracity of the emerging world order and the importance of sound and healthy relations with a view to exploit the opportunities to accelerate the economic development and settle the mutual differences in an amicable manner.

In order to successfully face the challenges of today's environmental realities and socio-political dynamics, it is incumbent on both the nations to act on the principle of "United we stand and divided we fall". This principle is not only confined to the geo-strategic realities of today's world order, keeping in mind the assertiveness of United States of America(USA) which is for the time being, the sole superpower of the world, but also the social, economic and regional realities. The enormous potential of India- China alliance needs to be tapped to ensure that both countries can speedily join the group of developed nations and also for the creation of a new world order to diffuse the sole superpower status of a single nation and guide the world towards a multi polar world. China, in spite of her growing status as a rising global power, needs to understand that in order to hasten the economic development her relationship with India must be cordial and accommodative. India, on the other hand, must make an endeavour to leverage the advantage of her geographic and historical closeness with China by consolidating her position as a rising economic and regional power in Asia. The path to success lies in complementary rather than competitive nature of relations. In order to derive a meaningful and fruitful relationship we need to delve upon various areas of convergence between both the countries which can act as milestones towards the pursuit of excellence jointly. In this chapter we would be analyzing multiple areas of cooperation between both the countries such as energy security, influence on world and regional forums (United Nations Organization (UNO), East Asia Summit (EAS), etc.,), trade and commerce to arrive at the deduction that both the nations need to put their past behind and forge cooperative associations to progress energetically towards peace, stability, economic development and long lasting strategic alliance in the emerging world order.

TRADE & COMMERCE

India is aiming to become one of the largest economies in the world by 2020. India is presently one of the fastest growing economies of the world and it is estimated that India's economy would be third largest economy in the world by 2050 just behind China and USA. Although it can be seen as a challenge to the Chinese growing economic influence but the prudence lies in cooperation not confrontation. In this regard, Beijing is now paying increased attention to India's drive towards attaining the status of economically developed nation. There has been a massive jump in the quantum of bilateral trade between the two nations. Beijing and New Delhi also signed the Bilateral Investment Promotion and Protection Agreement and set an ambitious bilateral trade target of $40 billion for 2010. The suspicious nature of ties between the two nations and uncertainty of border dispute is seen as an impediment in exploiting the tremendous potential of bilateral trade.

In 2000-01, Goldman Sachs had forecasted the exponential growth of emerging markets economies of India and China. Mutual cooperation between India and China will assist in exploiting the potential of globalization. Expanding trade ties have given the two sides a huge stake in keeping co-operation alive. In 1992, their trade totaled $338 million. By 2004, it had mushroomed to $13.6 billion, and by the end of this year is expected to reach a whopping $60 billion - more than quadruple the amount from the middle of the decade. Cooperation between the two economies holds potential for creating what is called 'Chindia', the largest economic powerhouse in the world. As a senior Chinese official once put it, "Chinese manufacturing plus Indian services, Chinese hardware plus Indian software, will create an ideal win-win situation for both countries."

They should strengthen cooperation and coordination, jointly deal with the challenges, and guard against attempts by the developed countries to shift the burden of climate change and other global issues of concern to these developing countries. The two countries should actively participate in the process of the reform of the international financial system and institutions like International Monetary Fund and World Bank to promote the building of a fair, equitable, inclusive, and orderly global economic system, and safeguard the common interests of developing countries.

Investments

Two way investment links between India and China are also growing at a rapid pace. These new investments are critical strategic moves aimed at profiting from the other country's expertise and enormous growth combined with the shortage of talent in crucial sectors in both the countries. The strengths of India and China are different from each other. China is an industrial powerhouse in manufacturing sector while India's advantage lies heavily in services sector. If both countries combine their respective advantages then it will not only greatly improve the economic strengths of both the countries in this sector but also lead to better relationship between both the countries in the emerging economic world order.

Manufacturing. India can take advantage from cooperation with China in restructuring her manpower intensive industries. Direct competition with Chinese manufacturers would facilitate India to push some significant reforms necessary to fuel their improvement and expansion. As the Chinese labour wages are rising steadily at a faster rate, India can take this opportunity to move in a bigger way into such labour-intensive sectors such as apparel, footwear and toys. India and China enjoy a surplus of low cost labour. Exports of labour-intensive products from both countries are growing rapidly and it would not be surprising that these two countries are bound to race with each other to sell such products in world markets. China has a distinct advantage in labour-intensive mass-produced goods whereas India's proficiency lies in its ability to produce differentiated niche products like handicrafts, handmade carpets etc. Intra-industry trade between the two economies is thus not only feasible but also is the need of the hour. Moreover, the rapid pace of economic globalization and consequently expansion of international trade and investment has extended the areas of influence of the production units in both the countries beyond national boundaries. Therefore, in spite of comparative advantage in similar sectors, such as processed metals and alloys, chemicals, machinery, equipment and textiles, there is enough space available to each other to grow in the world market. India and China thus can use their respective comparative advantages in similar products and can utilize these advantages for their inclusive growth. For example, competition between India and China in textile exports has pushed Chinese industries to carry out manufacturing and export of garments by importing textile materials from India. Hence, both countries can make the most of competition into opportunities for cooperation through intra-industry trade and investment.

Services. Services sector accounts for a major part of the GDP in both India and China. However, the importance of the sector in India has increased more rapidly than in China. Between 1995 and 2002, the contribution of services in India's GDP increased from 43.6 to 50.7 per cent and that for China from 30.7 to 33.5 per cent. The trade in services forms an important part of the agreed upon "Comprehensive Bilateral Economic Cooperation". The service and knowledge trade between India and China has particularly significant potential for both in areas like biotechnology, Information Technology (IT), health, education, tourism and financial sector. In an address to information technology professionals in Bangalore on 10 April 2005, Premier Wen Jiabao said that China and India should work towards bringing together Chinese hardware and Indian software, putting aside their historic rivalries. India's advantage in sectors such as outsourcing and IT can act as building blocks for enhancing economic relations between both the countries. The ongoing visit of Chinese Premier in India will definitely augment trade and commerce exchanges between both the countries.

In a nutshell, India need not be scared of the economic growth of China in geometric progression. India has an edge in services sector whereas China is the world leader in manufacturing sector. The time is ripe for both the countries to exploit their strengths to capture a major share of the world economy by showing an integrated front to ensure the increased flow of Foreign Direct Investment (FDI) in their respective economies and should not in any way act as puppets to the western world by showing a confrontationist approach. The path to glory and success lies in collaboration for mutual rise in the economic trajectory on the new world order.

Energy Cooperation

China and India are competing in the world energy market to secure their energy future in order to ensure unhindered economic growth and infrastructure developmet. India's ONGC Videsh Ltd (OVL) and the China National Petroleum Corporation (CNPC) have often been rivals in the race for overseas oil and natural gas in Central Asian Region, Middle East and Africa. In overseas bidding efforts since 2004, Indian firms have faced competition from Chinese firms and in three different instances India lost to China in the race to secure overseas hydrocarbon assets. Angola was the first instance, where India bid for 50 per cent stake of Shell in Angola's Block 18 field.

The bidding competition again surfaced when India wanted to buy the stake of Petrokazakhstan - a Canadian oil firm operating in Kazakhstan. The third incident was in the case of India's energy interest in Ecuador, where India and China competed for Encana's stakes.

After the Angola incident itself both sides realized that there is a greater scope and necessity for cooperation in their future search for overseas energy. This thought crystallized into bilateral meetings and exchanges of visits.

As part of Joint Declaration of 2005, both the nations agreed to fully implement the provisions of the Memorandum of Understanding on cooperation in the field of oil and natural gas in order to expand all round mutually beneficial cooperation. India's ONGC Videsh Ltd (OVL) and the China National Petroleum Corp (CNPC) are partners in producing oil and natural gas field in Sudan. Cooperation between the two countries would have far reaching implications on the global energy market. By pooling financial and technological resources, such a joint venture would become one of the largest state-owned bilateral joint energy efforts to address the energy security issues of two major energy consumers of the world. The primary areas of possible cooperation are:-

Pooling their investments and technology for energy exploration. Hydrocarbon transportation route - oil and gas pipelines -where they can bring energy through the shortest possible routes with minimum investment cost.

As China gets most of its hydrocarbon supply through the Indian Ocean Sea Lanes of Communication (SLsOC), it is important for her to cooperate with India to ensure the security of supplies arriving from Middle East. Entering into joint ventures in securing new sources of natural gas and oil in the untapped markets of Africa.

Climate Change

Climate change has emerged as a major international issue since 1992 Earth Summit which was held under the aegis of United Nations Organization (UNO) in Rio De Jenario, Brazil. Thereafter a legally binding agreement was signed at Kyoto, known as Kyoto Protocol which imposed Green House Gases (GHG) emission reduction provisions on the industrialized nations of the world.

However, developing countries were widely unaffected from any legal causes agreed upon to mitigate the Green House Gases (GHG) to reduce global warming under United Nations Framework on Climate Change (UNFCCC), apart from being benefitted in the form of carbon trading under Kyoto Protocol's flexible driving mechanisms like, Clean Development Mechanism (CDM).

Since Bali Summit in 2007, there was a growing resentment among developed or so called industrialized nations of the world regarding the tremendous economic progress made by developing countries such as China, India, Brazil and South Africa and consequently the rising emission levels of these countries.

Hence, the pressure mounted on these developing economies to accept the international norms in order to control the global warming and also carrying out financial contributions in reducing Green House Gases. Thus, the widening rift amongst developed and developing countries became the main point of conflict while trying to arrive at a common consensus towards addressing climate change in the Copenhagen summit in 2009.

Since both India and China share similar concerns and positions in addressing the climate change issue they kept close coordination and consultation with each other during the summit. India and China consider that it is important to keep pace with the economic development in spite of its adverse effect on climate in order to eradicate poverty and join the group of rich countries.

The developing countries like China and India firmly believe and rightfully so, that present climatic chaos is the product of so called developed nations and the developing countries are paying a heavy penalty in forms of natural calamities and global warming for no fault of theirs. Therefore, these countries' point of view is that such eco-friendly activities in developing countries should be mostly funded by developed countries.

Before the climate meeting in Copenhagen, India and China signed a broad agreement to cooperate in the fight against climate change and also underlined a common position on contentious talks for a tougher global climate deal. Such an agreement brought to light the tremendous potential which exists for cooperation on mutually beneficial issues at the world stage. US President Mr. Barack Obama announced prior to attending the Copenhagen Conference that U.S. will cut emissions of greenhouse gases (GHG) by 17% from 2005 levels by 2020. The day after the U.S. announcement, China issued a "carbon intensity target" reduction of 40-45% by 2020 to bring to Copenhagen. India, on the other hand is way behind in the per capita emissions of Green House Gases which is almost equal to about 1.65 tons of carbon di oxide or its equivalent gases. However, Prime Minister Mr. Manmohan Singh announced a National Action Plan for Climate Change in order to address the issue in a formalized manner. The present status is that China and India are putting a united stand in the negotiations going on under United Nations Climate Change Conference 2010 at Cancun, Mexico which is a healthy development for their bilateral relations and also for all developing economies of the world. The stand of China and India is fairly simple. These economies require massive infrastructure development in order to eradicate poverty and improve the quality of life for their countrymen. Therefore, it would be unfair to treat them at equal footing with other developed nations of the world such as USA, UK or other European Nations. Moreover, the double standards adopted by USA by not ratifying the Kyoto Protocol at the first place is another stumbling block which hinder any further progress towards achieving a globally accepted agreement regarding combating climate change. Therefore, in the light of recent developments, it is imperative on China and India to develop a common framework for them so as to carry on with the unhindered economic growth of both the countries while at the same time working towards use of eco-friendly technologies to preserve the nature for our future generations.

Strategic Cooperation

The prospect of a Russia-India-China strategic triangle's emergence has been the subject of continuing analysis by political and strategic analysts ever since Russia mooted the proposal in the late 1990s. The emergence of such a triangle, if and whenever it takes place, would alter the global strategic balance in a strikingly significant manner. The emergence of a Russia-India-China strategic triangle would herald the arrival on the global strategic calculus of a "Trinity of Three Asian Powers" which are all nuclear weapons states.

The main challenge to the emergence of an effective Russia-India-China strategic triangle lies at the base of this triangle. India and China, at the opposite ends of the base of this triangle have to forge strong bonding, overcoming the trust deficit that has existed ever since 1962. Expanding cooperation on regional and international stage was part of the joint declaration issued after the talks between Prime Minister Manmohan Singh and Chinese President Hu Jintao in Nov 2006.

At the regional level, there is a definite attempt by both the countries to enhance their strategic relations by involving in Indo-China military interaction and confidence building measures such as reducing the tensions along Line of Actual Control(LAC) as part of military diplomacy. China and India conducted their first mil-to-mil exercise 'Hand-in-Hand 2007' at the Kunming Military Academy in China's Yunnan Province in December 2007. Military diplomacy has led to the reduction in tension between China and India. Political relations have become less hostile and the Line of Actual Control between the two countries has become relatively stable compared to the Line of Control (LC) between India and Pakistan. Improved Sino-Indian relations at the military level may allay India's worst fears of the prospect of having to face a 'two-front' war with China and Pakistan.

INFLUENCE ON INTERNATIONAL AND REGIONAL ORGANISATIONS

General. India and China are the prominent members of the most of the world's institutions such as UNO, G-20 and various other regional forums. There is a need to analyze the mutual areas of cooperation for both the countries in these international institutes in order to increase their influence and also carve out a mutually beneficial association to forge greater strategic and economic cooperation in the emerging world order.

United Nations Organisation (UNO)

UNO is the world's premier organization with over 190 member countries under its umbrella. However, lately due to the dominance of USA it is considered as an organization without requisite powers to make its presence felt in significant terms in the present world order. The rise of China and India has acted as a counterweight to US's influence on world politics. After the Global recession USA was in the favour of budget cuts in UNO which was seen as a deliberate attempt to dilute the influence of UNO in global affairs. There's still a long way to go for countries like India and China to significantly tilt the balance of World from uni-polar to multi-polar world. The process can start in the form of financial contribution to world economic bodies like World Bank and International Monetary Fund for the development of poor countries of the world.

The reality is that in spite of meteoric economic rise of India and China, it will take almost two decades for these countries to start contributing significantly in these organizations. Therefore, China and India have to wait and watch for opportunities to significantly impact the UNO and its charter of duties in the new world order. Another aspect to it, is the issue of permanent membership in United Nations Security Council (UNSC). China is one of the five permanent members of UNSC. However, India is widely regarded as one of the strongest contenders for the same. China's reluctance in supporting India's cause is a thorn in the flesh for Indian Government. Therefore, it should be the endeavour of Indian Government to work towards reducing the trust deficit between both the countries to further own interests in this regard.

East Asia Summit (EAS)

East Asia Summit (EAS) is an off shoot of Association of South East Asian Nations (ASEAN) which was first held in 2005.

Therefore, in order to understand its significance we need to have a brief overview of ASEAN which is a geo-political and economic organization of 10 countries located in South East Asia. It includes the countries of Indonesia, Malaysia, Philippines, Singapore, Thailand, Brunei, Vietnam, Laos, Myanmar and Cambodia. Its aims include the acceleration of economic growth, social progress, cultural development among its members and the promotion of regional peace. In 1997, with an aim of widening the scope of ASEAN, the ASEAN member nations and the People's Republic of China, South Korea and Japan agreed to hold yearly talks to further strengthen regional cooperation in the form of the ASEAN plus Three meetings. In 2005 the "ASEAN plus Three" countries together with India, Australia and New Zealand held the inaugural ASEAN Plus Six Meetings or East Asia Summit (EAS).

It is a pan-Asia forum held annually by the leaders of 16 countries in East Asia and other major regional players in Asia. The relationship between the EAS and ASEAN plus Three is not cordial. Some countries are more inclined towards the narrower ASEAN plus Three grouping whereas others support the more inclusive EAS. However, with regard to India- China relations, the recent meeting of leaders of both the countries at Hanoi during ASEAN summit in 2010 speaks volumes of the growing realization of the growing trade and investment prospects in broader EAS member nations. This, in turn is acting as the binding factor for both the nations in spite of various areas of divergence. Hence it should be the endeavour of the politicians and diplomats of both the nations to utilize this regional forum to pursue their national interests and work towards building peaceful and prosperous relations between both the neighbours.

G-20 Summits

The Group of Twenty Finance Ministers and Central Bank Governors (G-20, G20, Group of Twenty) is a group of finance ministers and central bank governors from 20 economies: 19 countries plus the European Union, which is represented by the President of the European Council and by the European Central Bank. Their heads of government or heads of state have also periodically conferred at summits since their initial meeting in

2008. Collectively, the G-20 economies comprise 85% of global gross national product, 80% of world trade (including EU intra-trade) and two-thirds of the world population. G-20 summits commenced with effect from 2008 as a response to the global recession which shook the economic foundations of the entire world. In addition, it was also realized that the emerging economies such as BRIC nations are not playing an active role in global economic policy making.

The core issue for G-20 summits is to build greater transparency in the global economy and avoid protectionism. This provides an opportunity to India and China to work together to promote the cause of globalization which is ironically turning out to be a cause of concern for strong western economies. India and China has a big advantage of cheap labour and consequently utilized this advantage by exploiting it in manufacturing and services sector. Therefore, both the countries can exploit the potential of this forum to chalk their path towards economic development.

Shanghai Cooperation Organization (SCO)

Shanghai Cooperation Organization (SCO) is another grouping with global implications. SCO as an institution and as a concept represents the world's greatest potential. The SCO grew out of the Shanghai Five alliance of Russia, China, Kazakhstan, Kyrgyzstan and Tajikistan formed in 1996 on the basis of the Treaty on Deepening Military Trust in Border Regions to ensure border demarcation and security in an area of the world thrown into turmoil by the precipitate break-up of the Soviet Union five years earlier.

In 2005 India attended the fifth SCO Summit as an observer. Indian External Affairs Minister Mr. Natwar Singh announced India's desire to apply for its membership and also declared India's intention for a greater role in the organization. Russia is also encouraging India to join this elite organization keeping in mind the strategic imperatives and historical ties both countries share since India's independence. Also, India's military presence and deep interests in Central Asian Region's energy resources are major incentives for her to join it in spite of strong association of other regional players like Pakistan and Iran with this organization.

However, the most significant reason for India's keenness in having a greater role in this organization is to develop cordial and mutually beneficial relations with China and Russia in multifarious areas of cooperation like transportation, energy, telecommunications, security, military, economic, cultural, banking, anti- terrorism and prevention of drug trafficking. Global think-tanks is terming SCO as a counterweight to USA's superpower status. Hence, it is imperative on both China and India to maintain close coordination in making this organization more powerful in order to develop a secure, peaceful, stable and balanced world order.

BRIC

The acronym BRIC (for Brazil, Russia, India, China) was first used in a Goldman Sachs thesis projecting the economic potential of Brazil, Russia, India and China.

The 1st BRIC summit took place in Yekatarinburg in Russia in 2009 and discussed global issues related to trade, commerce, terrorism and other global issues. Between 2003 and 2007, BRIC countries carried 65% of the expansion of global GDP. In 2009, the combined PPP GDP of the BRIC countries was US$16.3 trillion, or 23.4% of global total. The second meeting took place in Brazilia, Brazil in April 2010 which was attended by heads of all the four countries. Indian Prime Minister called for closer cooperation in the fields of energy and food security, as well as tapping into the potential of other sectors such as trade and investment, science and technology and infrastructure.

However, the most crucial aspect of this grouping is India-China relations. Both heads of the state stated in the meeting at Brasilia that there is enough room for both the countries for inclusive growth in various areas such as economy, food security, energy security, science and technology. Mrs. Nirupama Rao, the foreign secretary of India, praised the diplomats of both the countries in her recent visit to China in effectively and efficiently pursuing the agenda of inclusive growth in various areas of convergence. Therefore, the groupings such as BRIC will play a greater and meaningful role in various international issues of long term significance such as environment, climate change, reforms in international financial institutions and nuclear non- proliferation which will also pave the path for greater cooperation between India and China in the new world order.

Misc Areas of Convergence

India and China has many other areas of convergence apart from various fields as discussed above, such as food security, maritime security, cultural and religious connections, combat against terrorism and extremism. The policy of engagement between both the nations also includes educational tourism. At Present over 7,000 Indian students study in China, and the Central Board of Secondary Education (CBSE) is set to introduce Chinese in the curriculum of schools from the next academic session.

Indians are going in large number as tourists either to marvel at the rapid economic growth of China or to find investment and trading opportunities in this great country. Also, similar to the lines of BRIC group of nations, India and China has partnered well in other grouping of BASIC (includes South Africa along with other BRIC nations).

In the geo-strategic front in immediate neighbourhood, both countries are wary of an unstable Pakistan and consequently the rise of Islamic terrorism which is affecting both Kashmir and Xinjiang province. An open, balanced and inclusive architecture to enable a transparent dialogue on these issues that concern security and stability in immediate neighbourhood involving Pakistan is in the larger interest of both growing military and economic giants.

This is an issue of convergence rather than divergence in present geo- political and geo-strategic reality. The present instability along with rapid expansion of Taliban makes it incumbent on India and China to promote stability and development in Pakistan with military forces under control of a strong democratically elected government. The other fields where Indians need to emulate Chinese genius is their tremendous sporting ethics and diligence with which they perform their best to showcase China and her culture to the world. China organized the best Olympics games ever in 2008 and their recent organization of Asian games along with the medals tally should inspire Indians that they can do lot better than what has been done in recently concluded Common Wealth Games in New Delhi.

Conclusion

To conclude, there is a really long list of areas of convergence and mutually beneficial relations between both the nations wherein, both the countries will gain a lot in terms of regional, financial, strategic and diplomatic interests in the emerging world order. Currently, both China and India are dedicated to national development and both are in great need of stable international and regional environment. China-India relations are in transition stage and are looking towards new opportunities for further progress. This year mark the 60th anniversary of the establishment of diplomatic relations between both the countries, coinciding with a China Festival in India and an India Festival in China. We should exploit this opportunity and further strengthen exchanges and collaboration in various fields, promote mutual understanding and trust and expand people to people partnership with a view to augment China-India relations to a new height. If we try to do a SWOT analysis and have an unbiased approach to India- China relations then, we will realize that it is more advantageous to have a cooperative and peaceful relations with China in order to pursue our national interests and carry on with socio- economic development of our nation state as a whole to attain our rightful place in the new world order.

CHINA'S RISE, AMERICA'S PIVOT, AND INDIA'S ASIAN AMBIGUITY

The year 2012 began with the U.S. President Barack Obama formally announcing the so called 'pivot to Asia' that involves rebalancing America's global military weight to Asia. The new U.S. strategy calls for deploying 60 per cent of all American naval forces in Asia in the coming years, strengthening its traditional alliances in the region and building new partnerships, including with India. This has opened simultaneously for India a rare opportunity to shape the Asian balance of power and the real danger of being drawn into the conflict between the world's foremost power and the rising challenger. The pivot is not just a new military strategy. It is complemented by a more active American economic and political engagement with Asia, which saw Obama embark on the first American presidential visits ever to Myanmar and Cambodia at the end of 2012. Although the Obama Administration insists that the pivot is directed at China, Beijing is quite convinced that the new policy is about preventing it from reclaiming its rightful place as the pre-eminent power of Asia.

China, which had its own leadership transition in 2012, is unfazed by the American pivot and signalled its determination to strengthen its own military capability and readiness to face up to potential confrontations with the United States. Meanwhile, the United States has declared that India is a 'linchpin' of the new Asian strategy and is urging Delhi to take a larger leadership role in Asia. Many countries of East and Southeast Asia want India to do more in providing security to the smaller states and promoting a stable regional balance of power. Beijing, meanwhile, would like to prevent Delhi from aligning with Washington and is teasing India with the promise of a stronger partnership. Is Delhi ready to join Asia's new power play?

Delhi, like the rest of Asian capitals, has been surprised by the rapid turn of events and is utterly unprepared to cope with the strategic consequences of China's rise and America's response to it. Willing to believe that the rise of China will most likely be peaceful or betting that small nations can socialize a rising giant, Asia is scrambling to cope with the evolving dynamic between Beijing and Washington. The United States, which encouraged its Asian allies to accept Communist China as a legitimate power after the rapprochement with Beijing in the early 1970s and facilitated its economic growth, now confronts a compelling rival on Asia's horizon. India, which was deeply uncomfortable with the western and Asian embrace of China in the past, now finds itself in a very different quandary as relations between China and America begin to deteriorate.

One reason for the sense of strategic surprise in Asia and America at China's rise has been the severe and prolonged nature of the global financial crisis. The economic slowdown in the West since 2008 and continued high growth rates in China have accelerated what would have been a slower but inevitable shift in the Asian balance of power in China's favour. While some current linear projections – of China overtaking the U.S. as the world's largest economy by the end of this decade – might not necessarily turn out right, the nature and direction of the Asian power shift is undeniable. So long as China hangs together as a purposeful state, its aggregate military weight and strategic impact on Asia will dramatically rise in the coming years despite its low per capita income and what that number implies about the unstable nature of its domestic politics.

A second reason, arguably, is the nature of international, essentially American, scholarship on China. Like those who devoted their lives to the study of the Soviet Union could not predict its fate in the 1980s, the army of China experts in the United States could not anticipate the kind of foreign policy that Beijing has recently adopted towards its neighbours in Asia. If India is near China-blind, thanks to the absence of a critical mass of national expertise on China, the American view of China seems cluttered by a surfeit of it. If the instinctive basis of India's engagement with China could turn out to be dangerous, American scholarship too has suffered from biases of its own. If America's Russia scholarship always exaggerated the threat from Moscow, both in the Soviet phase and after it, Chinese studies in the U.S. have tended to 'explain' away controversial actions of Beijing and downplay the strategic challenges from the PRC. Cleaning the lens through which we view China is as important as marrying technical expertise with a sense of political judgment on Beijing's future course.

More broadly, barring for a short period in the early weeks of the George W. Bush Administration, the prospect of a potential peer competitor threatening America's global and regional primacy has not animated U.S. policy making or its vast foreign and defence policy communities. Two decades ago, in the immediate aftermath of the Cold War, the national security strategy of the George H.W. Bush administration declared that the main objective of the United

States was to prevent the emergence of a rival power or a coalition of powers dominating the Eurasian landmass. This did not need any American follow through given the belief in the durability of the 'unipolar moment' reinforced by the Russian weakness and Chinese unpreparedness to contest the U.S. hegemony.

As a result the U.S. had the luxury of focusing on non-proliferation, terrorism, failed states, nation-building, promoting democracy, and the so-called non-traditional security threats in the last two decades. The U.S. military, with a sense of unchallengeable superiority, began to devote energies to such tasks as counter-terrorism, counter-insurgency, and counter-proliferation. The objective here is not to run down the importance of these issues; it is to highlight the point that this agenda was premised on the absence of a threat from another great power. America's exhaustion from the two wars in the Middle East and the rise of China, however, might be bringing the recent episode to a close.

At this juncture it is not unreasonable to assume that China is well on its way to becoming a great global power. Whether it is the material sources of power that are accruing to China or the unambiguous political will in Beijing to exercise power, it now has the upper hand in defining the evolution of the Asian balance of power. China does not have to match America's military strengths to alter the Asian balance of power. Beijing knows that with sufficient capabilities and an asymmetric strategy it can significantly limit Washington's ability to dominate its land and maritime peripheries. China's rise is likely to strain the nature of great power relations in Asia, stress the existing security arrangements, compel a modernization of military forces and doctrines, and undermine the current regional institutions. The following section outlines a few broad scenarios that help frame the debate on the nature of China's rise and its regional implications. The final section looks specifically at India's new policy challenges in dealing with a rising China and collaborating with the United States in structuring a stable Asian balance of power.

As we look ahead it is possible to imagine at least eight possible ways in which the rise of China could affect Asian regional security politics. The first is the prospect of a *Sino-centric Asian Order*. Many scholars including some in the United States have argued that there is something natural about Asia being reorganized around Chinese primacy. After a couple of bad centuries, we are told, China is reclaiming its place at the heart of Asia. China's new role as Asia's largest economy and the engine of its economic growth would provide the foundation for this Sino-centric order in Asia. While the economic logic seems convincing, it is not clear if many of the large countries of Asia, like India, Indonesia, Vietnam, and Japan are politically prepared to accept such an order.

A second possibility is the reinforcement of American primacy, which has been the source of order and stability in the region for decades. Even if the United States gets its economy up and running, and successfully sustains the pivot strategy, there is no certainty that the old order in Asia can be restored. For the scale and scope of China's power is such that America must either prevail over China in a costly confrontation or share power with Beijing. That brings us to a series of other possible outcomes.

The third, fourth and fifth possibilities are about different forms of accommodation between the United States and China. Before announcing the pivot, the Obama Administration signalled its willingness to accommodate a rising China if it was willing to play by the (American) rules. While many in Asia characterized it as the G-2, the fact remains that Beijing had no time for it and rejected it out of hand. Many leading lights in the U.S. strategic community like Henry Kissinger have warned that a confrontation with China will be disastrous for America and insisted that there is no alternative to their 'cooperation and coevolution'. The Chinese leaders have called for an entirely new type of a relationship with the U.S. that is different from the past pattern of conflict between rising and declining powers, and have set their own terms for accommodation with America. The problem, then, is about the price the U.S. is willing to pay for Chinese willingness to join the condominium, not the principle.

Besides condominium there are other forms of accommodation between China and the United States. The fourth scenario on our list is the prospect of an arrangement for separate spheres of influence. Much like Spain and Portugal agreed not to compete with each other, it is possible to imagine America and China demarcating their primary areas of interest and agreeing on the principle of no-contest in agreed spheres of influence. Another variant of this is the prospect for 'offshore balancing' by America. Similar to the British policy towards continental Europe, America could step back from its current role as a hands-on manager of the regional order, promote an 'in situ' balance of power in Asia and intervene only to restore when the shift in the balance threatens its interest. Many American scholars dismiss the possibility of the U.S. ever adopting such a role by citing the nature of Washington's strategic culture.

The sixth option is to consider the regional balance of power from a perspective that goes beyond the bilateral dynamic between America and China. After all Asia has many large nations with a massive power potential of their own and middle powers that shape the regional balance. The idea of a concert of Asian powers, including America, China and India, has gained some traction in recent years but faces many practical obstacles. Beijing has been resistant to the idea of a trilateral dialogue with Washington and Delhi, and there will be enough actors opposing any grouping of major powers that presents itself as a self-selected Asian concert. In the post-Napoleonic era, the Concert of Europe was formed by a set of roughly equal sized powers, all of them located within the old continent. In Asia, the varying size of the powers, the problems of limiting geographic scope and the pitfalls of excluding key players could complicate the challenge of constructing a concert of powers.

The seventh possibility is the hope that the current efforts to strengthen regional institutions will help mitigate the great power tensions in Asia and set the stage for cooperative regional security. The reality, however, is that the very construction of these regional institutions, defining their membership and mandate, has been subject to contradictions among the great powers. The evolution of the East Asia Summit initiated by the Association of South East Asian Nations underlines this. While ASEAN sought to draw in most other powers, including India, Russia and America, into the

EAS fold to broaden the playing field as it were, Beijing's emphasis has been on limiting the scope of the EAS and refusing to let it interfere with China's pursuit of its own national interests.

If the EAS has not done too well, neither the older institutions like the ASEAN Regional Forum nor the newer ones like ADMM Plus (which brings together the defence ministers of the EAS member states) are likely to be effective in coping with the historic redistribution of power in Asia. Their current focus on soft-security issues in EAS only underlines its inability to address the larger challenges coming to the fore. Meanwhile, the attempts at regional economic integration are being pulled in different directions with the ASEAN calling for a new Asia-wide free trade agreement that excludes the U.S. and the American initiative on the Trans-Pacific Partnership.

Finally, the most likely scenario for the near future is the slow but certain build-up of the Sino-U.S. rivalry in the region. China's assertiveness in the region and the U.S. response to it, in the form of military and diplomatic rebalancing of Asia, might have set the stage for a prolonged geopolitical contest in the region. It is a rivalry few in the region have wished for or can manage. The tension between the Chinese search for greater freedom of action in its Asian periphery on the one hand, and the American forward military presence and its long standing alliances on the other, is real and will have great bearing on Asia's international relations for a long time to come. The search for a regional balance of power will be different from the Cold War experience in Asia. Unlike the Soviet Union, which was isolated from the economic flows in the region, China is at the very heart of Asia's economic dynamism and is by no means amenable to a strategy of containment by other powers.

On the other hand, China's power naturally complicates the credibility of traditional U.S. alliances in the region. The current debate in Australia, one of the most loyal allies of the United States and a major economic partner for China, on how to cope with the Sino-American rivalry, is indicative of a larger trend. Japan and the Philippines fear that the United States might not stand by them when their territorial conflicts with Beijing turn into shooting matches. Meanwhile, the ASEAN, which has seen itself as the driver of regional institution building, is finding it hard to stay united amidst the assertion of Chinese power.

The new divisions across the region are further reinforced by the deepening schisms within the political elites of all major countries on how best to deal with China's assertiveness and how far their nations must go in working with Washington to constrain Beijing. These new dilemmas are clearly visible in India's own policy response to the changing balance between China and the United States. In Delhi they acquire greater complexity given India's own aspirations to play a larger role in Asia and its celebrated tradition of non-alignment.

On the face of it, the U.S. pivot to Asia is an extraordinary strategic opportunity for India. The unfolding Sino-U.S. rivalry has the potential to end India's prolonged isolation from Asian geopolitics and offer Delhi a chance to insert itself as an indispensable element of the new regional balance of power. That India has long sought to balance Chinese power is not in doubt. India's expanding security cooperation with the United States and its allies in the last few years and the attempts to raise its independent profile in East Asia points a clear Indian intent to balance China. Yet, at the very moment the U.S. moved to an explicit balancing strategy and is urging India to take the leadership role in Asia, India is sending ambiguous signals. Delhi has neither endorsed the U.S. pivot to Asia nor criticized it.

Nothing illustrates India's urgent need to balance China and the problem of doing so better than the expanding strategic gap between Beijing and Delhi in favour of the former. At the turn of the 1990s, China and India were roughly equal in terms of aggregate economic size and per capita income. By the turn of the second decade of the 21st century, China looms nearly four times larger. China, which has become the second largest economy of the world, also spends nearly four times as much on defence as India. This huge gap is unlikely to close any time soon.

Even if India produces its best historic economic performance of nine per cent annual growth rate – seen for a few years in the mid-2000s – it will stay behind China for a long time. Since 2010, the Indian economy has visibly slowed down to less than six per cent, and Delhi is perilously close to a macro-economic crisis amidst the widening trade deficit, falling rupee, high inflation and mounting burden of wide-ranging subsidies. The conditions for reducing the gap in the foreseeable future – a significant slowdown of the Chinese economy and a rapid acceleration of India's growth rates – may not present themselves easily.

India, of course, has the option of accepting the widening power differential with China, eschew rivalry, and tailor its policies towards greater accommodation. Such a course would seem largely unthinkable for Delhi. Given its own self-image as a natural leader of the developing world, India will find it hard to settle for a secondary place in a Sino-centric Asian order and an international system where Beijing plays a larger role in setting and enforcing rules. This could, however, change if Beijing could tempt India with a reasonable settlement on the boundary, addresses its concerns on Pakistan and cuts some space for the pursuit of India's own ambitions in Asia.

If China is not ready to accommodate India's geopolitical interests, Delhi has no alternative but to balance China. Balancing a larger power is usually done in two ways – internal and external. Internal balancing involves the full mobilization of domestic economic and military resources to maintain a measure of strategic parity if not strict equality. The other is an external balancing of strong power through alliances and partnerships.

On all the three counts, India faces a challenging period ahead. Internal balancing requires an extraordinary political will and executive capability in rapidly building comprehensive national power. India's chaotic internal politics naturally leads to much skepticism about purposeful actions to balance China. Despite the visible expansion of Chinese strategic capabilities across the spectrum – from transforming the border infrastructure to cyber warfare capabilities – Delhi's response has been slow, inconsistent and unimpressive. Whether it is the construction of border roads or modernizing the Indian military, whether it is upgrading its human resource potential or investing in advanced research and development, Delhi has not shown the purposefulness of Beijing.

On the question of external balancing, India has made some interesting moves in laying the foundations for strategic partnerships with the United States, Japan, Indonesia, Vietnam and others who are all alarmed to different degrees by the rise of China. Yet, India finds itself hesitant to follow through the logic of external balancing. Self-doubt, fears about losing strategic autonomy, apprehensions about being a junior partner and domestic political concerns have significantly limited Delhi's capacity for strategic cooperation with powers bigger than itself. If the ghosts of non-alignment impede India's partnerships with the U.S., an ingrained reluctance to offend Beijing has constrained what India can offer smaller powers like Vietnam seeking to balance China.

It is not that India is alien to balance of power strategies. After all, its *de facto* alliance with the Soviet Union during the 1970s was a classic balancing act against Sino-U.S. rapprochement. Delhi's problem today is not as much about the high principles of strategic autonomy or non-alignment but of finding the political skill to navigate the current regional turbulence, strengthen the partnership with the United States without courting a premature conflict with China and elevate India's standing in the Asian balance of power. China's emergence as a major economic partner for India adds a further wrinkle to the strategy of external balancing.

India is the last one in Asia to recognize the benefits of deepening economic integration with China. As in Asia and the United States, finding harmony between economic and strategic imperatives in dealing with China is already a big headache for Indian policy makers.

Finally, the idea of an asymmetric strategy towards China has barely begun to figure in India's strategic discourse. Delhi has seen the Pakistan Army implement the asymmetric strategy of cross-border terrorism during the last two and a half decades as a way to neutralize India's superior capabilities. India is witnessing China's similar approach to weaken the United States in the Indo-Pacific region. Despite the demonstrated virtues of an asymmetric strategy in dealing with a stronger power, India will take a long time in developing one, if at all.

In the end, it is not about choosing between the three options. India will have to move forward on all the three fronts even as it deepens economic partnership with China and explores a bilateral geopolitical settlement with Beijing. Internal balancing, alliances, and asymmetric approaches are as old as statecraft. They are not inventions of modern political thought from Europe or America, but date back to the era of Kautilya's *Arthashastra*. China's rise and America's response to it have laid before India its greatest geopolitical opportunity and the biggest diplomatic challenge since independence. It is up to the Indian policy community to rescue the debate in Delhi from empty slogans, return to the first principles of statecraft and reconnect it to inherited strategic traditions.

CHINA AND INDIA AS DRIVERS OF REGIONAL GROWTH

There is little doubt that China's rapidly growing exports to countries outside of Asia-Pacific in Asia has generated equally rapid growth in imports by China from other Asian and Pacific countries, not just from its neighbours in East Asia but also from Australia, India and Indonesia. According to Perlez (2003), Japan's current "recovery is being driven by a surge in exports to China. Australia's healthy economy is being kept that way by Chinese investments in liquid natural gas products.

China is now South Korea's largest trading partner... In Indonesia, Malaysia and the Philippines (and to a lesser extent in Thailand)... China's main interest is to scoop up what it can for its modernization. Indonesians call this new relationship with Beijing as 'feeding the dragon.'" Although India is by far the largest (and rapidly growing) market in South Asia, it is yet to have a major impact on the trade of its neighbours in South Asia in spite of the creation of the South Asian Preferential Trade Area (SAPTA) in 1997. To a significant extent, this reflects the hostile relations between India and the next largest market in South Asia, viz. Pakistan. Pakistan is yet to grant a most favoured nation status to India. Unless the relations between the two normalize, the prospects of SAPTA are not bright. However, India-Sri Lanka bilateral trade and investment have grown rapidly since the conclusion of a free trade agreement between the two became operational in March 2000. Recent signs of a warming of Indo-Pakistani relations, if they lead to their normalization, could make India the engine of growth for South Asia, as China already is in the Asia-Pacific region.

Foreign Direct Investment

China receives a much larger flow of net foreign direct investment (projected at $57 billion in 2003) than India's (under $4 billion in 2001-02). In Srinivasan (2002), I discussed some of the reasons for this difference. In short, as Luce and Kynge (2003) succinctly point out, "whether it is China's cheaper, more reliable power supply or the more rapid turn around at its ports, China remains an incalculably better environment for most manufacturing than India, which is slowly waking up to this." This environment and the bureaucratic obstacles at all levels of government in India in large part explain the huge flow of FDI to China relative to India. The Indian government has recognized FDI as key for achieving the Tenth Plan target of 8% annual growth and appointed a steering committee on FDI in 2001. It reported in 2002 with several recommendations for making India more attractive as a destination for FDI.

Exchange Rates and Foreign Reserves

Although China's trade surplus with the United States has been growing, its overall trade surplus is modest since it is running a growing trade deficit with Asia-Pacific countries that offsets in large part its trade surplus with the US. The economic logic that only a country's overall trade and current account balances have economic significance and not its bilateral balances with any one or a subset of trading partners, has never been understood by politicians anywhere, and in particular, in the US. As Japanese trade surpluses created an anti-Japan backlash in the eighties, it is now China's turn to be at the receiving end of US pressure. China has accumulated a substantial (projected at $383 billion by the end of 2003) foreign exchange reserves, exceeding its annual imports. India has done the same—its reserves, around $92 billion at the end of 2003, exceed by a substantial margin the likely imports of $60 billion. The issues of the appropriate level of reserves, and whether both countries have accumulated far too much relative to what would be needed to smooth volatility in export earnings and import expenditures and to contain any potential financial crisis like the one experienced by East Asia in 19975. Since neither the renminbi nor the rupee is convertible on capital account and capital controls are in place in both countries, prima facie the probability of an exchange rate crisis of the type experienced by countries with open capital account and fully convertible currencies is very low. This is not to say, of course, that a balance of payments crisis (BOP) that makes the prevailing exchange rate unsustainable cannot arise—after all, despite capital controls and an inconvertible (on capital account) rupee, India experienced a severe BOP crisis in 1991, which resulted in the devaluation of the rupee and other policy changes. Still, given that partial insurance from other sources of external funds (e.g., from the IMF) is in principle available, should self-insurance through reserves be pushed as far as the current level of reserves in China and India seem to have done?

Any attempt to determine the appropriate level of reserves has to be based on an analysis of the appropriate exchange rate regime for either country, and the related issue of whether the benefits from integration with the global financial markets outweigh the costs. Without doing such an analysis myself, let me cite Kenneth Rogoff of Harvard, the former Economic Councillor and Director, Research Department of the IMF, on the issue:

My interpretation of the evidence not just from Asia but from the whole world, from Europe's experience, from floating rates, from the Bretton Woods system, is that policy makers vastly overrate the risks of having volatile exchange rates and vastly underrate the indirect costs that can come from all the policies that they have to try to suppress them. Certainly I wouldn't say that India has gone too far at the moment in accumulating reserves, it has a very strong position but I think all the countries in Asia are reaching a point when they have to start asking the question how much is enough, that basically a lot of the reserves that the Asian economies are accumulating—even outside of Japan—we are talking about close to a trillion dollars, are basically low interest rate loans from the emerging markets to United States and Europe, and this is very costly. There are opportunity costs to the domestic economy. How much is enough and at what point should one risk letting the exchange rate appreciate. Knowing the multilateral aspects of it, I realize that there are some outside the IMF who call for greater flexibility in Asian currencies in order to strengthen demand from the rest of the world. I think that is an issue worth considering but it is not the one I want to focus on. From the Asian economies' own perspective, and this is true for India, it is true for China, it is true for virtually all the countries in the region, moving to a regime of greater flexibility would be something that is advisable, would not bring the cost many policy makers fear, and in fact would allow the economies to reduce the level of recession and that would have many positive growth effects (Rogoff 2003). Rogoff's conclusion does not imply that US pressure on China to revalue the renminbi was justified or that India should also let its rupee appreciate, but only that greater flexibility in exchange rates would be appropriate in both countries.

The Indian exchange rate regime is one of managed float (although Rogoff prefers to characterize it as a crawling peg), and it does allow some flexibility. It is possible to argue that the Indian central bank (i.e., Reserve Bank of India) has inappropriately intervened to prevent the rupee from appreciating, and this has cost the Indian economy in terms of foregone growth. But this is an argument that the flexibility inherent in the managed float regime has not been utilized appropriately. It is not the same as arguing that India should immediately make the rupee fully convertible and adopt a regime of clean float. The latter argument is not persuasive for the simple reason that domestic financial sector reforms are incomplete, and it is risky to open the capital account under the circumstances. In any case, there is no country in the world, developed or developing, that allows a clean float of its currency. On the other hand, there are long term benefits from a convertible currency and by credibly committing to a fully convertible rupee for at a not too distant and specified future date, the pressure to complete the financial sector reforms by that date would become significant. What about China? Again, the problems in the financial sector, particularly the overhang of NPLs are serious, and an immediate revaluation might worsen the problem. Besides, it has not been established by anyone, least of all by the US Treasury, that the current renminbi-dollar exchange rate is too far from a long-run equilibrium rate. If it is not, and China moves to a floating regime, that US Treasury might find, to its surprise, that the exchange rate does not move from its current level! Unfortunately, China is likely to succumb to the pressure to revalue if newspaper reports (*Financial Times*, February 10, 2004) are to be believed.

It is not unlikely that if India's reserves continue to climb, and outsourcing gathers further momentum, there would be charges of "currency manipulation" against Indian authorities, as the Chinese are currently being charged with. China and India should cooperate in resisting such accusations and pressures and decide on their exchange rate policies in their own interests. Finally, as Rogoff rightly points out, by continuing to accumulate reserves in terms of US dollar assets, China, India and other Asian countries are financing US current account deficits. As Alan Beattie (2003) points out: "In theory, Asians' role in financing the US current account deficit could give them enormous economic or even political leverage, since a sudden shortfall in capital inflows would spark a slide in the dollar and possibly a sharp rise in interest rates." But he rightly concludes that: "A wholesale flight from the dollar, if it drove up interest rates and forced the US into a rapid tightening of consumers' belts, would also hurt one of the principle buyers of Asia's exports." Chinese and Indian policy makers are sophisticated enough to realize this and can be expected to slow the accumulation of reserves, if appropriate, and allow greater exchange rate flexibility in due course.

INDIA FALLING BEHIND CHINA IN SOUTH ASIAN DIPLOMACY

India has always been a local superpower, being by far the largest country within South Asia, and is, in fact, the only one in the group that borders every other South Asian country except Afghanistan, which shares a border with Pakistan. But India's economic performance was stunted by years of state control of the kind now prevalent in Iran. Over the past 15 years, however, economic growth has been strong, enabling the country to have a much greater diplomatic reach than at any time since the 1950s when India briefly emerged as the leader of those countries that were being de-colonized by the European powers. Given this situation, it ought to have been the case that New Delhi would be preeminent in its own backyard. Instead, over the past two decades, India has lost the status of being the lead player in any South Asian country barring Bhutan, a country with which it still has a treaty relationship. In almost the entire region, China has overtaken India in that intangible quality - influence - especially in Nepal and Sri Lanka, while Beijing's existing alliances with Pakistan and Bangladesh are growing stronger.

This is not due to a lack of quality within India's diplomatic service. Instead, the Indian Foreign Service (IFS) has produced a modern corps of skilled diplomats, many experts in different regions of the world, and eager to do more to advance their country's interests. The wall they face is the ambivalence that has become second nature to the country's top policy makers, both within the political crust as well as the administrative backup. Phrases such as "going all the way" and "going for the kill" are inelegant. Yet they represent a reality that is that sometimes a country has to formulate and then determinedly implement a clear policy to be carried out till success is achieved.

In South Asia, such a quality was recently displayed by President Percy Mahinda Rajapaksa of Sri Lanka. He succeeded in wiping out the terrorist group known as the Liberation Tigers of Tamil Eelam (LTTE) where, over the past three decades, all his predecessors had failed. Unlike them, President Rajapaksa did not heed (well-meaning but disastrous) advice to slow down his offensive or agree to a cease-fire, the latter being a device that the LTTE used since 1987 to gain time to recover after having lost the initiative in the field. Once the LTTE recovered its strength, the ceasefire would be abandoned. This point was repeatedly made by Rajapaksa to the peacemakers who clustered around him, especially in the final months of the brief, brutal war against the LTTE that began with his coming to office in 2005.

Once India, because of political considerations such as the need to avoid alienating the country's sizable Tamil population, refused to give the Sri Lankan army equipment, Rajapaksa turned to Pakistan and China. Both countries opened their warehouses to him, and so built up immense capital both within Sri Lanka's Sinhala most importantity as well as the country's policy establishment. Rajapaksa showed none of the half-heartedness that has characterized so much of Indian policy and, as a result, emerged a winner. In the case of India, the desire to win brownie points with key international players (by heeding their sometimes incorrect advice) as well as an aversion to risk ensured that much of Indian diplomacy was too watered down to be effective. This is especially the case in its immediate neighbourhood.

This on-again, off-again excellence can be seen in Indian diplomatic policy towards Pakistan especially in regard to the long-term pattern of instituting confidence building measures (CBM) being followed - usually after a mass terror attack - with strong rhetoric and a withdrawal of contact. The reality is that in the case of Pakistan, conventional war may have ceased to be an option. This is because the Pakistan army has itself lost control of many of the jihadis that it has trained, equipped and funded for so long.

Instead of reducing the risk of a terror attack, going after the Pakistan military would inflame a large segment of the Pakistani population thus making them susceptible to recruitment in the ongoing jihad against India. Given that situation, it may have been preferable for Indian policymakers to publicly resort to a conventional war except in the case of a conflict started by Pakistan, an unlikely possibility. The military option would work only if (a) the Pakistan army controls the jihadi networks and (b) is comprehensively defeated in battle. Neither condition exists.

A "No War" declaration by India would remove the Pakistani military establishment's most frequently used excuse to station more than 60 percent of its army along the India border, even as the force is engaged in a life-and-death struggle with the Pakistan Taliban. Instead, even though New Delhi has no intention of going to war, the prospect of one is deliberately kept open especially after terror strikes such as Mumbai 11/26-28. Thus, the benefits of India's "No War" declaration are denied, while the other side is aware that the mock-aggressive posture is a bluff and hence will not change its behaviour as a result of the threat.

A glaring example of how promoting the idea that India would go to war over Pakistani provocations has hurt New Delhi can be seen in the 2002 standoff with Pakistan in the mountains separating the two. Ostensibly to scare the international community into putting pressure on Pakistan to call off its Kashmir jihad, the then-Vajpayee government mobilized two Indian army strike corps on the border, keeping them and their support units on a hair-trigger alert for the greater part of the year. Aware that the Indians were bluffing, the Pakistan government refused to budge from its policy of helping jihadists active in Kashmir. The long Indian army mobilization created a perception of regional instability that affected India's status as a safe investment destination even as it exhausted the elite army units on the front line. Given the information that India would not attack, the 2002 mobilization came at a horrendous cost and no benefit. In a system where posturing comes easily to the higher levels of the Indian policy establishment, Prime Minister Manmohan Singh has thus far resisted jingoism and has made it evident that India would not be stampeded into military action. In the case of Sri Lanka, the policy was to intensify conflict until victory. What is needed is a clear policy that is carried out effectively, not a zig-zag routine that confuses the international community and results in a loss of credibility for India.

Military sales can become an effective instrument of diplomacy, were they deployed by India. Within the region, including in Sri Lanka and Nepal, the military is a significant component of the policy process, often the crucial player. Because of New Delhi's longstanding policy of not permitting foreign military sales save for exceptional situations, China has been provided an opportunity to fill the gap. Had Bangladesh, Nepal and Sri Lanka been more reliant on Indian equipment and training for their armed forces, New Delhi would have been in a much stronger position to influence policy in those places than it is today. Instead, the "weapons gap" isincreasingly being filled by China.

The mantra of "non-alignment" has in most instances become a cover for lack of action. Even during the period of the Cold War, when India suffered many of the consequences of being seen as a Soviet ally, not a single Soviet soldier was ever stationed in India or trained here, nor did any Indian soldier undertake any sort of mission in the USSR. In contrast, there are regular exchanges of U.S. and Indian soldiers and joint training exercises have become routine. The warming of ties is because there is a natural fit between the two sides. India has a significant pool of trained (and trainable) manpower, while the United States has abundant stocks of equipment that could be transferred to New Delhi rather than mothballed or left under-utilized. This is especially the case with naval vessels, where India is now being made to pay $3 billion for a secondhand Russian aircraft carrier that it is finding it difficult to float and move at the same time.

Progress in U.S.-India military to military relatives has been slow and is still far below its potential in substantial part because of the wariness of the Indian establishment over China's reaction. Compare this with Pakistan which has built up close military ties with both China and the United States, its friendship with one not affecting the other. In the military field, the choice is between going with the United States or going alone, because a military alliance with China is not an option. Beijing sees New Delhi as a potential competitor and has repeatedly shown through its actions its commitment to a strategic policy that inhibits the growth of Indian power. Unfortunately, in this case, Indian ambivalence is now being matched by the United States under the Obama administration, which has downgraded ties with India to a level much below that set under President George W. Bush. It seems inevitable, however, that both countries will, hopefully within the present presidential term, awaken to the need for a partnership that can ensure that Asia does not fall under the sway of any single power.

The persistent Indian ambivalence in policy was visible in Sri Lanka, where India simultaneously called for a cease-fire while backing the unity of the island nation. As a consequence of simultaneously conveying two contradictory messages, neither the Tamil nor the Sinhala zealots have anything other than distaste for India, while the abundant provision of military supplies has led the Sri Lankan military towards becoming as close to Beijing as are their counterparts in Pakistan.

In Nepal, after first helping to get King Gyanendra to abdicate, New Delhi threw its support behind the Maoists, who promptly reacted by threatening to scrap the India-Nepal agreement and replace it with a similar deal with China. After its embrace of the Maoists, which ended only after their tilt to Beijing became manifest (by the end of 2008), no other Nepali party is willing to trust New Delhi and see it as a reliable partner, even the once-friendly Nepali Congress. Meanwhile, in a show of deft footwork, Chinese diplomats have been active in Kathmandu renewing ties with the non-Maoist parties that today run the government (after the departure of the Maoists), so as to accelerate the growth of PRC influence in Nepal.

Today, there are almost as many radical training camps located within Bangladesh as there in Pakistan, camps whose specific purpose is to replenish the stream of jihadis into India. Yet, unlike in the case of Pakistan, the Indian government is not posturing as if was is likely. A hostile Pakistan, an unfriendly Bangladesh, and Nepal and Sri Lanka heading towards the PRC. These are the wages of a diplomacy that refuses to go for the jugular in the pursuit of objectives, but almost invariably crafts a compromise that gives much less geopolitical benefit. India presents an example of how a most important power that avoids a clear policy line or a better deployment of its assets gives way to the other who is ruthless and willing to complete the marathon rather than slow down and stop before the finish line. Such a policy is the delight of politicians and anathema to statesmen, who understand the need for not just vision, but for will and perseverance.

2

ASEAN-India: The Threshold of a New Era

It is fortuitous that the first ever India-ASEAN summit took place in Cambodia where Indo-Southeast Asian cultural synthesis reached its glory. Today the vision for India and ASEAN is being crafted in such a manner that the future would also be as remarkable as our past.

THE FIRST ever India-ASEAN summit held in Cambodia early this month has been a landmark development heralding a new chapter in the relationship between India and ASEAN, a regional grouping of Southeast Asian countries. It is also heartening news that the ASEAN-India summit will be held every year. Given the fact that it was only a decade ago that India and Southeast Asian countries started the process of rediscovery and a serious dialogue began between the two, the gains are anything but significant. In pursuance of India's "Look East" policy, amply reciprocated by the members of ASEAN, the dialogue has moved from a limited sectoral one (1992) to full dialogue partnership (1995) and membership of the ASEAN Regional Forum (ARF) in 1996 to a summit this year. This process has led to closer evaluation and greater interest on both sides of each other's potential and capabilities while keeping in mind limitations and vulnerabilities.

Post September 2001, Southeast Asia has emerged as another hub of terrorism. Reports of a number of local terrorist groups operating in close league with Al Qaeda has created a major concern among the governments and people of the region. The heinous terrorist act in Bali a few weeks ago shocked people everywhere. A theatre of major power rivalry during the Cold War days, Southeast Asia had been witness to warfare and strife for several decades. One of the principal objectives of ASEAN has therefore been to create a haven of peace and stability in the Asia-Pacific in the fulfilment of which ARF, an ASEAN-driven security forum, has brought together major powers from all around the world. India's membership in ARF since 1996 and its active role is looked upon as a useful contribution to the maintenance of security especially in the western flank of ASEAN, fitting the description of the Prime Minister of Singapore at the summit that India is another wing of the "ASEAN aircraft."

The Malacca Straits through which bulk of the energy supplies to East Asia pass is a strategic waterway to ASEAN and major East Asian countries. The financial crisis of 1997-98 was a signal to the Southeast Asian countries as to how vulnerable their economic and social structures were in facing the thrust of globalisation. Partnership with India has been conceived as an on-going effort to create interdependence and linkage with a country with a large and liberalising market as well as a democratic and pluralistic polity which could respond positively to ASEAN's aspirations.

The question that will continue to engage the minds in India and ASEAN is how the latest interaction between the two at the highest level will lead to a better understanding and convergence of views, political, economic or social.

Undoubtedly, this would depend on the evolving situations in both regions as indeed on the commonalities and complementarities between India and ASEAN. The worldview of ASEAN and India and their priorities have differed in many ways in the past. Nevertheless, today there is much less divergence than what was seen during the Cold War period. India and ASEAN have now growing stakes in mutual stability, security and economic well-being. Closer understanding and cooperation on the issue of terrorism should therefore constitute a priority area in our future engagement. The "concrete programmes of cooperation" agreed to during the summit would expectedly include institutionalised mechanisms to comprehensively combat "non-traditional security threats" bilaterally with ASEAN members as also multilaterally within the existing framework of the ASEAN Regional Forum.

Free trade area

The announcement by Prime Minister Vajpayee and the ASEAN leaders to work towards an ASEAN-India Free Trade Area and enhance economic cooperation in different sectors marks the highlight of the interaction at the summit. India's initiative in proposing an FTA with ASEAN signifies its desire to develop close economic linkages. The setting up of an India-ASEAN Regional Trade and Investment Area as a long-term objective should be the main focus for the India-ASEAN dialogue in the coming months and years. Till such time an RTIA is set up, it should be the effort of ASEAN and India to enter into broad-based bilateral agreements in areas such as science and technology, biotechnology, IT, space technology application, financial services, human resource development, education, etc., the areas of recognised excellence of ASEAN members as well as India. The China-ASEAN agreement to create an FTA in the next ten years and the Japan-ASEAN Comprehensive Economic Partnership signed in Phnom Penh point out to the interest that regional powers such as China and Japan are taking in forging close economic ties with Southeast Asian neighbours.

The fruitfulness of our dialogue will depend on the attractiveness and competitiveness of both partners. No doubt there are complementarities; yet as developing countries we both are largely dependent on agriculture, commodities and primary goods. The Indo-ASEAN two-way trade grew by 30 per cent from U.S.$ 7.6 billion in 1999 to $ 9.88 billion in 2001. While the growth has been high, the volume is still small considering the vast potential for trade that exists among countries comprising over 1.5 billion people. Moreover, the trade is still quite imbalanced with India's exports at approximately 1:4 ratio with ASEAN's exports to India. Similarly, the level of investment flows on both sides is marginal though there is good potential to raise it to nearly $ 1 billion by 2007. The positive feature so far is that there have been investments from ASEAN to India as also from India to ASEAN countries unlike with the European Union or the U.S. Intensive efforts for promotion of trade, joint ventures, technology transfers would be necessary for improving the situation. In this regard the initiative to hold the first India-ASEAN Business Summit in New Delhi and Hyderabad on October 17 and 18, was a welcome step. This meeting addressed by Mr. Vajpayee and Prime Minister Mahatir of Malaysia and attended by a number of Ministers from ASEAN countries has given a boost to the promotion of business synergies on the two sides in areas such as infrastructure including roads and ports, IT, biotechnology, tourism, etc., and prepared a useful backdrop for the present summit.

Sub-regional cooperation

The continuing India-ASEAN dialogue at the highest level could also reinforce our efforts in sub-regional economic cooperation, namely Bangladesh-India-Myanmar-Sri Lanka-Thailand Economic Cooperation (BIMST-EC) and Mekong Ganga Cooperation in which India and five ASEAN countries namely Cambodia, Laos, Myanmar, Vietnam and Thailand are associated. Such cooperation as also the decision by Thailand, Myanmar and India to build a road linking Thailand to India through Myanmar would go a long way in developing connectivity and border trade possibilities for our Northeast with the adjoining Myanmar and the Mekong region countries beyond.

One major development which needs to be taken into account relates to the growing coherence between ASEAN and three major economies of Asia, namely China, Japan and South Korea. As was evident at the Phnom Penh meetings, the grouping, ASEAN + 3 has in a short span of two years acquired a structure in which policy coordination has begun to take place. In this arrangement one can see the beginning of an East Asian Economic Community. The contours of this community are still evolving, but they point towards possible formation of a new zone in East and Southeast Asia which could be one of the major economic entities in the world. India with its pattern of development, endowments and capabilities, and being one of the fastest growing economies can find important complementarities with the economies of this community. A harmonised and coordinated economic interaction between ASEAN + 3 and India could offer a mutually beneficial opportunity for the future. India's proposal at the summit to set up an FTA with ASEAN over a ten year period appears to be a step in the right direction.

ASEAN has already outlined its Vision 2020 and the Hanoi Action Plan which provides a roadmap for socio-economic development of the region in the coming years. In this, the focus of the Initiative for ASEAN Integration on CLMV countries (Cambodia, Laos, Myanmar and Vietnam) is an important one. India's political and cultural linkages with these countries are traditional and well-known. India's decision at the summit to extend $10 million line of credit to Cambodia and the three agreements signed with this country in the areas of trade, technical education and maintenance of the 1000-year-old Tam Pram temple marks a positive contribution. India has also announced greater tariff concessions to the less developed members of ASEAN namely, Myanmar, Laos, Vietnam and Cambodia. It is fortuitous that the summit took place in Cambodia where Indo-Southeast Asian cultural synthesis reached its glory. Today the vision for India and ASEAN is being crafted in such a manner that the future would also be as remarkable as our past. The summit provided an invaluable opportunity to that end.

CHINA AND INDIA STRATEGIC ECONOMIC DIALOGUE (SED): PROGRESS AND PROGNOSIS

India-China Strategic Economic Dialogue (SED) an institutionalized and established process now? The third round of the SED was held in Beijing from 17-18 March 2014, in which the two sides discussed at length issues concerning international, bilateral and domestic economic conditions and deliberated on how to expand their bilateral and international cooperation. They discussed firming coordination in BRICS, G-20, UN, enhancing cooperation in trade, investment and economic fields, and forging greater cooperation among the key industries between the two countries. While some of the sentiments expressed in this round are genuine and generate a new level of India-China interactions, it needs to be seen where and how exactly this interaction can go forward. This round was conducted with the assistance of five

Working Group mechanisms, namely, policy coordination; infrastructure; resource conservation and environmental protection; hi-technology; and energy. The Working Group mechanism has been key for progress and institutionalization of the SED. In May 2013 five Chinese Working Groups visited India and in September 2013 five Indian Working Groups visited China to prepare the ground for the third SED.

This essay analyses the significance of SED in India-China engagement. Besides this introductory section, it comprises four sections: *first,* it reviews the importance of SED; *second,* it delves into the areas of convergence and divergence; *third,* it explains how China's current economic and financial pre-eminence has overlooked addressing India's bilateral concerns, which creates unevenness in the SED. The essay concludes with the caveat that while the scope of the SED is relatively high today because of constant institutional engagement, it will remain limited unless the fundamental bilateral economic issues are addressed.

The SED Mechanism So Far

Usually held between the counterpart planning commissions of the two countries – the Planning Commission of India and the National Development and Reform Commission (NDRC) of China – SED is gradually becoming a mechanism of import. India and China are not only big economic powers, being the third and second largest global economies, but the panoply of their engagement has been upgraded to a new level of global and autonomous standing today. This is important when world politics has become more multipolar in nature and the two countries are engaged with each other in a range of bilateral, regional, cross-regional and global multilateral forums.

A range of dialogue mechanisms exists in India-China interactions, both at the official and non-official levels and at the political and non-political levels. The SED was first mooted in December 2010 when Premier Wen Jiabao visited India. Beijing hosted the first SED round on 26 September 2011 and New Delhi hosted the second round on 26 November 2012. The rise of emerging economies within Brazil-Russia-India-China-South Africa (BRICS) forum furthers the importance of the SED. The first SED round was led by Zhang Ping, the then Chairman of NDRC, and Montek Singh Ahluwalia, Deputy Chairman of India's Planning Commission. Some of the issues covered were the global economic condition and the macroeconomic situation at the domestic level; mid- and long-term developmental plans; energy efficiency, conservation & environmental protection; infrastructural cooperation; water use efficiency; and use of clean water technologies. The second round reiterated that the primary aim of this dialogue mechanism was to "improve macroeconomic policy coordination" between two economies. It emphasized global economic cooperation, enhancing mutual communication on macroeconomic policies, expanding trade and investment, and expanding cooperation in financial and infrastructural sectors.

It had been agreed to hold the third round in 2013, but the event was postponed. The tensions arising out of People's Liberation Army's (PLA) incursion in Ladakh in the India-China border region and Xi Jinping and Li Keqiang's assumption of power in China as new leaders may have been the reasons for this postponement. Nevertheless, the importance of SED was reiterated during the new Premier's visit to India, stressing its active role in promoting "macroeconomic policy coordination" and "pragmatic cooperation" in various fields. The two sides agreed to strengthen cooperation in issues concerning energy, environment, new and renewable energy and high technology cooperation. They also agreed to enhance collaboration in the railway sector, noted the vitality of the Doha Development Round, expressed their intention for a bilateral Regional Trade Arrangement and reviewed the state of Regional Comprehensive Economic Partnership (RCEP) negotiations. In the third SED, for cooperation in railways, three specific areas have been chosen: station development, raising the speed of passenger trains in India and for heavy haul freight. China will assist India in improving its railway tracks to enable faster movement. Besides, China is supposed to construct high-speed tracks in three sectors – Delhi-Agra, Delhi-Kanpur and Delhi-Chandigarh.

A number of factors explain the importance of SED interaction. *First,* both countries participate in various regional and global multilateral institutions and frameworks such as Russia-India-China (RIC), BRICS, BASIC and G-20. *Second,* they share a common interest in preventing protectionism in the multilateral trading system. They also share similar sentiments about reforming global financial institutions like the IMF, WTO and World Bank. Their interactions and deliberations are important not only for their individual stakes in these bodies but also for the rest of the developing world, such as improving voting rights. SED is an appropriate forum for this. *Third,* macroeconomic issues need joint deliberations, but bilateral consensus should be there in the first instance. As developing countries and two fastest emerging economies of the world, much of the global economic sustainability heavily depends upon both China and India. SED creates conditions for them to coordinate in regional and global economic dealings.

Need for Serious Global and Regional Prognosis

India and China have several dialogue mechanisms besides SED, such as India-China Financial Dialogue, India-China Defence and Security Dialogue, India-China Strategic Dialogue, and India-China Joint Economic Group (JEG) etc. On 20 August 2013, the fifth round of the India-China Strategic Dialogue was held in New Delhi. Bilateral issues like utilization of trans-border river waters, enhancing trade and investment contacts and trade imbalance and global issues such as the Bangladesh-China-India-Myanmar (BCIM) economic corridor project, possible cooperation under BRICS, emerging politics in Asia-Pacific and post-2014 Afghanistan politics were matters of discussion. In 2014, in the sixth round of India-China Defence and Security in New Delhi, the two sides discussed bilateral, regional and global security issues of strategic substance and of mutual concern, involving security conditions in South Asia, Asia-Pacific and the Indian Ocean. The two sides have also conducted six rounds of financial dialogue regarding multilateral cooperation in bodies like G 20 and Asian Development Bank (ADB). The three key issues in the dialogue have been infrastructural investments, sustaining Asia's economic growth conditions and establishing closer coordination between developed and developing economies to address the global economic situation. While most of these mechanisms overlap each other, there is no denying that India-China interaction today is more methodological: these mechanisms involve stronger global, regional cross-continental and bilateral dealings in a range of economic, security and strategic issues.

As regards the SED, this dialogue mechanism requires particular focus on two aspects: *economic multilateralism* that is linked to various geo-political issues, and *political multilateralism* that is linked with geo-economics. Greater cooperation in global financial bodies such as the IMF, WTO and the World Bank is one aspect that needs careful discussion in SED in the future. The principal outlook on forging a common perspective on "developing country" and "emerging economies" phenomenon needs serious debate, at least from India's perspective. China today is a leading country in many global financial institutions and has also emerged as a big donor in a number of international agencies. India needs to be assured by China that the "developing country" formula will continue to be common to both countries in terms of vision and strategy in the coming times. Currently, there is a question mark on this aspect, considering that the new Chinese leadership is pushing forward the idea of a "new type of major power relations", promoting China's status as a power equivalent to the USA. This is being promoted concurrently with the strong US-China Strategic and Economic Dialogue (SE&D).

The India-China SED needs to discuss seriously the issue of reforming the global financial bodies. Both countries have for long advocated their reform, but common and decisive joint perspective is still missing. Besides, a solid understanding between the two is required for improving voting rights and quota in the IMF. Despite being the second and third largest economies in world ranking, their voting rights and quotas are far from impressive. Climate governance is another important issue that SED could discuss seriously in future. Climate change is not simply an issue of governance today but a macroeconomic issue that involves economic and political multilateralism. In the BASIC (Brazil-South Africa-India-China) climate grouping, the two sides have viewed climate change as a "threat and challenge" to humanity and to the goal of sustainable development. Greater deliberation is needed between the two on how to address "sustainable development" that is linked to "poverty eradication" in both India and China. Greater consensus is also needed on sustainable development where the two countries must take a lead along with other BASIC and BRICS members on the COP18/CMP8 on Doha principles, which is to be concluded by 2015. Further, working group on environment in SED must delve into where and how the two countries can cooperate in line with Rio principles of sustainable development.

Cooperation on financing projects and obtaining loans from various international banks also needs discussion and closer understanding between the two. Mr. Saumitra Chaudhuri, Member of India's Planning Commission, raised this issue during the third SED round, stating that greater cooperation is needed in multilateral forums like G-20 and ADB. The matter of the ADB is particularly significant here. In 2009, China's foreign ministry opposed strongly India's loan application in the ADB for infrastructure development in its state of Arunachal Pradesh in terms of the "Country Partnership Strategy for India (2009-2012)". Qin Gang, the then foreign ministry spokesperson of China, expressing strong objection over the issue, stated that 'ADB as a regional development agency must not interfere in political affairs of its members'. China has enormous clout in the ADB: by 2009, it was the third largest donor to it after the USA and Japan. It has been five years after this issue raised its head, but no India-China dialogue mechanism has addressed it, including SED. It needs to be stressed that the SED mechanism loses much of its significance if it cannot de-link the security aspects from the economic aspects. The SED is the most appropriate forum to discuss this issue of ADB as it has two working mechanisms: *policy coordination* and *infrastructure*. Prime Minister Manmohan Singh in his speech on India-China relations at the Central Party School in Beijing (24 October 2013) stressed the issue, saying, "... we need to pay much greater attention to the expansion and modernization of our infrastructure. India plans to invest one trillion U.S. dollars in infrastructure in the next five years and we would welcome China's expertise and investment in this sector". The concern on both sides is on how to facilitate flow of investment from China in the Indian market and vice-versa.

The BRICS Development Bank, on which BRICS members have failed to build consensus so far despite several rounds of deliberations, is another issue that needs serious deliberation in the SED. The onus is on India and China primarily because these two are the largest economies in BRICS.

Currently, there seems to be contention regarding the location of the bank's headquarters, type of projects that this bank will finance and its source of funding. BRICS Development Bank is an idea that is linked to North-South politics, whether it will act as a plausible alternative to the Bretton Woods institutions. China, it appears, wants to hog the scenario, to have headquarters of this bank in a Chinese city, probably Shanghai. China also has a disproportionate number of billionaires, prompting it to demand a big slice of the cake in the bank. India is somewhat cagey about this possible development.

Security and strategic issues need serious deliberation in SED too, especially because these issues involve economic and strategic nuances. Maritime security, China's recent "maritime Silk Road" proposal, security situation in Afghanistan, terrorism, and the geo-political implications of the recent Ukraine crisis need serious discussion in SED.

As regards China's invitation to others to join in the "maritime Silk Road" programme, before India decides to accept the offer, it is crucial to discuss in clear-cut terms Beijing's perspective on India's initiative for oil exploration in the South China Sea with the Southeast Asian countries, which China has so far opposed. SED must discuss and review the regional economic nuances that are attached to various issues that have arisen in the current international scenario that affect the region vitally.

It also needs to discuss issues such as revitalizing the Russia-India-China (RIC) forum and the RCEP. China also needs to reconsider its current opposition to India's partaking in the ASEAN+6 mechanism when it comes to the issue of regional economic integration in East Asia. A greater level of dialogue in the SED on RCEP and its negotiation process will help them to proceed much faster in terms of a possible future free trade agreement (FTA) between themselves.

Bilateral Concerns

Addressing macroeconomic issues and forging a stronger understanding in regional and global outlook can be attended better if bilateral economic grievances can be addressed easily. Trade imbalance, which in the last few years has widened in favour of China, is for India a disquieting issue.

India has regularly sought to convince China particularly to open its domestic markets in areas like Information Technology (IT), pharmaceuticals and engineering products. The Joint Economic Group (JEG) dialogue mechanism is supposed to address this issue and the SED is supposed to look after macro issues in India-China economic engagements.

This, however, creates a doubtful atmosphere for the progress of the SED. It is necessary to discuss the trade imbalance issue in SED as most of the India-China economic dealings today carry both strategic and economic ingredients. The two countries have set a target of $100 billion trade target by the year 2015, but their bilateral trade has declined in the last couple of years, from US$74 billion in 2011 to $66 billion. During the third SED, India also raised the issue of mutual investment flows to address to some extent the trade imbalance between the two countries.

Border trade is another matter that can be discussed in future India-China SED interactions.

The two countries are linked in the BCIM economic corridor project. Enhancing trade, transit and investment linkages are important aspects of the BCIM agenda. *Xinhua* reported in December 2013 that there was a sharp rise in India-China border trade in Renqinggang, which is located in Southwest China's Tibet Autonomous Region (TAR), that the trade figures there reached 86.3 million Yuan (approximately $14.3 million), a 23.3 per cent rise over the previous year. To what extent the declining value of the Indian Rupee has contributed to this rise in the border trade is not known.

These questions need serious deliberations in the SED, as these issues have strategic and economic nuances that involve greater India-China sub-regional dealings and cross-border engagements.

Summing Up

The three rounds of SED have, no doubt, built a strong momentum in the India-China institutional engagement, but the challenge is how to upgrade the level of dialogue, bring maturity to the interaction and make it a distinct and regular affair without making it just another talk shop. China has a similar dialogue mechanism with the USA. Initially started as US-China Strategic Economic Dialogue (SED), now a special "strategic track" and "economic track" has been added to this and it is known as US-China Strategic and Economic Dialogue (SE&D). The India-China SED has not really matured as a trusted bilateral mechanism to discuss the regional and global complexities of economic and strategic substance yet. Attempts need to be made to make it much more regular and systematic and to encompass issues for open discussion of not only India-China regional and global relations but also their foreign policy objectives.

China currently has strategic dialogue mechanisms with many countries and regions, such as with the African Union (AU), European Union (EU), and with ASEAN at the think-tanks level, but the US is the only other country with which China has a SED dialogue. New Delhi needs to make a special note of this seriousness on Beijing's part where China is concerned. There is no dearth of issues that the SED can address, but the success of the mechanism will depend upon how openly and candidly the two countries discuss them. The next SED round is supposed to be held in 2015 in India. New Delhi will by then have a new government in place. For India, the challenge is not only how to give new momentum to this mechanism but also how to persuade the Chinese to address the trade deficit issue.

3

ASEAN Power and China

For the ASEAN countries, being surrounded by the big powers is an unalterable geographical reality. At the same time, ASEAN can change or shape its strategic environment. ASEAN can co-dance harmoniously with the big powers by relying on the concerted efforts from within together with the international situation, as well as via creating and implementing both the strategy of 'check and balance' among those powers and the strategy of East Asia cooperation. As a result, a regional new order can be established that features peace and prosperity. Along this course, China can offer help and support to ASEAN to fulfil its goals and resolve its problems, so as to achieve a 'win–win' outcome in the region.

Put another way, the success of ASEAN in forging a new security framework to a large extent relies on strategic support from China, which is a firm supporter of ASEAN integration. While some countries seek to dominate the process of East Asian cooperation, China is actively maintaining the leadership status of ASEAN. China was the first big power to negotiate the establishment of FTAs with ASEAN, to join TAC, to establish a strategic partnership with ASEAN, and to bring 'smile diplomacy' to Southeast Asia. It also hopes to become the first to sign the *Treaty on the Southeast Asia Nuclear Weapon Free Zone*. The positive role of China has drawn other counterparts to show their goodwill to ASEAN, which has enabled the proper performance of the balance strategy and the regional cooperation strategy of ASEAN. With the joint efforts of China and ASEAN, other powers have begun to approach Southeast Asia in a similar manner, so as to achieve cooperation, a 'win–win' outcome, and equality, which is objectively conducive to multipolarity in the region. To help others and to achieve this 'win–win' outcome at the same time, the China-ASEAN relationship has become a good example of how to develop and handle international relationships.

Over the past 15 years, having helped ASEAN tide over the 1997–98 Asian financial crisis and the Severe Acute Respiratory Syndrome (SARS) outbreak, China then attempted to control the H5N1 influenza through joint efforts with ASEAN. Over the next 15 years, the risks confronting ASEAN from modernisation and globalisation will not diminish. For China, the next 15 years will also be a period in which strategic opportunities and protruding contradictions abound. The deepening strategic partnership between China and ASEAN calls for sharing the risks as well as the gains. In the future, the joint mission for the two sides will be how to avoid strategic risks and take economic and social risks under control. In essence, as China helps extricate ASEAN from risks and worries, a 'win–win' outcome for the region can also be achieved.

Judged from the development of bilateral relations between ASEAN and China since the end of the Cold War, China and ASEAN have achieved a 'win–win' relationship. China's relations with ASEAN and with ASEAN's members respectively have all reached the most positive point in history. The two sides witnessed positive developments simultaneously in many aspects: the coincidence of China's rise and ASEAN's ascendant status in the international community; and the coincidence of China's greater influence and ASEAN's more dominant role in the region. In a word, ASEAN and China go forward in tandem. The phrase 'Strategic Partnership Relationship' indicates that China's relations with ASEAN as a whole have risen to an unprecedented height, which will not be surpassed by China's relations with other regions.

The progress of China-ASEAN relations brings the feelings of stability, sureness and accomplishment to China's neighbour policy. This is the first time that such feelings have characterised China's relations with Southeast Asia. The benefits from this good relationship are wide-ranging: China can deal with the North Korean problem, China-Japan relations and the Taiwan issue attentively; it can, together with ASEAN, promote the development of East Asia regional cooperation, or even pan-Asian cooperation including Central Asia and South Asia; and it can associate itself with ASEAN's strategy of balancing powers in a natural way, and thus reduce the worrisome attitudes of other powers (such as the United States and Japan) toward China. Meanwhile, ASEAN has gained weight and influence from its good relationship with China. For example, China supports the process of integration within ASEAN and its dominant role in the development of East Asian cooperation on the basis that this does not harm the interests of other regions. This kind of relationship is a comparatively stable situation, resulting from complex interactions in a global context. As a result, there is great rationality and vitality within this relationship.

In view of the above, China's future strategy should include the following points. First, China should continue to support ASEAN's process of integration, and seek to link it with the three communities within ASEAN, which are still in the construction phase. Second, China should advocate ASEAN's dominant role in the development of the East Asia Cooperation, and realise China's own strategic interests while helping ASEAN to achieve the ideal regional structure. Third, China should be fully aware that it is only one part of ASEAN's strategy of balancing major powers. In future, big powers, such as the United States, Japan, India and Australia will definitely increase their strategic presence in this region. In this circumstance, China should not treat other regional powers as enemies or exclude other big power interests from the region. Rather, China should share its interests with the other big powers in the region.

BEIJING UNVEILS NEW STRATEGY FOR ASEAN-CHINA RELATIONS

Earlier this month, Chinese President Xi Jinping and Premier Li Keqiang embarked on high-profile trips to five Southeast Asian nations to attend the latest round of Asian summitry and commemorate a decade of the strategic partnership between China and ASEAN (the Association of Southeast Asian Nations). During their respective tours of the region, the two also revealed the new leadership's policy declaration on Southeast Asia for the next decade, known as "the 2 + 7 cooperation framework". But while Beijing's diplomatic offensive provided a good window into the new leadership's thinking about Southeast Asia and also produced some impressive initial results, there remain limits to ASEAN–China relations in both the economic and security dimensions that could continue to bedevil ties for years to come.

ASEAN–China relations have improved dramatically over the past decade since the inking of their strategic partnership on August 29, 2003. Two-way trade increased more than six-fold over the last ten years to top $400 billion last year, while investments exceeded $100 billion during the same period (Xinhua, October 17). As of last year, China was ASEAN's largest trading partner for the third year in a row, while the region was Beijing's third largest trading partner. More generally, ASEAN–China cooperation has grown to cover over 20 areas from agriculture to disaster relief, and the two sides have set up 12 ministerial mechanisms and a range of cooperative platforms like the China–ASEAN Expo and the China–ASEAN Business and Investment Summit. Though differences still exist on some issues, most prominently over Beijing's handling of the territorial disputes in the South China Sea, Chinese officials have repeatedly emphasized that these should not overshadow what is otherwise a largely successful relationship.

At the ASEAN–China Summit in Brunei on October 9, Chinese Premier Li Keqiang put forward the "2 + 7 cooperation framework," a new policy declaration on developing ASEAN–China relations over the next decade. It consists of a two-point political consensus and seven proposals for cooperation. The two-point political consensus held that the basis for promoting cooperation is deeper strategic trust and good neighborliness, saying that the key to deepening cooperation is focusing on economic development and expanding mutual benefit (Xinhua, October 10). The seven-point proposal included some interesting ideas for further cooperation, including inking a treaty on good-neighborliness, upgrading the

China–ASEAN Free Trade Area (CAFTA) to raise trade to one trillion dollars by 2020, setting up an Asian infrastructure bank to finance mushrooming regional connectivity projects, and building a 21st-century "maritime Silk Road" (Xinhua, October 10).

While the specifics of these proposals are still unclear, Premier Li and President Xi have already begun to expand cooperation bilaterally with several ASEAN countries during their Southeast Asia trips. Premier Li's three-country tour saw the birth of new cooperative endeavors with respect to joint exploitation of energy resources in Brunei, high-speed rail technology in Thailand, and potentially even maritime exploration in the disputed South China Sea via a newly conceived working group in Vietnam (Xinhua, October 11). Meanwhile, President Xi's visits to Malaysia and Indonesia resulted in an elevation of Beijing's relations with the two countries to the level of a comprehensive strategic partnership, with notable improvements not only in economic ties but defense and security cooperation and people-to-people links as well (Xinhua, October 9). The optics of the visits reinforced their substance, with Premier Li and President Xi delivering rare, high-profile addresses to the Thai and Indonesian parliaments respectively.

The initial reception of ASEAN states to the economic components of the 2 + 7 cooperation framework has been largely positive. In particular, both Indonesia and Brunei welcomed China's proposal for an Asian infrastructure investment bank prioritizing ASEAN projects, even though it came a little earlier than expected. It was originally scheduled to be announced next year when China hosts APEC. That is no surprise, since China's initiative dovetails with ASEAN's effort to enhance physical connectivity among its members through a series of infrastructure projects (ASEAN Secretariat). As one seasoned ASEAN observer pointed out, as of late last year, the grouping was only been able to raise a few hundred million dollars for the Master Plan for ASEAN Connectivity, far short of the Asian Development Bank projections, which say the region needs a whopping $60 billion a year over the next decade to make the proposal a reality.

The other two economic ideas in the cooperation framework have already been discussed previously and are considered important by Beijing and Southeast Asian states as they build on previous achievements in ASEAN–China relations. While CAFTA has been successful thus far in reducing tariffs, both sides agree that there is much room for improvement, whether through cutting non-tariff barriers or focusing more on the areas of services and investment (Xinhua, October 8). At the Special China–ASEAN Foreign Ministers Meeting in August, Singapore's foreign minister K. Shanmugam said that all ASEAN members supported the initiative (Xinhua, August 30). The proposal to further enhance ASEAN–China financial cooperation, which initially grew out of the 1997 Asian financial crisis, has also been welcomed, particularly in the wake of economic uncertainty amid the European debt crisis and a slow U.S. recovery (Caixin Media, October 16; China Radio International, October 15).

But while Southeast Asian countries may laud some of Beijing's fresh initiatives, their view of the long-term trajectory of ASEAN–China economic relations is also tinged with caution, for two reasons. First, as the Singaporean commentator Simon Tay has noted, China's economic size and power has grown tremendously relative to Southeast Asia since the 1990s, and this asymmetry alone worries some in the region today. Second, and on a related note, ASEAN countries may worry that being overly dependent on China economically would allow Beijing to use its dominance to undermine their foreign policy autonomy. The consequences of overdependence on China were on full display during ASEAN deliberations in Cambodia in July 2012, when Phnom Penh was pressured by its largest trading partner and investor to shape the agenda which eventually resulted in the organization's unprecedented failure to issue a joint communiqué (Asia Times, July 27). Given these fears, some Chinese commentators and diplomats have emphasized that boosting economic ties with ASEAN requires more than just new economic proposals, but "enhancing political mutual trust" as well.

ASEAN's reaction to some of the political-security initiatives in the 2 + 7 cooperation framework has been more cautious. Its response to the newly proposed Treaty of Good Neighborliness, Friendship and Cooperation exclusively between China and ASEAN in the ASEAN–China Summit joint statement was a nuanced one, noting it with appreciation but also signaling a preference for a more open and inclusive agreement by mentioning Indonesia's hope for a similar pact that includes "a wider Indo-Pacific region, beyond ASEAN and China" (ASEAN Secretariat). ASEAN Secretary General Le Luong Minh also later told *The Straits Times* in an interview that the Chinese proposal "has to be studied carefully first". ASEAN also appeared cool to Beijing's proposal for an informal ASEAN–China defense ministers meeting in China, choosing to leave this to "a convenient time in the future" in the statement. And while the Chinese proposal to strengthen exchanges and relations in the security field may be a good idea in general, experts noted that even the recent enhanced defense ties Malaysia and Indonesia agreed to with Beijing during President Xi's trip represent more continuity than change in what is still nascent cooperation.

ASEAN's caution is not surprising. Greater economic cooperation with Beijing since the 1990s has failed to spill over into the political-security realm, and Southeast Asian states continue to be concerned to varying degrees about China's growing military capabilities and its lack of transparency about its intentions. Beijing's renewed assertiveness over territorial and maritime disputes with ASEAN countries in the South China Sea since 2009, including the imposition of unilateral fishing bans, harassment of vessels from other nations, and its saber-rattling at sea with the Philippines over the Scarborough Shoal, has only compounded these fears. This unease has manifested itself in various forms over the last few years, from Singapore's founding father Lee Kuan Yew's speech in October 2009 urging the United States to balance a rising China to investments in naval capabilities by South China Sea claimants Vietnam, the Philippines, and most recently Malaysia.

Meanwhile, totally absent from China's new framework was any mention of dealing with the South China Sea with ASEAN as a region, although this dispute has been the main irritant in Beijing's relations with Southeast Asia. Instead, Chinese officials at the recent round of Asian summitry repeated their mantra: that the disputes should be addressed bilaterally and that other external actors should not interfere (*The Straits Times*, October 11). Beyond the rhetoric, Beijing's actions on the issue over the past few weeks have been worrying to say the least. Beijing disinvited Philippine president Benigno Aquino from the ASEAN–China Expo in Nanning, in apparent punishment for his government's decision to turn to the United Nations to challenge China's extensive maritime claims. More generally, experts say China has continued its foot-dragging on a binding code of conduct with ASEAN. Chinese officials continue to say that consultations should only be pushed forward in a step-by-step fashion, even as they work to delay meaningful progress by insisting that the issue be tackled by lower-level officials within the ASEAN–China Joint Working Group and proposing the establishment of an experts' group to address technical issues (*The Straits Times*, October 1). But as one Chinese commentator correctly noted, distrust of China will linger in Southeast Asia unless Beijing demonstrates its willingness to address key security issues head-on rather than hoping that economic cooperation will spill over into other areas (*Global Times*, October 15).

While these are serious obstacles to better ASEAN–China relations, they are not insurmountable and the new Chinese leadership is at least trying to overcome them. One way to mollify concerns about China's economic might, for instance, is to grant partners generous and customized concessions like the early harvest program Beijing offered to Southeast Asian states before the initial conclusion of the CAFTA. Premier Li appeared to employ a similar tactic on his visit to Thailand when he said Beijing would buy Thai rice and rubber—both of which the government has been struggling to sell (Associated Press, October 11). And in the security realm, progress on Beijing's proposed working group on joint exploration in dispute areas with Vietnam could at least demonstrate that there are alternative ways to approach the South China Sea issue aside from confrontations at sea or contentious arbitration the United Nations.

Ultimately though, if Beijing truly wants to forge an ASEAN–China "community of common destiny," as President Xi told

Indonesia's parliament, then it will require much more. The two-point political consensus embedded in the new leadership's cooperation framework holds that promoting cooperation should be based on strategic trust and good neighborliness, while deepening cooperation should be focused on advancing joint economic development. The problem for China, simply put, is that its relationship with ASEAN lacks strategic trust due to lingering security concerns, while prospects for joint economic development are limited by ASEAN's fear of domination by its larger neighbor. At the ASEAN–China Expo earlier this year, Chinese premier Li Keqiang described the past decade of ASEAN–China relations as a "golden decade" and said both sides have the power to create a "diamond decade" in the next ten years. But all that glitters is not gold. Indeed, China's diamond decade may quickly lose its shine if Beijing does not address ASEAN's concerns in a comprehensive fashion.

ASEAN'S RELATIONS WITH CHINA

In a series of meetings involving the Association of Southeast Asian Nations earlier held this month in Kuala Lumpur, China's moves to strengthen its effective control of disputed territories in the South China Sea — including land reclamation — took center stage. But the discussions also exposed ASEAN's limitations and weakness as a group as it failed to adopt a strong, unified stance against China, apparently due to internal divisions among members. It will be important for countries concerned, including the United States and Japan, to work out strategies to reduce regional tensions by taking into account the positions of individual ASEAN countries.

The Philippines and Vietnam are the most vocal in their criticism of China's recent actions, while Thailand and Malaysia take a softer attitude toward Beijing, probably because China has offered infrastructure-related assistance to these countries — a move apparently intended to divide ASEAN members.

A joint statement by the ASEAN foreign ministers was released Aug. 6 — two days after their meeting. It stated that they "remained seriously concerned over recent and ongoing developments in the area" — a reference to China's land reclamation activities around reefs and the construction of such facilities as radar towers and airstrips. On the basis of satellite images, the U.S. think tank Center for Strategic and International Studies says that China is engaged in land reclamation on Fiery Cross Reef in the Spratly Islands with the aim of building a 3,000-meter airstrip. The islands are claimed by Brunei, China, Malaysia, the Philippines, Taiwan and Vietnam. The center also says that an airstrip of the same length is nearing completion on the Spratly's Subu Reef, which is close to an area where Filipinos are living. These airstrips will be long enough for the takeoff and landing of strategic bombers. However, the foreign ministers refrained from naming China in their communique.

Although the foreign ministers stated that the land reclamation activities "have eroded trust and confidence, increased tensions and may undermine peace, security and stability in the South China Sea," they only "took note of the serious concerns expressed by some ministers" on the issue — an apparent reference to the foreign ministers of the Philippines and Vietnam.

An earlier draft of the statement expressed concern over the slow progress in the talks between ASEAN and China for a legally-binding code of conduct (COC) in the South China Sea to ease tensions in the area. But that part was deleted in the final statement, apparently out of consideration for China. The communique noted "progress in the consultations" on the COC and "reiterated the importance of the expeditious establishment of an effective COC."

In a meeting of the ASEAN Regional Forum (ARF) between members of the group and other Asia-Pacific countries, the U.S. and Japan expressed a strong concern over China's actions in the South China Sea. China reacted strongly by saying that countries located outside the area should not intervene in the matters of the area. The ARF consists of the ASEAN countries and countries around Southeast Asia, including China, Japan, the U.S., North and South Korea, Australia, Canada and Russia.

The U.S. is expanding its military exercises near the South China Sea in response to China's growing assertiveness in the area, while Japan has carried out a joint drill with the Philippines. In pushing his security bills in the Diet deliberations, Prime Minister Shinzo Abe emphasizes the threat from China in the East China Sea and South China Sea as a factor that necessitates the legislation. But both Tokyo and Washington need to realize that the ASEAN countries themselves are not monolithic in their dealings with China. Even countries engaged in territorial rows with China hesitate to have a head-on confrontation with Beijing due to their economic interests. Attempts by the U.S. or Japan to encircle China through closer ties with ASEAN might cause friction between them and the group, and possibly increase tensions in the area. Both countries should be aware of that risk and explore ways to defuse tensions in the area through dialogue with Beijing.

BALANCE OF POWER IN ASIA-PACIFIC

Behind the collapse of the Soviet Union and the disappearance of the four-decade-long Cold War structure, the entire nature of the geopolitical landscape in the Asia-Pacific region has dramatically changed. The bipolar equilibrium of the two superpowers broke down. As a result, regional players have commenced *a new game of balance of power.*

One of the main features of the regional strategic chessboard is the emergence of a new balance of power. The question of just how a balance of power is formed and what direction this new balance is moving in remains complicated, unpredictable, and even arguable. Nevertheless, it is likely characterized as an evolution in which no major conflict occurs, and the new power equation appears *as a flexible five-power equilibrium* in which no single power becomes a hegemon, while the United States and China play dominant roles. The relationships among the five Great Powers in the region (United States, China, Japan, Russia and India) are now geared to *both cooperation and competition,* instead of collusion and confrontation.

Under these circumstances, how should the future role of an expanding ASEAN, as middle-sized game-players in the Asia-Pacific region, be viewed and assessed? In other words, how will the new correlation of forces affect the interests and strategic posture of the states of Southeast Asia? Answering these questions would undoubtedly help identify various policy options that can best serve the benefits of ASEAN. This is of significant importance for ASEAN states, especially as we enter a new century.

The purpose of this chapter is to look into and understand a variety of factors, particularly the relationship between the United States and China, and how it affects the rallying of forces and the shaping of a new balance of power in the Asia-Pacific. Based on this, an attempt is made here to arrive at a critical evaluation of ASEAN's current posture, the problems that may arise, and the policy options taken by ASEAN that can contribute to the strengthening of its role and position.

The subject of the research is addressed in three parts. Part one deals with the concept of balance of power and the present balance of power in Asia-Pacific in the post-Cold War era. Part two concentrates on assessments of the US-China relationship, the trends of its future evolution, and its effects on the rallying of forces in the region. All ideas and observations relating to ASEAN's role and posture, its opportunities and challenges, as well as its strategic options in a new regional game, are contained in the final part of this paper.

PERCEPTION OF BALANCE OF POWER

In general, there are two main theoretical schools of international relations: *realism* and *liberalism*. *Realism* identifies the entire system of state relations based on criteria such as strength, power, geopolitics, geostrategy and the correlation of forces largely among Great Powers. *Liberalism* emphasizes other factors, such as economic interdependence, "soft" sources of power, and the role of international institutions and multilateralism.

According to many scholars, while various approaches could be considered supplementary, realism is the more dominant theoretical tradition since the policies of Great Powers and their relations have so far strongly influenced international affairs. Moreover, the regional and multilateral institutions would not be able to function without the participation of Great Powers.

The theory on balance of power is associated with realism and remains the most fundamental framework for understanding international relations. The concept of balance of power has historically been used to explain the actions of states in an insecure environment. The system was first formed and operationalized among the applied though debate on it continues.

Balance of Power: Meaning

Balance of power is perceived *as the basic concept in the relations among states*. Modern theory on balance of power is connected to the Newtonian conception of an universe in equilibrium. The substance of this theory is: *Under normal circumstances, all states always seek to maximize their power and international positions through various methods and techniques, and because of the adjustments of the "invisible hand", no one gains hegemony and an equilibrium in the international relations systems is maintained.*

This definition suggests a mechanism in which any attempt by any state to expand its power and attain dominance or hegemony that would allow it to impose its will on the other states will be resisted. No state, therefore, will be in a position to determine the fate of others.

Thus, a state of equilibrium in the international relations system is one in which no state becomes an absolute dominant power; more powerful states, in spite of pursuing various strategic interests, are satisfied with the existing territorial, adjustments may take place, no powerful state (or group of states) seeks to change the system fundamentally, as it would not yield additional benefits commensurate with the anticipated costs.

Consequently, the Great Powers have frequently supported the balance of power system throughout history, because they have both greater capacity to influence outcomes and the largest stake in the established order. In effect, balance of power mirrors the Great Powers' compromises on the distribution of benefits and spheres of influence in the world on the basis of their correlation of forces.

Rules of the Diversion

The aim of countervailing power is the protection of each state's security and the system in which these states exist as a whole. Therefore, the way to ensure each state's security is to prevent the emergence of any preponderant state that would lead to an upset of the existing status of equilibrium.

As Wolfer puts it, in balance of power terms, these rules can be stated in the following manner:

(a) Watch a potential adversary's power and match it.

(b) Ally oneself with a weaker state to restore the balance of power.

(c) Abandon such alliances when the balance has been restored and the common danger has passed.

(d) Regard national security interests as permanent; alliances must therefore change when a new threat rises.

(e) *Do not treat defeated states harshly through punitive peace treaties (today's adversary may be tomorrow's ally).*

Change of Balance

An international system is not maintained in a state of stable equilibrium when important shifts in the array of forces among states occur. There are two basic elements leading to the attempts to change the balance of power system:

- Differential growth in political, military and technological power that creates a change in the array of forces among states.
- Shifts in states' domestic political coalitions may necessitate redefinition of their "national interests" and foreign policies.

An equilibrium can be altered if there is a shift in political, military and technological capabilities of states and, as a result, *the expected benefits exceed the expected costs of bringing about a change in the system.* Victorious state or states would create the new peace settlements and status quo reflecting the redistribution of power in the system. The hegemonic wars in this view included the Thirty Years War from 1618-1648, the wars of King Louis XIV from 1667-1713, the Napoleonic Wars from 1792-1814, World War I from 1914-1918 and World War II from 1939-1945. However, resolution of crises is still possible through peaceful adjustment of the systemic disequilibrium, by compromises or moderation of the ambitions of emerging Great Powers. Essentially, it is the sharing of costs and benefits in keeping the status quo among the existing Great Powers.

The determinants of whether or not to create and maintain the international balance of power are the cost-benefit calculations that a state (or states) will make in the determination to change the existing equilibrium. The material environment (e.g., economic growth, demographic change, military technologies, communications and transportation conditions), the international system structures, and "internal" factors (e.g., leadership personalities, national identities, political-economic interests of groups and others in the society) provide incentives or disincentives for a state to attempt to change the international system.

Meaning of Implement a Balance of Power Policy

As J. Spanier explains, all states are very concerned about their strength or power for survival. To prevent an attack, a state must be *as powerful as potential aggressors; a disproportion of power may tempt another state. A balance of power is thus a prerequisite for each state's security.* When the balance is disturbed, the tendency is to take responsive action to return to a position of equilibrium. If states disregard the operational rule that power must be counterbalanced, they place their own security in jeopardy.

As Kissinger argues, *the balance of power serves to restrict the ability of states to dominate each other and to limit the scope of conflicts.* Kissinger views the balance of power not as an automatic mechanism, but instead as one of two possible outcomes of a situation in which states are obliged to deal with each other. One state can become so powerful that it dominates the others, or else the "pretensions" of the most aggressive member of the international community are kept in check by chosen by prudent leaders.

Harman, when studying the significance of theory on balance of power, asserts that *prudent states do not amass more enemies than they can effectively counter or handle at any one time. If states must deal with two or three adversaries, it would be wiser to concentrate on the strongest one by isolating and separating it from the others.* This principle is called the "conservation of enemies".

Chessmen on the New Strategic Chessboard

On the international strategic chessboard, the ranks of "chessmen" are classified by geopolitical, demographic, economic, military and traditional criteria in which geopolitics has significant importance. Generally, two ranks are identified: the first rank comprises *Great Powers,* whose scope of interests and capability of intervention reaches out beyond their borders. The second rank is comprised of *Middle and Small Powers,* which do not have (or have only a very few) of these roles to act, while the Middle and Small Powers are acted upon.

The "chessmen" positioned on the strategic chessboard in the Asia-Pacific are ranked as follows:

- *First* is a group of Great Powers that includes the United States, China, Japan, Russia and India. These are the chief game players in the strategic chessboard. Their positions, however, are not necessarily equal to one another:
  - The United States is currently the single superpower having political, economic and military might, and global influence.
  - China is an emerging power with an increasingly important voice in the regional economy and greater political influence in the Asia-Pacific. -Japan is an economic power whose political and military stature are not commensurate with its economic abilities.
  - Russia's international prestige declined sharply after the collapse of the Soviet Union. In spite of this, however, Russia still has a strong military force, including nuclear weapons.
  - India is now exercising its clout mainly in the South Asian region and is also viewed as a rising power.
- *Second* is a group of Middle Powers. These countries do not have great influence on the developments in the region, but they play an important role in balancing power, as they occupy strategic geopolitical positions and are the Korea, and Vietnam.
- *Third* are Small Powers (Laos, Cambodia, Singapore) and some very small states like Brunei (with a population of

300,000 people), and the Marshall Islands (with a population of 40,000 people). Those countries can only make worthwhile stands when they are engaged in alliances or alignments with other actors.

- *In addition,* some scholars of liberalism have flirted with the idea that new transnational actors, such as international and regional organizations, NGOs and multinational corporations, are gradually playing a greater role in international affairs.

EFFECTS ON OTHER GREAT POWERS' POSITION

The United States, China, and the other Great Powers do not want to see this scenario occur, as they all will be placed in a very difficult situation in dealing with one another. However, if this case should come about, *the process of rallying forces will be followed by two blocks, with one block comprised of the United States and its allies, the other block comprised of China and its allies, and with the rest in between the two sides.* Specifically:

- Polarization is in place, with the United States and Japan on the one side (based on US-Japan Security Pact), and China and Russia on the other.
- China seeks alliances with other Asian nations (based on cultural and religious similarities), which may lead to a loose coalition between China and India and Japan (the US-Japan Security Pact to be nullified by China) to limit US influence in the region.

When China becomes more powerful and more aggressive, other Great Powers may ally with the United States to curb China's ambitions.

Regarding options taken in dealing with the United States and China, two hypotheses can be put forward:

- Russia, Japan, and India improve their relations with both the United States and China, thus making *a concert of power.* Coordination among Great Powers is formulated in solving regional and international issues in which the United States and China play leading roles.

- After the establishment of strategic partnerships, the United States and China attach less importance to their relations with other Great Powers or even compromise on each others' interests. The consequent gradual decline of the role played by Japan, Russia, and India in the strategies of the United States and China therefore compel them to regroup to struggle for their balanced interests.

As the US-China relationship is largely driven by a mixture of cooperation and competition, both countries must attach greater importance to broadening their relations with external forces so that other countries will have more policy choices that conform to their own interests.

Effects on Middle and Small Powers' Status

The Middle and Small Powers often have less opportunity to act rather than be acted upon by the adjustments of Great Powers' strategies in complicated international relations. In Asia, the relations of neighbouring countries with China and the status of its relations with other Great Powers.

Middle and Small Powers in dealing with Great Powers:

- To ally or align with one single Great Power and rely on security, political, and economic protections from that Power.
- To participate in the games, but keep balanced relations with all Great Powers.
- To stay out of the games and keep neutral like Finland and Switzerland (the mode called "Finlandization").

Because of the widely diversified interests of all countries, there is a variety of behaviors. In view of many fundamental changes in the world today (e.g., the existence of multipower balance, growing globalization, highly interdependent conditions), *alignment is likely to be seen instead of the classical alliance, and no nation is likely to stay outside or be "neutral."*

Dibb observes that in these uncertain circumstances, Middle Powers in the region are likely to view their own interests as best served by preserving an equilibrium among Great Powers. He cites Amitav Acharya, who notes that the ASEAN states' preferred approach to regional order seems to lie in the maintenance of a regional mechanisms remain critical to the prospects for regional order in the post-Cold War era. The Middle Powers are likely to feel threatened by the domination of the Asia-Pacific region by any one Great Power, and to regard some measures of checks and balances on each by the other as the condition of their own security. According to Dibb, *all the Middle and Small Powers in the region seek ways to avoid tendencies of either a keen rivalry or confrontation or a concert of Great Powers,* because these scenarios leave them less space for maneuver.

It is anticipated therefore that whatever US-China relations develop, *Middle and Small Powers naturally opt to participate in the balance of power game, maintaining balanced relations with the Great Powers, especially with the United States and China on the one hand, and regrouping themselves to raise counterweights in dealing with those Great Powers on the other.*

EFFECTS OF US-CHINA RELATIONS ON THE BEARING OF ASEAN COUNTRIES

ASEAN is an association comprised of all ten Southeast Asian nations that are not regarded as powerful states having dominant influence on developments in Asia-Pacific or in the world as a whole. However, ASEAN captures an important position in Great Powers' strategies as *ASEAN states are ranked Middle Powers (some of them have become newly industrialized countries) and are geographically situated in sensitive areas in the region.* Brzezinski argues that these Middle Powers are "geopolitical pivots" that have very significant political and cultural consequences for more active neighbouring geostrategic players. Moreover, the landscape in Southeast Asia today is strikingly different from that of the Cold War period. For the first time since 1945, Southeast Asia is a relatively peaceful and stable region, where a state of confrontation in the relationships

All ASEAN states are now actively involved in a regional integration process for the benefit of their own development, and the association has emerged as a noticeable political and economic centre in Asia-Pacific. In spite of new challenges posed by ASEAN's expansion, its remarkable achievements recorded in all fields over the past three decades are undeniable, and up to now ASEAN has basically preserved its solidarity, cohesion, regional self-reliance and self-resistance identities. ASEAN is also a unique regional organization in a developing world, which successfully attracts all major Centres and Great Powers to engage in regional political, security, economic forums.

For that reason, *ASEAN asserts itself as an indispensable element in the establishment of a new balance of power and regional order in Asia-Pacific in the post-Cold War era.*

Some are of the view that ASEAN's position in the regional strategic chessboard is no longer considered as important as before, when "certain arrangements" were directly made by Great Powers. Even so, it is obvious that the international game today is entirely changing. If all chessmen had to entrust their fates to one general on the board during the Cold War, they are now in mixed positions. Every chessman, even a pawn, has its own soul, fate, and moves on the board, though growing international posture, ASEAN's role will be increasingly enhanced.

Location of ASEAN in the US Asia-Pacific Strategy

Stemming from the strategic requirements of the United States as well as ASEAN's political role and economic dynamism, ASEAN constitutes a considerable element in the US policy vis-a-vis Asia-Pacific, particularly in the context of the higher priority given to this region and China's rise as a new power. Furthermore, this region is also capturing increased attention from other Great Powers.

Given these considerations, the United States wants to see a continued prosperous and American-influenced Southeast Asia serving the political and economic interests of the United States in the region and becoming a counterweight to China and Japan so as not allow these countries to control the region and modify the balance of power. Economically, ASEAN is viewed as an attractive potential market with enormous trade and investment opportunities (the region consists of 500 million people and a total GDP of $600-1000 billion), and the United States has great interest in promoting economic ties with ASEAN.

Accordingly, the Unites States has reaffirmed its continued commitment to the region, applauding ASEAN's position economically and politically, and has encouraged ASEAN to be a driving force in building up regional security mechanisms. Recently, the United States has devoted further attention in assisting those ASEAN countries affected by economic crises in overcoming difficulties, thus preventing the danger of spreading regional disturbances, and limiting the negative impacts on the US economy.

Position of ASEAN in China's Asia-Pacific Approach

China's consistent strategic objective is to become a powerful political, economic and military state in the world, first and foremost in Asia-Pacific. To realize this goal, China on the one hand seeks to develop cooperative relations with all countries, especially the United States and other Great Powers, just as it takes advantage of other countries' constraints and difficulties to enhance its own role in the region. Southeast Asia is perceived as China's traditional "backyard" and ASEAN is an important competing object that China needs to win over in order to strengthen its position and create a counterbalance to the other Great Powers in Asia-Pacific.

Over the last few years, China's ties with the Southeast Asian states have been continuously fostered and developed into full-fledged partnership, while China's relations with other Great Powers have been complicated. Remarkably, China has undertaken a series of activities aimed at consolidating and building up a comprehensive cooperation programs in political, economic, security, military, cultural fields for the twenty-first century, marking a new milestone in the China-ASEAN relationship.

However, China has reaffirmed on several occasions since 1991 its claim to sovereignty of the Spratly Islands, and has projected military forces there (adoption of state law on territorial waters in 1992; proclamations of basic lines in 1996; economic special exclusive zones and continental shelves with an area of over 3.5 million square kilometers; construction of structures in Mischief Reef; a ban on fishing in the Spratly Islands). Some scholars have argued that China has taken advantage of US preoccupation with

European affairs to vigorously expand its own role in Asia and Southeast Asia.

ASEAN's opportunities and challenges originate from its position on the regional strategic chessboard.

CONSTRUCTIVE CONDITIONS AND OPPORTUNITIES FOR ASEAN

From a balance of power perspective, ASEAN states currently enjoy fundamentally favourable conditions for the implementation of their foreign policies. With the end of the Cold War, peace and development have prevailed in the international relations in the region. Great Powers, namely the United States, China, Japan, Russia and India, have been willing to compromise and seek coordination, creating a relatively balanced and stable framework of their relations. All these factors have contributed to an ongoing favourable environment. Moreover, the Great Powers' possession of nuclear weapons constitutes, to some extent, a deterrent balance in the region. In the next fifteen to twenty years, China still needs to maintain stable international relations, especially with Great Powers and its neighbours, to realize its four modernizations (i.e., agriculture, industry, culture and military). The political and economic advances that ASEAN has made over the last thirty years, as well as the international prestige, have helped lay solid foundations for ASEAN's future.

At present, ASEAN is not tied to any Great Power military alliance and an no longer be dragged into any balance of power game as in the Cold War. *Thus, ASEAN has considerable choices and scope to maneuver in the regional game.*

Difficulties and Challenge for ASEAN

The first challenge is ASEAN's inescapable "security dilemma." The security of ASEAN is closely linked to that of the Asia-Pacific region and to the global policy considerations of the Great Powers. As a consequence of its geography and historical background, any single gesture made by ASEAN in its relations with the United States or other Great Powers is understandably very "sensitive" to China, just as any further improvement in ASEAN's relations with China is understandably very "sensitive" to the United States, Japan and other Great Powers.

Faced with unceasing fluctuations of the array of forces among Great Powers and unpredictable complexities while the Asia-Pacific region still lacks region-wide comprehensive cooperation and security mechanisms to regulate potential rivalries, how to build a more balanced relations with Great Powers and to limit their shoulders in the conduct of international relations.

The second challenge is ASEAN's ability to "manage" sources of conflict with Great Powers. While other regions were able to develop peacefully after World War II, the ASEAN states had to face the sufferings and consequences of continued wars and conflicts. Besides that, the sources of conflict that existed in the region remain unsolved, as illustrated by various forms of territorial and natural resource disputes, and differences on levels of economic, historical, cultural and religious development. The crucial challenge for ASEAN therefore lies in its ability to manage these sources of conflict without the possibility of provocation from Great Powers, and to restrain the conjuncture of being affected, controlled, or even imposed upon with a "rule of the game" by Great Powers.

The third challenge is the question of the Indochinese peninsula, which is tacitly understood as the "sensitive" zone of Southeast Asia. For the Southeast Asian region, Indochina is of great geostrategic importance and often draws the Great Powers' special attention. This fact is demonstrated by those complexities of Great Powers' deep involvement throughout the Cold War period.

This is a difficult math for both the Southeast Asian mainlanders and islanders in seeking a policy on balance of power among Great Powers for the common sake of the association.

4

China Playing a Rising Role in ASEAN Business

Being export and investment-oriented, the Association of Southeast Asian Nations economies have benefited from the Chinese market, which has fostered the bloc's rising momentum in both of its economic growth drivers, experts said. ASEAN member countries, including Malaysia, Singapore and Thailand, are considered to be the world's most burgeoning economies at a time of global economic fluctuation. It started a new era of its cooperation with China in 2010, when the China-ASEAN free trade zone was launched.

The free trade association, benefiting a population of 1.9 billion and with a GDP of nearly $6 trillion, also signals China's new steps toward the bilateral coordination mechanism. The two sides plan to increase bilateral trade to $1 trillion by 2020. Zhang Hemin, a Malaysian- Chinese, came to Nanning, the capital city of Guangxi Zhuang autonomous region, during China's National Day holiday to sell rubber products.

"Because China's domestic demand is booming, we expect to set a foothold in the huge market and, more importantly, to gain from China's efforts to promote trade with ASEAN trading partners," Zhang said.

From $55 billion in 2002, bilateral trade between China and ASEAN increased to $400 billion in 2012. Over the past decade Sino-ASEAN trade has jumped more than 600 percent. Malaysia has been China's largest trading partner among ASEAN members since 2009. China has overtaken Singapore to become Malaysia's largest export market.

Rubber is one of the main exports from Malaysia to China. While, Zhang's company is only one of thousands from ASEAN member countries tapping into the Chinese market and exporting various goods ranging from agricultural, electronic to textiles. China's ongoing structural transformation and upgrading is not only being conducted as a key way to maintain sustainable economic growth but also to act as a big attraction to foreign trading partners.

"Since the global financial crisis, ASEAN economies have suffered a slowdown. But the Chinese market has fueled and helped drive the economic growth of the community," said Mei Xinyu, a senior researcher at the Chinese Academy of International Trade and Economic Cooperation.

"China has already become a stabilizer of the economic development of ASEAN members," Mei added. Former ASEAN Secretary-General Surin Pitsuwan said China is such a huge market that everyone wants to enter it so ASEAN economies will grow alongside China.

"We should also get involved in China's supply and production lines," he said. At the opening ceremony of the 10th China-ASEAN Expo in September, Premier Li Keqiang vowed to further reduce tariffs, initiate service trade negotiations and ease market access in the investment area as main measures to upgrade the Sino-ASEAN Free Trade Association.

The China-ASEAN FTA is the world's third-largest. Since it was launched, bilateral economic cooperation has become a model for international trade exchange globally. The growing convergence of southeast Asian economies has become a real attraction for foreign investors to enter the emerging economy. Li also said China would like to reach a long-term agreement on agriculture trade with ASEAN and actively increase imports of competitive products from the association.

Apart from that, the government also plans to promote bilateral investment to $150 billion within the next eight years. The China-ASEAN FTA brings benefits in terms of both trade and investment, according to Pitsuwan. By the end of 2012, accumulated bilateral investment between China and ASEAN reached $100.7 billion, of which investment from China accounted for 23.4 percent and that from ASEAN was 76.6 percent, according to the China-ASEAN Business Council. In 2012, China's investment in ASEAN economies was $4.42 billion, up 52 percent from a year earlier. Bilateral investment was valued at $11.49 billion, of which Chinese investment accounted for 38.5 percent.

"China's investment in ASEAN economies witnessed a faster-pace of growth than ASEAN's investment in China last year. The proportion in total has been rising in recent years," said Xu Ningning, executive secretary-general of the business council. By the end of 2012, Singapore had become the destination where Chinese companies invested most among ASEAN members, followed by Cambodia, Burma, Indonesia and Laos, according to data from the business council.

"Thanks to China's good economic momentum, competitive Chinese enterprises have actively invested in developed and emerging economies, driving global economic development. Many Chinese companies have expanded their businesses in Singapore," said Tan Lui Hai, economic counselor at the Singapore Embassy in China. Tan said China is the center of Asia and Singapore would like to be a gateway for Chinese investors' global expansion.

Ong Chong Yi, minister counselor for economic affairs at the Malaysian embassy in China, said that over the past three years Chinese investors have been active in the construction sector in Malaysia but have less presence in the service sector. "The liberalization of the country's service sector gives Chinese companies opportunities to explore new areas of business," Ong said. "Factors including strong complementary trade, broad market access and rich reserves of natural resources in ASEAN economies have boosted Chinese investment flowing to them in recent years," said Xu at the business council.

US, CHINA ROLE PLAY FOR ASEAN

Southeast Asian policymakers looking north to the Asian mainland and east across the Pacific Ocean see two major, different, and complementary assets to their region: China's biggest-in-the-world economy and America's best-in-the-world military. This is not to underestimate the economic importance of America to Southeast Asia. For all the hype about China's rise and America's fall, measured by the value of trade and investment flows, the Association of Southeast Asian Nations (ASEAN) economies' interactions with China and the United States in 2009 were equally robust.

China and the United States each imported 10.1% of the total value of ASEAN's exports. As for inflows of foreign direct investment into the ASEAN economies, of that total in 2009, China and the United States accounted for almost identical shares - respectively 10.4% and 10.8%. But a snapshot is not a film. These equalities filled a single frame in an ongoing video of progressively greater disparities in the relative importance of China and America to ASEAN's economies. Back in 2003 America took in more than three times the share of ASEAN's exports absorbed by China - 19% versus 6%. Seen from Southeast Asia, that American advantage over China has since disappeared. From 2003 to 2008, China's share of all Southeast Asian trade burgeoned at an astonishing 26% average annual pace - a rate that the American market could not match.

China's economic importance to its southern neighbors will only increase in future as Western economies retrench, barring a Chinese financial crisis to come. China will not escape collateral damage if the eurozone implodes and political paralysis in Washington allows American budget deficits and national debts to spiral unchecked toward an estimated worst-case US$22 trillion over the next decade. But China could still emerge from such extreme turbulence relatively better off than Europe or America, and thus better equipped to cushion the shocks to Southeast Asia.

Southeast Asians are by no means giving up on the American market, on American investment, or even on American financing. All of the policy analysts I have met so far on this trip through Southeast Asia want American economic engagement. There is nevertheless a tendency in Southeast Asia to think of Beijing and Washington as playing specialized roles: China the economic partner who facilitates prosperity, America the security provider who guards the peace.

Such a dichotomy is understandable. It captures the comparative advantage for Southeast Asia that each outsider has to offer: China's booming economy, America's matchless military. It avoids the risk - many Southeast Asians would say the folly - of entrusting regional security to the People's Liberation Army Navy, or PLAN, let alone the PLA.

Whether China seeks hegemony over the region is a matter on which many disagree. But ASEAN will not willingly invite China to replace the American security role in Southeast Asia, not if Beijing continues to assert forcefully its control over nearly the entire South China Sea - or, as some Vietnamese and Philippine activists would like it to be called, the Southeast Asia Sea.

As for valuing America more for its might than its market, Southeast Asians want to trade more with America, attract more of its investment, and benefit more from its technology. But they fear that America's domestic woes and partisan politics may turn its priorities inward, away from Asia. What they want from the United States is protection from harm not harmful protectionism. They know that only following a prolonged struggle did the Barack Obama administration finally persuade Congress to approve a trade agreement with South Korea. Exaggerations of America's economic decline make China look all the more like the future.

Competing communities

Reinforcing this ostensible division of labor is the economic success of China's preferred regional vehicle, ASEAN Plus Three (APT), which excludes the United States, compared with the prominence of security on the evolving agenda of the East Asia Summit (EAS), to which both China and the United States belong.

Beijing prefers the East Asia-only APT to the larger EAS where its influence is diluted. China sees the APT, which also includes Japan and South Korea, as a nascent East Asian Community based on trade and investment, a vision that ASEAN shares. Located as it is on the "wrong" - eastern - side of the Pacific, America is obliged by geography to cultivate a trans-Pacific space.

America's then-president Bill Clinton expressed that oceanic - westward - American priority when he hosted the first-ever meeting of the leaders of the Asia-Pacific Economic Cooperation (APEC) forum, which includes China, in the west-coast city of Seattle in 1993. That Pacific outlook was even more evident in the Hawaiian location of the APEC leaders' meeting just hosted by President Obama. But APEC has not lived up to its original promise as the basis for a trans-Pacific economic community - a Free Trade Area of the Asia Pacific (FTAAP).

Two questions arise: Should the economy-focused APT aspire to play a security role? Conversely, should the EAS privilege security alone, or should it also develop an economic agenda? Underscoring the timeliness of these questions is the consecutive scheduling of the APEC leaders' meeting in Honolulu on November 12-13 and the EAS here in Nusa Dua, Indonesia on November 19. Under present conditions the APT will not enlarge its footprint to encompass traditional security. China has not pressed for such an expansion of the APT's terms of reference, and the ASEAN states are too suspicious of Beijing to go along. China will eventually play a hard-power regional security role of some kind, welcome or not. But for now, Southeast Asian leaders do not want to jeopardize the economic success of the APT by adding visceral issues of sovereignty and security to its agenda.

ASEAN hopes that China will someday sign what still does not exist - a binding Code of Conduct on the South China Sea. But even if that happens, ASEAN will not willingly ask Beijing to be the sole sponsor of regional security in East or Southeast Asia. In this delicate context, a security focus for the EAS amounts to a hedge against unwanted Chinese assertion. That hedge is still purely symbolic, however. To the extent that the United States credibly underwrites Asian-Pacific security, it does so through treaties and ties that are bilateral not multilateral, and the EAS to date has been little more than an annual conversation.

If APT will not soon evolve into a full-spectrum outfit by adding security to economic concerns, how about the EAS? Will its purview expand in the opposite direction, adding the regional economy to regional security as an object of its attention?

No full-service venue

Chinese officials did not welcome the formation of the EAS and appear reluctant now to incorporate economic affairs into its terms of reference. Beijing is loath to further empower a vehicle through which the United States and its democratic friends outside East Asia - India, Australia, and New Zealand also belong to the Summit - could frustrate Chinese goals. If China is already *primus inter pares* among the 13 APT economies and is becoming the hub of the global economy, some in Beijing may see in the 18-member EAS the next concentric circle in which to augment Chinese economic influence. But China's current priority is to grow APT into an East Asian economic community that reflects and projects China's own comparative advantage.

Like the Hu Jintao administration in Beijing, but for very different reasons, the Obama administration does not want the EAS to become an economic summit. APEC already is one; why duplicate the "E" for "Economic" in that forum's name? More recent, and conceivably more important, is what American policymakers perceive to be the accelerating momentum of a novel arrangement that is still being negotiated: the Trans-Pacific Strategic Economic Partnership Agreement, or Trans-Pacific Partnership (TPP).

Not long ago, when the TPP first appeared on their horizon, policy wonks rushed to Wikipedia to find out what it was. Its Lilliputian size and odd geography made it hard to take seriously. A 2005 agreement between Brunei, Chile, New Zealand, and Singapore seemed far too thin and dispersed to be the end of a larger wedge.

Since then, however, five more countries - Australia, Malaysia, Peru, the United States, and Vietnam - have agreed to participate in negotiations with a view toward joining the group. Canada, Japan, the Philippines, South Korea, and Taiwan have also expressed interest in possibly signing on. A juggernaut the TPP is not. The high quality of the agreement helps to explain the low quantity of its members, who must commit themselves to comprehensive economic liberalization, including provisions on intellectual property, labor, and the environment. This high bar to entry may well enhance the agreement's impact, and it appeals to American politicians averse to "unfair" trade.

But its provisions will be harder to endorse in countries that protect agriculture, repress labor, appropriate technology, and resent the costs of "greening" their economies. Its rules on intellectual property are especially controversial. This would matter less if the TPP were content to be a club of the few. But the Agreement expressly aims (in Article 1.1.3) "to support the wider liberalization process in APEC consistent with its goals of free and open trade and investment." This mandate opens the TPP to interpretation as a would-be vanguard of freer trade in that far larger and less welcoming context.

Linked as the TPP is to APEC, the Obama administration would rather encourage that vanguard role in a two-track division of labor between the TPP/APEC (economy) and the EAS (security).

Deterrence in Darwin?

As I write this, President Obama is in Darwin, Australia, en route to attend the 6th East Asia Summit here in Bali on November 19. But Darwin is more than a convenient stopover between Australia and Indonesia. The Obama administration and its counterpart in Canberra have agreed that 2,500 American marines will eventually be rotated through that north-coastal Australian city every six months or so for exercises and training with the Australian Defense Force. From Darwin, Indonesia's own coast is less then 500 miles away. "New US Base in [Indonesia's] Backyard" ran the disapproving front-page headline in The Jakarta Post on November 17.

The American contingent will be available for rapid relief should a natural disaster strike Indonesia. But in answer to a question on the Darwin deployment at a press conference prior to Obama's arrival in Bali, Indonesian foreign minister Marty Natalegawa did not mention this positive aspect of the American presence.

He emphasized the strictly bilateral nature of the Australian-American agreement to post the marines to Darwin - in effect, distancing Indonesia from the decision. He made no mention of

China. But clearly he was thinking of Beijing when he said that he "would hate to see" the marines' stationing trigger a "vicious cycle of tensions and mistrust" in the region.

In contrast, a Philippine official called the American troop move useful, and he did not have disaster relief in mind. The move, he said, "bolsters our ability to assert our sovereignty over certain areas, yes" - strengthening Manila's hand in negotiations with Beijing over the South China Sea. This was probably not what the other Southeast Asian claimants to parts of the Sea would have wanted to hear.

Beijing's first responses to the Darwin decision were muted. A foreign ministry spokesman did nevertheless link economy to security when he observed that "it may not be appropriate [for the United States] to intensify and expand military alliances at a time when [its] economy is still recovering." Read with just a hint of*Schadenfreude*: The deep-in-debt Americans can't afford to raise their security profile in Asia.

America is not and does not wish to be seen as a half-super power in Asia, consigned only to a security role. It is not in the interest of the United States for Southeast Asians to go to the Americans for ships, but to the Chinese for sales - as an American here in Bali expressed it. However warranted it may be in other contexts, the Darwin decision has reinforced this association. It has also increased the chance that Washington could be seen as siding with this or that claimant in the dispute over the South China Sea. It does not help in this context that in Manila recently Secretary of State Hillary Clinton called this body of water the "West Philippine Sea".

In 2008-09 then-prime minister of Australia Kevin Rudd proposed a full-spectrum framework equipped with a summit that could address problems with both economic and political causes, results, and interactions. His idea was not well conceived or presented at the time. But the absence of such a venue may be regretted nonetheless, as the latest financial crisis continues to illustrate so painfully the elusiveness of global financial security, the need for transnational coordination and governance reform to speed economic recovery, and the rising role of the Pacific Rim in seeking and sustaining long-term solutions. The Obama administration deserves credit for having pivoted toward Asia and involving itself adroitly in the multilateral economic and security architecture that it found here. That American involvement may be harder to focus on and fund, however, as confrontational domestic politics in the run-up to next November's elections and fiscal restraints in response to the financial crisis make a high worldwide profile on security harder to afford.

Drawdowns in Iraq and Afghanistan should help. So, too, will a more concerted effort to rebalance America's profile toward greater and more productive engagements with Asians in economic terms.

5

China and ASEAN: Negotiating a New Approach to Security

China and ASEAN are currently engaged in "negotiations" of two security arrangements, Treaty of Good Neighborliness, Friendship and Cooperation between China and ASEAN countries and the Code of Conduct of Parties in the South China Sea (COC).

ASEAN will establish the only sub-regional Community in the Asia Pacific by the end of 2015. And China is the biggest emerging and second largest economy in the world. Thus the security arrangements between China and ASEAN will have significant impact on the evolution of the regional order.

The paper argues that the consultation and negotiation of the two documents are part of the trust-building process between China and ASEAN, which formally started with China's accession to the Treaty of Amity and Cooperation and the signing of the Declaration of Conduct of Parties in the South China Sea (DOC).

Such process is more about trust-building than conflict prevention/resolution.

The two documents will embody and enhance ASEAN's norm of cooperative security and China's norm of developmental security. They will complement the regional security network and co-evolve with the U.S. security alliances and other security arrangements in shaping the regional order.

CHINA AND ASEAN: EFFORTS TOWARD REGIONAL SECURITY

Since its establishment in 1967, ASEAN has managed to maintain peace not only among its members, but also with its partners. Its security-community building efforts started with the Treaty of Amity and Cooperation in Southeast Asia (TAC) and were sustained through pragmatic cooperation process in the ASEAN Way of consensus, comfort level and minimum institutionalism. The establishment of ASEAN not only guaranteed peaceful resolution of disputes among its five founding members, but also prevented them from falling into the victims of the bipolar confrontation. In the late 1980s and early 1990s, ASEAN expanded to include all countries in Southeast Asia, engaging those of different political systems in building one community and hence peace becoming an inherent norm. In shaping a larger region, ASEAN has applied an "ASEAN +" institutional structure, played a "soft balancing" strategy among major powers, and socialized outside players in the building of a region toward peace, prosperity and progress.

Despite the general perception that China's security cooperation with ASEAN lagged behind its economic engagements, China was the first major power outside ASEAN that committed itself to ASEAN way of regional security and China has become increasingly active in regional security cooperation. China was the first major power outside ASEAN that signed TAC, established strategic partnership with ASEAN, and expressed willingness to sign Treaty on the Southeast Asia Nuclear Weapon-Free Zone. In 2002, China signed DOC with ASEAN countries, which has played a significant role in nurturing the habit of maintaining peace and cooperation at sea and laid important foundation for the consultation and negotiation of the COC. At the institutional level, China joined ASEAN Regional Forum initiated by ASEAN in 1994 and has become increasingly active in preventive diplomacy. Entering the second decade of China-ASEAN strategic partnership, China initiated the consultation and negotiation of the Treaty of Good Neighborliness, Friendship and Cooperation with ASEAN countries, proposed China-ASEAN Defense Ministers Meeting, advocated a concept of common, comprehensive, cooperative and sustainable security and supported the "dual track" approach in resolving disputes and maintaining peace in the South China Sea.

LOCALITY AND SECURITY NORM

In their efforts toward a secure region, ASEAN and China have developed distinctive ideas and norms of regional security, which are embedded in the local context. Acharya argues that local normative hierarchy is key in determining whose norms matter. For both ASEAN and China, non-intervention is fundamental in their normative hierarchy. Therefore, it is not surprising that ASEAN has transformed the "international" norm of "common security" into local norm of "cooperative security", that none of the treaties or declarations signed by China and ASEAN have strong legally binding force, and that a collective security institution like NATO was not implanted in East Asia.

Adhering to cooperative security, ASEAN has maximized its security through cooperation within itself and with outside partners. And with greater security, ASEAN can continue to consolidate, expand and upgrade cooperation. "Non-intervention" of internal affairs and separation between regional and domestic security have allowed maximum cooperation among members of diversified cultures and political systems and with inadequate strategic and political trust. And China, by advocating sustainable security, actually is contributing a new element to the regional security norm based on its own experience, that is, developmental security.

The basic idea of sustainable and developmental security is that there is no guarantee of security without social and economic development, and hence in the cooperation for greater security, priority should be placed on development.

For instance, maritime cooperation for pragmatic benefits is a major part of the DOC. Cooperation and development can also be expected to be key elements of the COC and the Treaty of Good Neighborliness, Friendship and Cooperation. Both treaties can be more institutionalized and more legally-binding than "declarations". But trust-building is still to outweigh conflict-resolution and the local elements of cooperation and development are likely to remain fundamental.

Patchwork, network and evolution of security order

Victor Cha argues that a regional architecture of complex patchwork is emerging in East Asia, which is fluid and inclusive, with all bilaterals, trilaterals and multilaterals threaded together by the U.S. security alliance. However, the East Asian regional architecture is more like fluid and ever-expanding network than patchwork.

What threads and connects the nodes in the complex network is not alliance, but norm, norm-defined security arrangements and norm-nurtured identification. China and ASEAN are making progressive efforts in deepening and institutionalizing security cooperation for a more secure region. The consultation and negotiation of the COC and the Treaty are thread-weaving efforts in strengthening the network. Cooperative and developmental security will co-evolve with collective security and "security alliance" in shaping the regional security order. And compatibility and integration of the networking processes depends on agency of all stakeholders in the region.

TRADITIONAL SECURITY THREATS

Three Major Potential Clashes in the Region

The unfinished civil wars between North and South Korea, as well as between mainland China and Taiwan, are legacies of the Cold War in the Asia Pacific. "These tense areas of political conflict stand out as the greatest threats to regional stability in East Asia for the foreseeable future." Given the significance of these potential conflicts, as well as that of the Spratly Islands in the South China Sea, each will be addressed in some detail.

The Korean Peninsula

The situation on the Korean peninsula has been described as "perhaps the most urgent security challenge in the world." Little progress has been made in peacebuilding since the signing of the Armistice Agreement in 1953. The two sides remain technically at war, divided by the most heavily armed border in the world. The North Korean regime, with its starving population, remains internationally isolated. Predictions as to what will happen on the peninsula range from the imminent collapse of the North Korean regime to a gradual reunification based on incremental economic change.

The sudden collapse of North Korea would likely result in massive refugee flows to South Korea, Japan, China, and Russia. Threatened by the internal instability that such large population movements would create, one or more of these countries may reach the conclusion that it is in their national interests to send in troops to restore order. Also, a sudden collapse might prompt members of the North Korean regime to engage in armed conflict, if only to improve their negotiating position in later reunification talks. This scenario has been referred to as "the suicide-threat option."

A more immediate concern is that South Korea will be unable to finance the two light water reactors promised to the North as part of the Agreement to disband its suspected nuclear weapons program. Some officials are worried that, should the South be unable to fulfil its promise, the North will resume its nuclear program. That the North may become a nuclear power is not only a threat in and of itself, but it could prompt a nuclear arms race in the region as countries tried to bolster their sense of security.

China and Taiwan

Another matter that continues to be a source of concern is the conflict between mainland China and Taiwan. In 1996, China engaged in large-scale military exercises in the Straits of Taiwan during Taiwan's presidential elections. While the confrontational rhetoric has since been tempered, tension between China and Taiwan continues. Predictions as to what China will do are hard to make, since, as with the Korean situation, the range of opinions varies widely. While some authors see the build up of the Chinese military as a harbinger of invasion, others doubt that such a direct move will be made and instead predict continued low-level military intimidation over a long period of time..

The South China Sea

A third potential source of conflict that has been drawing a considerable amount of attention is the land claim dispute that has arisen in the South China Sea, especially over the Spratly Islands. Six governments – Brunei, Malaysia, the People's Republic of China (PRC), the Philippines, Taiwan, and Vietnam – have all laid claim to all or some of the region. The islands in question are considered important for strategic security reasons, commercial shipping, fish, and, potentially, hydrocarbons. This last resource is particularly important as it is often by granting hydrocarbon concessions in disputed zones that claimant states exercise jurisdiction.

Competition to assert sovereignty has led to numerous occupations and low-level military confrontations between the several claimants. This dispute is not likely to be resolved soon. Despite their small size these islands are very important, not only for the reasons already mentioned but because they lie astride the principal sea lines of communication linking the Indian and Pacific Ocean. Should one country succeed in gaining control of all the Spratly Islands, there would be a significant shift in the balance of power in the region.

Internal Armed Conflicts

Each year, the Stockholm International Peace Research Institute (SIPRI) identifies the thirty largest armed conflicts in the world. In the 1997 edition, four of the thirty conflicts identified by SIPRI were located within the Asia Pacific region. Specifically, large armed conflicts exist within Indonesia, Myanmar (Burma), Philippines, and Cambodia. Although these conflicts are considered to be the major ones, they, unfortunately, do not represent all the existing armed conflicts in the area. Appendix 4 lists the internal (intrastate) conflicts in the Asia Pacific region.

"In each of these cases, we have soft states. Economic and social development occurred at a very impressive rate in very impressive ways throughout Southeast and East Asia. What lagged behind was the state.... The problem is one of state building." The significance of internal conflicts for regional stability must be recognised. Mr. Martin Rudner (Professor, Norman Patterson School of International Affairs, Carleton University) told the Committee that the weak state is perhaps one of the greatest challenges to the Asia Pacific region. While economic and social development occurred at a very impressive rate throughout Southeast and East Asia during the age of the "Asian Miracle," institutions, such as parliaments and legislative systems, lagged behind in development. Mr. Rudner pointed out that the electoral processes remained underdeveloped and political party systems, in all cases, were compromised by patron-client relationships. Today, a minimal public infrastructure and negligible social amenities exist in most of these countries, and the states are, for the most part, unable to respond to the demands of their citizens. Despite this lack of institutional development, it was possible to function during the period of economic growth; however, when the countries in the region were hit by the economic crisis, the legitimacy of even the states themselves came to be questioned.

The collapse of states from within is a security risk: when a state loses its ability to govern effectively, it invites external intervention. Efforts by a weak state to defend itself, combined with efforts of the stronger state to exploit the cleavages in the weakened state, can lead to intensified interstate strife.

The situation in Indonesia, the fourth most populous country in the world, is of particular concern and therefore warrants elaboration. Within Indonesia, there are a number of groups fighting for autonomy: in Northern Sumatra, East Timor, Irian Jaya, Aceh, Sulawesi, and Mandura. The economic crisis has not only exacerbated internal tensions, but also has led to mass protests and food riots. Ms. Shannon Selin (Research Associate, Institute of International Relations, University of British Columbia) presented the Committee with a number of explanations as to how conflict within Indonesia could have negative repercussions for the region. First, there is the danger that the small-localized disturbances will grow into widespread unrest. Second, she pointed out that should a strongly pro-Islamic government come to power in Indonesia – the largest Muslim country in the region - it could have political implications for Indonesia's neighbours as well as for access to regional waterways by Western countries. Third, Indonesia is considered the diplomatic leader of ASEAN; the internal turmoil within Indonesia may lead to a power vacuum in the region's only multilateral institution. Fourth, internal instability could lead to a flood of refugees, which would strain relations with Indonesia's neighbours. The last time there was upheaval in Indonesia, Singapore and Malaysia almost went to war with Indonesia. Fifth, if the victims in Indonesia are mainly ethnic Chinese, China might intervene to protect them. Not only would Chinese ships in Indonesian waters heighten tensions but also suspicions against ethnic Chinese in other Southeast Asia countries would be heightened. Sixth, 40% of the world's shipping tonnage passes through Indonesian territorial waters. The straits are critical for the passage of oil supplies to Japan and are also the route that American warships use as the quickest between American bases in the Pacific and the Gulf. These potential consequences of violence within Indonesia not only draw attention to this country in particular but serve to highlight the importance of interstate security in general.

Growth of the Business Involvement of Asian Armed Forces and the Spread of Weapons

Ms. Selin drew the Committee's attention to the fact that over the last 10 to 15 years there have been significant changes in the region's military forces. Armies have moved well beyond providing subsistence for themselves to large-scale involvement in non-military sectors of the economy. As a consequence, local economies are distorted because the army is receiving subsidies, tax breaks, and special legal treatment denied to other businesses. Military involvement in the local economy also adds to corruption and crime, and creates an "off book" source of revenue for the military budget. Further, there has been a dramatic change in the types of technology that are available, a fact that has an impact, not only on the way in which war can be waged but also on how peace can be maintained.

The last decade and a half has also seen an increase in weapons purchases by many countries of the region. Mr. David Dewitt (Director, Centre for International and Security Studies, York

University) described the Asia Pacific "as the sink for weapons, both old and new, recycled and cutting edge" (34345:10). According to Mr. James A. Boutilier (Special Advisor (Policy), Maritime Forces, Pacific Headquarters, Department of National Defence) the region has also seen a growth in navies, probably as a consequence of the large number of unresolved maritime disputes. In addition, the traffic in arms from Cambodia via Thailand to other countries has been a major concern for security planners in the region. Recently, the economic crisis has led to a decrease in government purchases of weapons, which some would argue is a positive outcome as it may help foster an atmosphere of peace. Colonel John B. Roeterink (Director, Asia-Pacific Policy, National Defence Headquarters, Department of National Defence) told the Committee that the decrease in weapons purchases allows Canada time to develop new policies and strategies to deal with the increased military arsenals of many countries in the region. Others, however, argue that the reduction in military spending in such places as South Korea sends a dangerous message of vulnerability to hostile neighbours.

NON-TRADITIONAL SECURITY THREATS

Economic Security

In many ways, the recent financial turmoil in Asia has deprived the region of the stabilizing influences it used to take for granted: strong economic growth and rapidly rising standards of living. The crisis has illustrated clearly that a country's security is not determined solely by the presence or absence of traditional external and internal threats. The food riots and looting which broke out in Indonesia after its economy began to collapse threatened the internal stability of the country. Many middle classes Indonesians who watched the value of their currency drop 75% within six months abandoned their support of Mr. Suharto and pushed for a change in leadership.

The instability brought about by the economic crisis is not unique to Indonesia. Migrant workers throughout the region have become victims of the economic crisis. Once tolerated and even accepted illegal workers in countries such as Singapore and

Thailand were sent back to their home countries with little prospect of finding work. The consequence has been a surge in dislocated workers throughout the region. In Malaysia, the government took strong measures to avoid illegal immigrants landing on its shores. The potential negative impact of the mass migrations of workers, as well as residents, seeking to escape the failing economy has been drawing considerable attention. It is important to note that the people who are migrating or are refugees do not necessarily constitute a threat in and of themselves; indeed, they are the victims of the immediate problem. But, obviously massive influxes of people can have a destabilising effect on a nation and may lead to conflict.

The Asian economic crisis has also forced regional players to focus closely on their domestic economies. Consequently, multilateral initiatives to bring about peaceful resolutions to such conflicts as the Spratly Islands, Cambodia, and North Korea will take a back seat. Bilateral efforts to resolve territorial and border disputes will also be put on hold while governments concentrate on nursing their country's economic health. Further, as has been the case with President Kim Young Sam of South Korea, President Suharto of Indonesia, and Prime Minister Hashimoto of Japan, the economic crisis has eroded the legitimacy of leaders in the eyes of their people, with further domestic instability as a result.

Finally, the tolerance between ethnic and religious groups, which was fostered during prosperous times, has been eroded by the economic crisis.Increased tensions brought about by financial strain may lead to conflicts between groups looking for an available scapegoat. These types of small-scale disputes could have the potential to escalate into much larger conflicts.

Environmental Security

The traditional definition of security – security from outside threats – does not address the very real threats produced by environmental degradation. It is estimated that the planet's human population will surpass nine billion within the next fifty years. Consequently, the rapid environmental degradation which already is apparent may itself create social turbulence which could undermine the political frameworks necessary to maintain a stable, strong state. The literature on environmental security has identified three ways in which environmental degradation can threaten state and regional security: (a) environmental hazards can jeopardize the economic livelihood of populations; (b) intense competition for declining or degraded resources can create conflicts within or among states, and (c) environmental degradation may force people to migrate, thereby creating conflict over scarce resources in the receiving areas.

Four factors contributing to environmental degradation that are of special concern to Asia are urbanization, rising sea levels, desertification and drought, and deforestation. Urbanization of the Asian population represents a serious – some would say the most serious – threat to the environment.

Effective solutions to urban waste problems, as well as water and air quality shortcomings, need to be found. Most notable among the Asian countries that may be affected by rising sea levels are China and Vietnam. Both have urban concentrations on delta plains and, as a consequence, millions of people might be displaced by a rise in sea level. More frequent and more destructive floods and tropical storms, which cause death and displacement, are expected as the sea levels rise.

Erosion and deforestation contribute to economic hardship and can bring on insurgency and rebellion. For example, in China there is little space to increase irrigated and arable land, water and fuel wood are extremely scarce, especially in the country's interior and northern regions.

These dire environmental circumstances are partially responsible for the estimated 100 million to 130 million Chinese who currently are on the move within that country. Experts are very concerned that these environmental scarcities may lead to serious internal conflicts as people fight for scarce resources.

The fires which burned throughout Indonesia and cast a haze over the region, are perhaps the best example of how the consequences of environmental degradation know no borders. The environmental damage wreaked by one country affects not only its own citizens but also the citizens of other countries. This type of large-scale damage could easily sow the seeds of conflict.

Transnational Crime

Terrorism undermines human rights, economic well-being, and the rule of law. Terrorism can act as a catalyst for internal war and possibly international conflict; as such, terrorism is a threat to regional security. Terrorism has been growing in the Asia Pacific region, particularly among countries of Southeast Asia such as Thailand, Indonesia, and the Philippines. Much of this terrorist activity is related to separatist campaigns in these countries. However, it is also linked to international terrorism by Islamic extremists. There is some concern that extremists are gaining a foothold in the region from which to carry out terrorist activities against the West (particularly the United States) and anti-Islamic elements in Asia Pacific.

With respect to drug trafficking, Southeast Asia continues to be a major producer of opium, despite government efforts to eradicate illicit opium poppy cultivation. Indeed, reports indicate that people and even governments short on hard currency have turned to this illegal cash cow in the wake of the economic crisis. Increasingly, other countries in the region are becoming transit points along the drug trade route to Australia, Canada, the United States, and Europe. In addition, the illicit manufacture of, traffic in, and abuse of amphetamines in many Asian countries is a serious concern. From a Canadian domestic perspective, Ms. Selin told the Committee that the majority of the 300 drug overdose deaths per year in British Columbia are believed to be the result of heroin coming out of Burma's Golden Triangle.

The impact of Asia Pacific security threats – such as the flow of illegal drugs, the spread of AIDS, the influx of illegal immigrants, gangs and terrorism – on Canadian society is a serious concern of the Committee. Mr. Dewitt drew the committee's attention to on-going projects undertaken by the international security and intelligence community to develop ways for countries to protect themselves against these cross-border threats. He pointed out that despite the importance of such initiatives, there is, at present, very little financial support for these projects in Canada. Witnesses suggested that the Canadian government increase its support of working groups on transnational crime (e.g., drugs, car smuggling, etc.) and that it consider the recommendations made by the Immigration Legislative Review Advisory Group concerning smuggling and illegal immigration.

CHINA-ASEAN MARITIME COOPERATION: PROCESS, MOTIVATION, AND PROSPECTS

The majority of ASEAN members are maritime countries, and so the ocean is the common bond for China and ASEAN. During his visit to Southeast Asia in 2013, Chinese President Xi Jinping shared that China hopes to "vigorously develop maritime partnership with ASEAN in a joint effort to build the Maritime Silk Road of the 21st century". This is a strategic vision based on the Chinese government's consideration of the region's big picture and the prospects for a community of common destiny with ASEAN countries. Deepened China-ASEAN maritime cooperation not only conforms to the common interests of China and ASEAN countries but can also help maintain regional peace and stability.

How China-ASEAN Maritime Cooperation Has Evolved

Maritime cooperation between China and ASEAN started in the 1990s. So far, the process of China-ASEAN maritime cooperation can be divided into the following stages:

The first stage lasted from 1991, when the China-ASEAN dialogue relationship was established, to 2001 when the two sides completed consultation on the Declaration on the Conduct of Parties in the South China Sea. This was a stage featuring multilateral and bilateral exploration, constraint, and contact. In the early 1990s, with a view to both developing relations with ASEAN and striving to improve bilateral ties with ASEAN countries, China fully restored or established diplomatic relations with ASEAN countries. In 1997, China and ASEAN decided to establish a good neighborly partnership of mutual trust that is oriented toward the 21st century, laying the foundation for promoting maritime cooperation between the two sides.

At this stage, both sides made the first step to explore sea-related cooperation, which paved the way for future maritime cooperation. First, discussions on maritime cooperation were held through the ASEAN Regional Forum (ARF). According to the 1995 edition of the ASEAN Regional Forum: A Concept Paper, maritime cooperation mainly refers to non-traditional maritime security cooperation, such as the prevention of naval vessel collision, climate monitoring, maritime search and rescue, marine environmental protection, and marine scientific research. In March 1997, China and the Philippines co-hosted the ARF inter-sessional meeting on confidence-building measures in Beijing, which attracted great attention from the international community and laid the foundation for later ARF inter-sessional meetings on maritime security.

Second, the two sides agreed to settle the South China Sea issue through peaceful means. After the publication of the ASEAN Declaration on the South China Sea in 1992, China responded that maritime disagreements should be resolved through peaceful negotiations. If conditions for negotiation are not ripe, related parties can shelve disputes and seek joint development.

The third aspect is negotiating territorial disputes and delimiting maritime boundaries bilaterally. China and Vietnam reached consensus on carrying out delimitation and development cooperation in some sea areas and signed the China-Vietnam Agreement on the Demarcation of Territorial Waters, Exclusive Economic Zone, and Continental Shelf in the Beibu Bay (2000) and the Agreement on Fisheries Cooperation in the Beibu Bay (2000), setting a shining example of settling maritime disputes and advancing maritime cooperation in the South China Sea.

Finally, the two sides jointly completed the UN's Regional Program for the Prevention and Management of Marine Pollution in the East Asian Seas (1994). China, together with some participating ASEAN countries, prepared the Sustainable Development Strategy for the Seas of East Asia, and finished the maritime cooperation demonstration program.

The second stage lasted from 2002 to 2011, when the China-ASEAN Maritime Cooperation Fund was established. This was an important stage that witnessed prodigious development in China-ASEAN relations, which was upgraded from a "good-neighborly partnership of mutual trust" (1997) to "a strategic partnership for peace and prosperity" (2003). Meanwhile, the China-ASEAN free trade negotiations started and saw an early harvest in 2004. In 2010, China and ASEAN formally completed the world's largest free trade area for developing countries.

China-ASEAN maritime cooperation was promoted in this new era. In 2002, China and ASEAN countries signed the Declaration on the Conduct of Parties in the South China Sea, which agrees in principle to promote five kinds of cooperative activities: marine environmental protection, marine scientific research, safety of navigation and communication at sea, search and rescue operations, and combating transnational crime, including but not limited to trafficking in illicit drugs, piracy and armed robbery at sea, and illegal traffic in arms.

Although the two sides put forward programs related to maritime cooperation the following year, practice showed that China-ASEAN maritime cooperation was not promoted under the framework of the Declaration on the Conduct of Parties in the South China Sea, but the framework agreement of strategic partnership signed in 2003 and its action plan (2005-2010), which included maritime cooperation in the field of "transport", one of the 10 major cooperation fields, and progress made was as follows: 1) identified the priorities of maritime cooperation, such as ship transport, Lancang River-Mekong River international shipping, maritime safety, the formulation of a strategic plan on transport and shipping cooperation, and human resources training; 2) established the minister-level coordination management mechanism – the China-ASEAN Transport Ministers' Meeting, which put maritime cooperation onto the track of government administration; 3) promoted cooperation on maritime affairs, which guaranteed the rights and interests of crew members, navigation security, sea water cleanliness and shipping convenience by establishing the China-ASEAN Maritime Consultation Mechanism (2003); 4) developed a shipping cooperation plan. On the basis of the Joint Statement on China-ASEAN Port Development and Cooperation (2007), the two sides signed the China-ASEAN Agreement on Maritime Transport in 2008, which designed a national cooperation plan to further develop maritime transport, including port cooperation, maritime transport infrastructure building, and human resources development in terms of modern logistics technology and management, which served as an institutional guarantee for the connectivity of maritime transport policies, plans, and implementation of agreements between China and ASEAN, improved the capability of managers of maritime transport and logistics, and enhanced capacity building for maritime transport cooperation; 5) strengthened training of, and exchanges between, sea-related personnel on both sides. China provided human resources training for maritime personnel of ASEAN countries, which greatly improved the management capacity of officials in charge of maritime affairs departments.

In the same period, China and some ASEAN countries jointly promoted bilateral or trilateral maritime cooperation, and achieved positive results as follows: 1) In the wake of the Indian Ocean tsunami at the end of 2004, China participated in disaster prevention and relief activities in Indonesia and other countries. 2) From 2005-2008, China, Vietnam, and the Philippines jointly collected two-dimensional and three-dimensional earthquake data and carried out test activities in an agreement zone as large as 143,000 square kilometers. 3) China and Indonesia advanced bilateral maritime cooperation, including exchange and cooperation on marine fisheries, marine scientific research, marine environmental protection, and island protection. 4) China and Vietnam carried out bilateral maritime cooperation, including China-Vietnam sea wave and storm tide forecast cooperation and cross-border joint sea oil and gas exploration in the Beibu Bay. 5) China and Malaysia carried out marine science and technology cooperation. The two sides signed the Marine Science and Technology Cooperation Agreement in 2009, which was the first inter-governmental agreement on marine science and technology cooperation signed between China and other countries around the South China Sea. 6) China and Thailand carried out maritime cooperation. The two sides signed the Memorandum of Understanding (MOU) on Maritime Cooperation Between the State Oceanic Administration of the People's Republic of China and the Ministry of Natural Resources and Environment of the Kingdom of Thailand, which further advanced marine science and technology cooperation between China and Thailand.

At this stage, significant progress was made in terms of bilateral cooperation between China and ASEAN as well as some of its member states. Since ASEAN proposed the connectivity plan in 2010, China has taken enhanced connectivity with ASEAN as an important approach to develop its ties with ASEAN countries and raise the level of economic integration between the two sides. Maritime connectivity has become a priority field and key direction in China's maritime cooperation with ASEAN. In 2011, China established the China-ASEAN Maritime Cooperation Fund valued at RMB3 billion, pushing maritime cooperation to new heights.

The third stage, starting from 2012, continues to the present day. Under the new diplomatic concept of "making proactive plans and striving for progress", China has been actively promoting maritime cooperation with ASEAN countries. In 2012, China proposed the establishment of a China-ASEAN maritime partnership, and issued the International Cooperation Framework for the South China Sea and Other Neighboring Sea Areas. In 2013, the country proposed the strategic plan to build the 21st Century Maritime Silk Road with Southeast Asia as its hub. In 2014, China set up the $40-billion Silk Road Fund. In 2015, it officially launched the Year of China-ASEAN Maritime Cooperation.

It is worth noting that relevant documents of this period reveal that, as both sides hope to raise maritime cooperation to new heights, maritime cooperation at this stage has improved significantly: 1) The two sides have promoted maritime cooperation through deepening political mutual trust. The frequency of meetings between the leaders of China and ASEAN countries has increased, while maritime cooperation has become a major topic in the diplomacy of government officials. 2) The two sides have reiterated that, in principle, maritime cooperation should be promoted under the framework of the Declaration on the Conduct of Parties in the South China Sea. It has been advocated that maritime security cooperation should be continuously enhanced, navigation freedom safeguarded, and the China-ASEAN maritime partnership developed, including properly using the China-ASEAN Maritime Cooperation Fund, and strengthening cooperation in fields such as connectivity, fisheries, marine science and technology, environmental protection, navigation security, search and rescue at sea, and maritime culture. 3) Bilateral maritime cooperation has witnessed stable development. Based on previous cooperation, China and such countries as Indonesia, Thailand, Malaysia, Vietnam, and Singapore have continued to sign a series of sea-related bilateral agreements or MOUs. 4) While carrying forward cooperation programs in the transport field identified previously, the two sides have expanded the scope of cooperation, increasing the number of programs supported by the China-ASEAN Maritime Cooperation Fund to at least 17.

According to the above three stages, the characteristics of China-ASEAN maritime cooperation can be summarized as follows:

First, maritime cooperation has evolved from a sub-field to a strategic pillar of the China-ASEAN partnership. For a long time, it was regarded as part of China-ASEAN transport cooperation, one of the 10 major fields of collaboration between China and ASEAN. The two sides promoted maritime cooperation as a sub-field of transport, instead of within the framework of the Declaration on the Conduct of Parties in the South China Sea. This situation was not reversed until 2012, when both sides recognized the significance of building a maritime partnership from a strategic point of view. The International Cooperation Framework for the South China Sea and Other Neighboring Sea Areas (2011-2015) launched by China focuses on maritime cooperation around the South China Sea. This plan has charted the course for the China-ASEAN maritime partnership.

Second, there has been an increasingly integrated approach to maritime cooperation. At the early stage, the partnership was fairly disjointed. Entering the new century, relevant parties still failed to focus and make concerted efforts to achieve progress. For instance, the cooperation programs identified in the Declaration on the Conduct of Parties in the South China Sea were implemented separately – three programs for each side – rather than joint implementation of six programs by China and ASEAN together. This inevitably led to some negative effects, one of which was the fact that maritime cooperation could only be placed in a sub-field of transport. According to the second Plan of Action to Implement the Joint Declaration on China-ASEAN Strategic Partnership for Peace and Prosperity (2011-2015), the two sides agreed to, based on the principles set by the Declaration on the Conduct of Parties in the South China Sea, establish mutual trust through cooperation before the disputes over territories and marine jurisdiction rights are peacefully settled and work with standard terms in accordance with international laws and norms. They also agreed to focus cooperation on non-traditional security issues and make efforts to strengthen dialogue and cooperation in areas such as maritime economy, disaster prevention and relief at sea, marine scientific research, marine environmental protection, safety of navigation and communication at sea, search and rescue at sea, humanitarian treatment of people who encounter danger at sea, and anti-transnational crime at sea, with a view to building an ocean of cooperation, harmony, and peace.

Third, multilateral and bilateral cooperation has been advanced side by side. Since the very beginning, China has consistently reached out to and communicated with ASEAN. China believes that ASEAN is an important regional organization and should play its due role. But ASEAN, in principle, should be a platform, which means that it should not take the place of sovereign states to lead the maritime cooperation operations supposed to be led by those states. For example, under the framework of the Declaration on the Conduct of Parties in the South China Sea, the two sides agreed to solve disputes in the South China Sea through consultation and negotiation with relevant parties, rather than introducing ASEAN to lead the settlement of disputes over territorial sovereignty and delimitation of maritime territories. Meanwhile, the regulations of the ASEAN Charter and the practice of intra-regional state-to-state relations show that ASEAN, a regional organization established by sovereign states in Southeast Asia, has provided a platform for exchange and cooperation between member states and those outside this system. ASEAN can play an active role in promoting regional maritime cooperation, but it should by no means weaken the sovereignty of its member states. Reality shows that maritime cooperation at the bilateral level between states is rich and diverse, but this kind of bilateral cooperation does not necessarily need the approval of ASEAN.

It can be seen from the process and characteristics of China-ASEAN maritime cooperation that sea-related cooperation has both enriched the strategic partnership and deepened existing cooperation, enabling the two sides to move beyond the 10 major fields. Maritime cooperation has also played a remarkably important role in consolidating the progress of China-ASEAN political and economic relations.

Motivates China and ASEAN to Cooperate at Sea

To explain the motivations behind China-ASEAN maritime cooperation, it is necessary to analyze recent developments from the perspective of broader international political and economic relations.

First, China's strategic motivation for continued progress is to build a more integrated China-ASEAN community of common destiny. While analyzing maritime cooperation processes, one fact can be discerned above all else: in any period since the end of the Cold War, the development of China-ASEAN relations requires the two sides to attach importance to maritime issues from a strategic perspective, making maritime cooperation a major aspect of the overall partnership between the two sides. This was true after China and ASEAN started a dialogue, after the good-neighborly partnership of mutual trust was established and after the partnership was upgraded to a strategic partnership. It is also true in today's new round of maritime cooperation. Though at times, due to special causes, the level of maritime cooperation was limited, both sides still include it in the framework and mechanism of comprehensive cooperation. Promoted by Chinese President Xi Jinping, maritime cooperation has become a strategic part of China-ASEAN high-level diplomacy. In addition to being an important topic for the development of overall China-ASEAN relations, it should also be an indispensable new pillar to build a more solid China-ASEAN community of common destiny.

Second, building the Asian maritime cooperation mechanism is the inherent motivation for the promotion of China-ASEAN maritime cooperation. China attaches great importance to this mechanism. President Xi has pointed out that we should "enhance the building of maritime connectivity, promote the construction of the Asian maritime cooperation mechanism, and advance cooperation in fields such as maritime economy, environmental protection, disaster management, and fisheries, making the sea a peaceful, friendly and cooperative bond among Asian countries". ASEAN has made the connectivity of institutions its core. By establishing platforms like the ASEAN Maritime Forum, ASEAN wishes to coordinate maritime political and security relations among various parties and settle maritime disputes in Southeast Asia.

However, against the backdrop of the involvement of forces outside the region, maritime disputes in Southeast Asia tend to be more complicated. China and Southeast Asian countries should adopt approaches such as diplomatic coordination, regional cooperation, international conferences, and the conclusion of international agreements to establish Asia's order for maritime cooperation, so as to avoid further escalation of regional maritime disputes into conflicts and confrontation. Jointly establishing corresponding cooperation mechanisms in sea-related fields is the institutional motivation for China-ASEAN maritime cooperation.

Third, strengthening functional cooperation is the pragmatic motivation for continued progress in China-ASEAN maritime cooperation. In the 1990s, cooperation programs between the two sides were relatively scattered. Most of the programs during this period were sea related functional cooperation. Since the beginning of the new century, with the rapid growth of China's economy, ASEAN countries have become more reliant on China economically and they need support from China in terms of maritime connectivity. ASEAN's connectivity plan includes physical infrastructure construction, consisting of two systems: a land transport system composed of road-railway networks on islands or peninsulas and a maritime transport system composed of shipping lanes. In fact, no line is drawn between the two systems of maritime and land transport. In the two systems, islands, ports, roads, and railways are integrated and connected with each other, forming a maritime economic belt of connectivity unique to the Southeast Asian region.

ASEAN countries' maritime economy has resulted from maritime geography and the awareness of "one sea," which is also deeply rooted in China's efforts to build the 21st Century Maritime Silk Road. In the field of sea-related capacity, China's and ASEAN countries' connectivity building plans are consistent with each other. For example, the realistic need to promote new industrialization is evident in the joint construction of port industrial parks between China and some ASEAN countries, and the infrastructure building undertaken by ASEAN countries aimed to enhance connectivity among islands, and even in some development bottlenecks such as maritime energy and communication. Most of these fields involve functional cooperation. On the way to becoming key to the development agenda of both sides, cooperation in these fields is the fundamental motivation to further deepen China-ASEAN maritime cooperation.

Fourth, promoting Asia's maritime culture is a realistic demand of the relationship. On the surface, China and ASEAN countries seem to be deliberately avoiding maritime geopolitical factors. But in fact both sides have ignored the historical and geographical impact of maritime culture on their relations. For several millennia, the maritime cultures of China and Southeast Asia have coexisted, carried out mutual learning, and prospered together. A maritime exchange system featuring peace and harmony has been established in East Asia. China and ASEAN countries oppose the colonial mentality in Western culture. Rather, they advocate the core idea of establishing maritime politics in the new century and promote maritime cooperation.

Challenges and Potential Solutions

Maritime cooperation is becoming a new highlight of China-ASEAN cooperation. The latest signs show that this momentum for cooperation is by no means a simple addition to existing programs as maritime cooperation between the two sides is no longer limited to transport. It should be an urgent task to explore broader realms. In this context, it is necessary to pay attention to several challenges.

First, the "trust deficit" is noteworthy. According to current trends, relations between the two sides involve maritime political factors, including sensitive issues such as territorial disputes and the intervention of powers outside the region. These pose political and even military challenges to maritime cooperation between China and ASEAN countries. For example, the Philippines has decided to introduce U.S. and Japanese military forces to respond to the perceived "maritime security threat" from China. Actions of countries like the Philippines have led to the emergence of a trust deficit between China and some ASEAN countries, which brings unnecessary political challenges to China-ASEAN maritime cooperation.

Second, there is also the problem of determining the level of cooperation. Since 2012, when it proposed to establish a formal maritime partnership with ASEAN, China has consistently put forward a series of preferential programs, fully demonstrating how serious the country is about its efforts to promote maritime cooperation. Leaders of ASEAN countries appreciate the sincerity and friendship of the Chinese side. However, that has not been enough to break through institutional limits. In reality, operations still depend on the transport field. Although new cooperation projects keep on emerging, they have to be arranged in a scattered way. This is the result of the structural obstacles hindering efforts to deepen maritime cooperation. Without a timely assessment and remediation, China-ASEAN maritime cooperation is likely to be fragmented.

Third is the problem of unilateral actions. It must be admitted that cooperative actions should be actions featuring joint promotion, exploration, and management. They are not supposed to include unilateral actions, in which only one party undertakes a project or two parties undertake one project separately. This having been said, China-ASEAN maritime cooperation has witnessed some unilateral actions. Sometimes there have even been situations where only one side is active and the other appears passive. This is not conducive to further promoting maritime cooperation.

At present, the overall momentum of China-ASEAN maritime cooperation is strong. In the context of more mature and stable relations, advancing maritime cooperation is conducive to a win-win relationship. China and ASEAN countries need to seriously address the aforementioned challenges to attain further progress.

First, the 21st Century Maritime Silk Road initiative should be regarded as a new driving force for China-ASEAN maritime cooperation. Southeast Asian countries were the first to receive the maritime cooperation proposal by the Chinese government. When it was proposed, besides new dynamics in the regional security environment, relations between China and some related ASEAN countries were faced with serious difficulties because of the South China Sea issue. While carrying forward the Silk Road spirit of peace, cooperation, and mutual benefit, the Maritime Silk Road initiative would not like to see the South China Sea issue affecting overall friendly cooperation between China and ASEAN.

Second, maritime cooperation should be an important new area of comprehensive cooperation between China and ASEAN. Chinese Premier Li Keqiang has stressed that maritime cooperation should be an important part of the China-ASEAN 2+7 Cooperation Framework, expressing the need to raise the level of China-ASEAN maritime cooperation. According to the current timetable, the second action plan of China-ASEAN strategic cooperation is going to expire soon. Maritime cooperation should be enshrined in the action plan for the next five years (2016-2020) as a major area of cooperation between the two sides, thus opening up new opportunities for the growth of the China-ASEAN comprehensive strategic partnership.

Third, maritime cooperation calls on both sides to abandon unilateral actions and align their operations. Maritime cooperation consists of joint actions in sea-related fields. Therefore, both sides should make efforts to strengthen policy coordination and strive to enhance program cooperation. Efforts should be made in the following areas: 1) coordinating development strategies. China's 21st Century Maritime Silk Road can be coordinated with ASEAN's development blueprint; 2) integrating programs, with a focus on maritime economy, connectivity at sea, maritime environmental protection and scientific research, search and rescue at sea, fisheries, anti-piracy cooperation, etc; 3) aligning marine industries. The

China-ASEAN Free Trade Area version 2.0 aims to deepen mutually beneficial economic relations and foster interdependence across the board. The capacity of some ASEAN countries with relatively backward infrastructure needs to be enhanced through industrial promotion and capacity building. It is suggested that China join hands with one or some ASEAN countries to set an example of maritime infrastructure cooperation.

ASEAN ENGAGES CHINA

The ASEAN nations have always viewed China with both suspicion and some cautious optimism. Their threat perceptions are influenced by history, geography, and cultural factors. In the former sense, being small states vis-à-vis China, they have always harboured a suspicion of their giant northern neighbor for two reasons. One is historical precedent, in particular Beijing's past support of the insurgent movements in their countries; the other is uncertainty about how China will use its power in regional affairs. China's preponderance and its growing weight in the post-Cold War era create additional concerns. Territorial disputes in the South China Sea and China's military modernization programs, together with perceived U.S. drawdown of forces have further heightened the sense of insecurity. But ASEAN countries also recognize that, given their limited capabilities, they need to live with China, and one way of ensuring that China will act responsibly is to encourage greater integration between China and the region, thus increasing the stakes. Indeed, ASEAN has been pragmatic enough to recognize the importance of engagement rather than confrontation and hence adopted a strategy that aims at integrating China gradually into a regional web of economic interdependence, political dialogue, and security dialogue processes. They also reject the strategy of containment as the best way to deal with a rising China.

ASEAN's active engagement of China played a critical role in removing suspicions and encouraged Beijing to full participation in the regional multilateral security arrangement. Specifcally, three outstanding issues of particular concern to the Southeast Asian states were to be addressed: potential economic competition coming from China, territorial disputes, and lack of transparency in China's defence spending. Beijing began to address these concerns, winning ASEAN's confidence in the process.

There is no question that the ARF has performed a critical role in exposing and socializing China to the ideas of cooperative security, multilateralism, consultation and dialogue, consensus-building, and noncoercive ways of settling disputes. Beijing's early concerns fell in four areas: that the regional forum would be dominated by the United States or otherwise could provide the justification for Washington to intervene in the region's affairs; concern over the internationalization of territorial disputes; concern that the Taiwan issue might be brought on the table, hence interfering China's internal affairs; and concern that China would be pressured to display greater military transparency.

ASEAN has been instrumental in engaging China and sensitizing Beijing to the values of the so-called ASEAN Way. This process has served to change China's perceptions of its interests and its policy choice preferences, leading to more moderate behaviour as contrasted to its earlier assertive posture.

Over time, through participation in various ASEAN-led multilateral dialogues, China has moved from its early suspicion and resistance to gradual acceptance and embrace of the idea of cooperative security and multilateralism. However, China's interpretation of multilateralism is a rather limited one, in that it is considered to be a supplement, rather than a replacement of the traditional bilateral approach. It also has resisted the more formal institutionalization of the ARF, as desired by the western countries. Beijing's comfort level clearly has increased with the understanding that ASEAN will remain in the driver's seat, and the forum will not touch on issues of vital importance to China.

Indeed, while ASEAN could be credited with socializing China to the concept of multilateralism, one must acknowledge that the multilateralism Beijing embraces remains conditional, selective, and largely a way to counter U.S. power politics. State sovereignty is still the core of Chinese foreign policy and on fundamental issues such as territorial disputes and Taiwan, China's positions continue to be more realpolitik than receptive of multilateralism.

What China pursues remains a notion of multipolarity, in which it will be recognized as an important actor. For ASEAN, this remains an issue to be reckoned with, but for the time being at least, Beijing is trying to reassure its southeastern neighbours.

The 1997 financial crisis significantly weakened ASEAN's position. However, continued uncertainty in Sino-U.S. relations and their perceived competition for influence and primacy in Asia have given ASEAN some leverage, in so far as China's diplomacy is concerned. This has enabled the organization to remain in the driver's seat in regional security arrangements such as the ARF.

At the same time, ASEAN also is reluctant to join U.S.-led military alliances due to ethnic sensitivity, as Southeast Asia is home to a large Islamic population. At a time when Beijing's relations with Tokyo also are experiencing difficulties, the value for Beijing of a better relationship with ASEAN has increased steadily. Beginning in the second half of the 1990s, the two sides moved to develop a number of institutionalized mechanisms to deepen bilateral relations, including the ASEAN+1, among others. In 2003, China and ASEAN signed the Joint Declaration on Strategic Partnership for Peace and Prosperity.

The Prevarication Strategy

International Relations theories long have debated the policy options of states facing an emerging power or hegemon. They invariably would either choose to balance (internally and/or externally) against the dominant power or bandwagon with that power. The latter is divided further into bandwagoning because of fear or bandwagoning for profits. In recent discussions, a new concept of hedging has emerged as yet another policy option for states facing uncertain international security environments. Denny Roy has further characterized the ASEAN strategy of hedging as "low-intensity balancing" that both seeks U.S. support and works with China. They encourage the United States to maintain a military presence in the region and provide support and base access but decline to form formal military alliances with Washington.

In Southeast Asia, hedging has been a particularly useful strategy for the region's small powers to manoeuvre among major powers to secure their interests. According to Robert Ross, the continental ASEAN and maritime ASEAN member states would have different attitudes toward China. The new ASEAN, which consists of Vietnam, Laos, Cambodia, and Myanmar, for instance, has special relationships with China due to history, geographical proximity, as well as unsettled issues.

Wherever possible, ASEAN member states try not to be forced to choose sides, but opt for developing and maintaining good working relationships with as many major powers as possible. They all recognize the inevitability of China's rise and see in it both opportunities and challenges. In a certain way, ASEAN states realize that they cannot by themselves form an effective alliance to check China's rise; but neither do they want to ally themselves with external powers such as the United States for fear of provoking China. In addition to engagement with China, they therefore also seek to persuade the United States to stay engaged in the region to balance China's rise and to develop a network involving all major regional powers so they have stakes in regional order.

As pointed out above, since the end of the Cold War, ASEAN has pursued a dual-strategy of retaining U.S. security involvement in the region, including a military presence, and engaging China in diplomatic-political terms and expanding economic ties. While all member states recognize the importance of continued U.S. security involvement in the region, they also are concerned with Washington's penchant for unilateral use of force, in particular after the September 11, 2001 (9/11), terrorist attacks on the United States. Regarding China, ASEAN members have tried to refrain from identifying China as a threat; rather they talk about challenges and concerns, and their chosen strategy remains that of engagement rather than isolation, let alone containment. However, ASEAN also has reservations and appears uncertain about what a rising China will mean for them.

If one could argue that ideology, overseas Chinese living in Southeast Asia, economic competition, and territorial disputes are the four key elements that could affect China-ASEAN relations, then it is clear that the first two, by and large, have been addressed, with the latter two constituting the remaining major challenges.

But even here, the implications may be different for ASEAN member states; the more developed may see less of economic competition in a rising China but more opportunities; countries that have territorial disputes with China may view Beijing's policies and activities more suspiciously. This may explain why ASEAN member states have adopted different approaches, and applied the hedging strategies with varying degrees, in their handling of China. For instance, some look for closer U.S. ties, while others seek greater engagement with China; still others, living in China's shadow, are making the best of their situations.

Although China has developed extensive ties with ASEAN on political and economic fronts, Beijing also has maintained close relationships with specific member states, which remain essential in China's regional diplomacy, especially where territorial disputes are concerned. At the same time, it should also be understood that ASEAN itself has yet to develop its own identity apart from agreements on general principles and processes. Each member state has unique historical experiences dealing with China, with varying threat perceptions regarding China's rise, and has adopted different strategies in its respective China policy. ASEAN countries' threat perceptions of China vary depending on history, geography, and the extent and nature of unresolved disputes.

SINO-MYANMAR RELATIONS

Myanmar was one of the primary countries to recognise the People's Republic of China in 1949. But the relations had suffered set back in the 1960s when anti-Chinese riots broke out in Yangon. One observer has briefly divided the China-Myanmar relations since diplomatic recognition in 1949 until today into the following phases: "first, ambivalent peaceful coexistence: 1949-1961; second, temporary setback: 1962-1970; third, improving relationship: 1971-1988; fourth, closer entente since 1989".

The US and its European allies imposed broad sanctions on Myanmar when the military Junta of Myanmar cracked down on the pro-democracy activists across Myanmar in 1988. It created a void in Myanmar's foreign relations and China stepped in to fill up the void. It is alleged that despite the sanctions, China provided

Myanmar with aid and weapons and strengthened existing trade ties. It is also opined that China provides broad diplomatic support to Myanmar's military government. However, Sino-Myanmar relations suffered a blow in August, 2009, when 30,000-50,000 ethnic Chinese, who had emigrated to Myanmar and are mainly traders, fled back to China following a crack down on the Myanmar National Democratic Alliance Army (MNDAA) in Kokang. MNDAA is a predominately ethnic Chinese militia group in the Kokang region of the Shan State, Myanmar. Media reports stated that about 1500 Kokang militiamen also retreated to China following the conflict. This incident was a shock to Beijing.

Myanmar is strategically very important for China. Myanmar provides China critical access to the Indian Ocean. The maritime aspect is very significant and gives Sino-Myanmar relations a strategic angle, not only for imports of natural resources (mainly oil and gas) and exports from landlocked southwestern Chinese provinces, but also "potentially for military bases or listening posts". Over time, China has built naval facilities, radars and signal-intelligence (SIGINT) posts along the Myanmarese coast and in Coco Islands. Media reports suggest that China is assisting Myanmar to modernise, improve and militarise naval port facilities in the Bay of Bengal at Akyab (Sittwe), Kyaukpyu and Mergui, and constructed a major naval base on Hainggyi Island near the Irrawaddy River delta.

According to an editorial published in the state controlled newspaper in Yangon, The New Light of Myanmar, bilateral cooperation between the two countries has expanded in various sectors, especially in the agriculture, hydropower, industrial, mining, oil and gas sectors and infrastructural building industry in the recent years. According to Chinese official statistics, China-Myanmar bilateral trade amounted to US$ 2.6 billion in 2008, which is 26.4 percent higher than in the year before. Until the year 2008, China's contracted investment in Myanmar amounted US$ 1.33 billion. Today, China is officially Myanmar's third-largest trading partner (after Singapore and Thailand) and the largest foreign investor.

Sino-Myanmar defence cooperation is also burgeoning. China is a major supplier of Myanmar's military hardware and training.

According to various sources, in recent years Beijing has provided billions of dollars in military assistance to Yangon, including fighter, ground-attack and transport aircraft; tanks and armoured personnel carriers; naval vessels and surface-to-air missiles. Chinese Vice President Xi Jinping, during his recent visit to Myanmar, met with Than Shwe, Chairman of the State Peace and Development Council of Myanmar and both leaders pledged to improve traditional friendship of the two countries.

Despite the recent developments and positive trends in the Sino-Myanmar relations, observers have often labeled the entente as "uneven, asymmetrical, but nevertheless reciprocal and mutually beneficial". The Sino-Myanmar strategic entente and economic relations are regarded as "a marriage of convenience".

SINO-PAKISTAN RELATIONS

Since establishing diplomatic relations in 1951, China and Pakistan have enjoyed a close and mutually beneficial relationship. Pakistan was one of the first countries to recognise the People's Republic of China and to break ties with Republic of China, based in Taiwan. Sino-Pakistan relations have evolved amid the period of Beijing's international isolation in the 1960s and early 1970s. Sino-Pak cooperation ranges from economic, military and technical exchanges to supporting each other at various global forums.

Many believe that Sino-Indian rift in the 1960s also played a critical role in bringing China and Pakistan closer. Today, rise of India is unsettling for Pakistan and is also equally discomforting for China. This reminds us of the age old adage: enemy's enemy is my friend! "A strong China means a strong Pakistan," said the Pakistani President Asif Ali Zardari when he visited China in October, 2008. It was his maiden foreign trip after he came to power in 2008.

Many analysts term Sino-Pak relations as "all-weather friendship". Trade and commerce between China and Pakistan are growing rapidly. Trade between the two countries was about US$ 7 billion in 2008, and both sides have a target to soar bilateral trade to US$ 15 billion by 2011. In recent years, Chinese investment in Pakistan has grown, with Beijing investing in heavy engineering, power generation, and mining and telecommunication sectors in Pakistan.

China and Pakistan have a strong strategic alliance. China is helping Pakistan to build a deepwater sea port in Gwadar, in Baluchistan Province. Apart from its economic value, analysts believe, the port has significant strategic importance. It can be militarised in the future, "providing China with a base to defend Persian Gulf oil shipping lanes. India regards the port with discomfort". The port has been a major concern for India. India believes that the Gwadar port would become the westernmost 'pearl' in China's "string of pearls" strategy.

Sino-Pak military cooperation is also witnessing an upward trend. Very recently, China (on July 31, 2009) delivered the first of the four state-of-the-art F-22P frigates to its "all-weather ally" Pakistan in accordance with contracts signed between the countries four years ago. The Sino-Pak relations reached a new height when news came out that China has agreed to sell 36 J-10B fighter jets to Pakistan.

The Chinese J-10 aircraft are known to be one of the most advanced weapon systems made in China. Pakistan will be the first country to receive technologically advanced J-10B Chinese combat aircraft. This arms deal indicates the depth of the strategic alliance between China and Pakistan. China has also offered Pakistan military assistance to fight terrorist activities in Pakistan. China and Pakistan have been jointly conducting R&D in the defence sector for many years. For instance, in January 1990, Pakistan and China formally agreed to jointly design, develop and manufacture MBT-2000 *Al Khalid* tanks for Pakistan army.

SINO-INDIA RELATIONS

"President Hu and we also discussed our mutual interest in security and stability of Afghanistan and Pakistan. And neither country can or should be used as a base for terrorism, and we agreed to cooperate more on meeting this goal, including bringing about more stable, peaceful relations in all of South Asia." (Joint Press Statement by President Obama and President Hu of China in Beijing, China.)

The joint statement issued by President Obama and President Hu during Obama's visit to the China has raised concerns in India regarding the future role of China in South Asia. Obama's calling for a greater Chinese role in South Asia has caused raised-eyebrows in the Indian political and strategic arena. Many analysts believe the joint statement was meant to accord China an important role in Indo-Pak relations. This development is contrary to New Delhi's official position that the India-Pakistan relationship is exclusively bilateral. It would be quite interesting to watch how this development shapes the course of Sino-Indian relations in the coming days.

The Indian State of Arunachal Pradesh remains the bone of contention between the two countries. When Indian Prime Minister Manmohan Singh made his maiden visit to Arunachal Pradesh as Prime Minister in January 2008, he proclaimed the disputed state as "our land of the rising sun." The Chinese government quickly expressed its protest over Manmohan's claim. In a recent move, the Indian Government has endorsed raising four new mountain divisions of the Indian Army along the 4,056 km long disputed Line of Actual Control between India and China.

According to Indian media report, Indian Army Chief General Deepak Kapoor in a seminar in December 2009 in Army Training Command, based in Shimla, India, stated that Indian army is revising its war doctrine for Pakistan and China. The Times of India, an influential Indian national daily, on December 2009 reported that Indian army is bringing about changes in its war doctrine to face challenges of a "possible two front-war with Pakistan and China", along with a host of other fourth generation warfare strategy reformulations. This is a significant development in the South Asian security realm and only exacerbates Indo-China tensions. Pakistani Army Chief, General Ashfaq Parvez Kayani, responded sharply terming the Indian move as "an adventurous and dangerous path, the consequences of which could be both unintended and uncontrollable." We are yet to hear Chinese reactions to Indian Army Chief's statement. Sino-India maritime competition is leaving a footprint on the relationship between the two countries. China is extending and establishing maritime cooperation with South and Southeast Asian states with a view to securing its foreign oil and trade routes. It is China's realisation that maintaining formidable maritime cooperation with Pakistan, Sri Lanka, Myanmar, Bangladesh, Thailand and Cambodia through investment and port development is essential to establish Chinese influence in the Indian Ocean, Strait of Malacca and the South China Sea. Therefore, China has taken up the 'String of Pearls' strategy quite seriously and it has become a major concern for India. There is a growing fear in India that the Chinese "Pearl" ports would be used for military means in the future to curtail Indian maritime influence in the region.

India bounced back in 2007. During that year, Indian navy, along with the navies of the US, Australia, Japan and Singapore, conducted a massive naval exercise, codenamed "Malabar-07-2", in the Bay of Bengal. Thirty-four ships and submarines of these five countries took part in the six-day war game. Two aircraft carriers of the US navy - USS Nimitz and USS Kitty Hawk joined India's only aircraft carrier, the INS Viraat, in the drill. According to Indian navy spokesman Captain Vinay Garg, this drill was perhaps the biggest ever peace-time joint naval exercise in Asia. While Indian Defence Minister A.K. Antony told that there was no military alignment, many analysts believed the exercise was an attempt by these countries (including India) to contain China's growing presence in the Indian Ocean. China registered its concerns over the war games.

Both China and India have great power ambitions. Both are on the fast track to development and are in competition with each other. Despite the suspicion and competition, Indo- China cooperation in various sectors is also being witnessed. India-China trade has burgeoned from US$ 2 billion in 2000 to an expected US$ 60 billion in 2010, exceeding the trade between India and the United States.

THE CHANGING FACE OF CHINESE DIPLOMACY

One of the most curious and underexamined features of the evolving North Korean nuclear crisis is the active and leading role played by China in the last nine months. Breaking with years of traditional Chinese passivity on global-security challenges, Beijing has helped to walk both Pyongyang and Washington back from the brink, surprising even China's critics.

Chinese diplomats were instrumental in bringing about a first round of tripartite discussions and six-party talks. Since then, senior Chinese officials have shuttled between Pyongyang and Washington to maintain momentum for the next round. Beijing has also used coercive measures such as a reported temporary suspension of oil supplies, an "inspection" of a North Korean ship in a Chinese port and shifting troop deployments on the China-North Korean border.

Beijing's consistent efforts to resolve the North Korean nuclear subject is one of many indications of a broader evolution in China's diplomacy. In recent years, Beijing's foreign policy has begun to reflect a more sophisticated, confident and, at times, constructive and proactive approach toward regional and global affairs.

For many previous decades until the mid-1990s, China regularly criticized the structure of the international system and complained that other powers colluded against its interests. Beijing now increasingly appears to be embracing the current constellation of international institutions, rules and norms as a means through which to promote and pursue its national interests. China is now working within the international system as opposed to criticizing and challenging it.

Evidence of the changes in Chinese diplomacy abound. China has expanded the breadth and depth of its bilateral relations, joined numerous regional and international agreements and increased the quality of its participation in multilateral organizations. Beijing's embrace of multilateral institutions represents one of the most dramatic shifts in its foreign relations. In the early 1990s, China was wary of such forums as venues that would criticize and constrain China. Beijing now views participation as a means to shape international rules, improve relations with neighbouring countries (especially in Southeast Asia) and limit what it perceives as undue U.S. global influence.

In East Asia, China has actively engaged the Association of Southeast Asian Nations and the Asean Regional Forum. Beijing has taken a series of calculated steps to reassure Asean states that

China's rise doesn't threaten their economic and security interests. In 2001, China proposed the establishment of a China-Asean Free Trade Area, the first of its kind. To allay regional fears about its territorial ambitions, China also agreed to a Declaration on a Code of Conduct for the island disputes in the South China Sea. And Beijing most recently signed the Treaty of Amity and Cooperation, one of the first non-Asean states to take this step, signaling its acceptance of their norms of conflict resolution.

Elsewhere in the region, China led the establishment of a multilateral organization focused on regional security in Central Asia, known as the Shanghai Cooperation Organization. The group now has six members who cooperate on border demilitarization, counter terrorism and trade.

Beyond Asia, China initiated an annual meeting with the European Union in 1998 and recently approached the North Atlantic Treaty Organization about starting an annual dialogue on strategic perceptions and regional security threats. This effort stands in stark contrast to China's traditionally critical approach to U.S.-led security alliances. In the U.N. Security Council, China voted in favour of the November 2002 U.N. Resolution 1441 on weapons inspections in Iraq. This was only the second time since China joined the U.N. in 1971 that it supported a Security Council resolution of the U.N. Charter, which authorizes the use of force. Through the 1990s, while it generally did not block U.N. action, China abstained on similar votes, including during the first Gulf War. More recently, China has voted in support of resolutions relating to the rebuilding of Iraq.

Over the past 10 years, China has sign several key arms control and nonproliferation treaties. Beijing has also subjectd numerous domestic export control laws in an effort to enforce these new nonproliferation commitments. While differences in interpretation of the regimes and problems with implementing controls on sensitive technology exports continue, the overall trend is encouraging. China has also actively addressed numerous territorial disputes that historically soured its regional relations. Since 1991, it has resolved disputes with Laos, Russia, Vietnam, Kazakhstan, Kyrgyzstan and Tajikistan. In these settlements, China often received less than half of the disputed areas. In addition, China has instituted troop reductions and confidence-building measures on border security with key neighbours such as India and Russia.

Likewise, the execution of China's diplomacy has become more sophisticated, as Beijing seeks to shape world opinion. At an individual level, China's third and fourth generation of leaders have sought to personalize China's diplomacy by traveling abroad far more than previous leaders.

More broadly, China has subjectd well over a dozen "white papers" outlining the government's official position on domestic and international policy subjects. The Foreign Ministry's and State Council's Web pages include an impressive trove of basic data on Chinese positions, new policy developments and official statements. Perhaps most surprising, Chinese officials have started providing the international press with Western-style "background briefings" before and after most important diplomatic events.

Within the last few years, and especially since September 11, 2001, even more dramatic shifts have occurred in China's thinking about its role in the international system. Influential Chinese analysts have begun advocating that China abandon its long-held victim mentality and instead promote the adoption of a "great-power mentality."

An important manifestation of these ideas is that Chinese strategists increasingly see their interests as more akin to most important powers and less associated with those of developing nations. This change alone represents a significant perceptual shift from the 1990s, when many Chinese still viewed their nation as disenfranchised by globalization, the other most important powers, and multilateral forums. Reflecting this change, President Hu Jintao was the first Chinese leader to attend a dialogue meeting of the Group of Eight leading nations this past summer.

Chinese diplomats and political leaders now talk about "shared global responsibilities" and improving cooperation among "great powers" (which includes China) to combat global security threats. This thinking stands in stark contrast to China's previously narrow view of its national interests, its identity as a most important power and its role in the international community. A final, most important element of China's new thinking is a recent, if grudging, acceptance that the world is for the moment unipolar and that U.S. preponderance will persist for decades. Although Chinese leaders publicly tout multipolarization as the trend of the times (and condemn American unilateralism), Chinese analysts also acknowledge that their country cannot (and will not) challenge U.S. global dominance anytime soon.

While all these trends are important, China still faces serious obstacles to becoming a high-profile, much less a dominant, player in the international community. Even as the country's diplomacy becomes more active, Chinese leaders need to grapple with severe political, social and economic challenges. China's new diplomacy presents Asian and American leaders with both opportunities and challenges. China's active participation in international institutions creates more chances to elicit its assistance on key subjects. Recent examples of this trend include U.S.-China cooperation on counterterrorism, counternarcotics and nonproliferation.

However, policy makers should remember that even as China becomes more engaged, it is also growing more adept at using its foreign policy and foreign relations to serve Chinese interests. Today's China is certainly smarter and more sophisticated – but not necessarily kinder or gentler. Beijing's new skills may at times frustrate Washington's objectives, as China is potentially becoming better equipped to challenge the policies of the U.S. and its allies. China's ability to consistently outmaneuver the U.S. at the U.N. Human Rights Commission in recent years should serve as a wake-up call.

China is dissatisfied with some features of the international system, such as U.S. preponderance and especially the status of Taiwan. Washington should remain aware of these frustrations and shape its ties with Asian nations in a way that recognizes the reality of China's expanding regional role. China is rapidly emerging as the engine of growth in Asia, which affords it increasing influence and leverage. Washington needs to pay consistent attention to managing relations with regional friends and allies, if it hopes to maintain its pull.

A longer-term task for the entire international group of people is to ensure that China's new diplomacy is consistent with regional stability and security. China's top political leaders have deemed the next 20 years a strategic opportunity to develop their country. An opening exists for the international community as well, and policy makers should use it wisely, to manage China's emergence as a diplomatic power.

SECURITY DISPUTES, NUCLEAR DOCTRINES, AND PROLIFERATION TRENDS

To begin with, proliferation issues in South Asia must be understood in context of vertical and horizontal proliferation. Vertical proliferation takes place as nuclear states modernize their nuclear arsenals with more reliable delivery systems and warheads. Countries including the United States, China, India, and Pakistan, are in the process of modernizing their arsenals through actions such as proposals for "a reliable replacement warhead" (as in the case of the United States). In the context of South Asia, nuclear modernization is mainly a function of prevailing threat perceptions arising from security dilemmas. Modernization of arsenals includes the development and testing of longer-range missiles-such as the tests of the Agni-III by India, and the Shaheen-II by Pakistan in the first half of 2007. Horizontal proliferation is the spread of nuclear weapons technology from nuclear states to other entities, including aspiring nuclear weapon states, as well as non-state actors such as terrorist groups. Horizontal proliferation generally involves a significant role for WMD supply networks that may or may not have a connection to official entities in a nuclear state. In the South Asian context, this variant of proliferation is especially pertinent, given the history of the A.Q. Khan network and its assistance to states such as North Korea and Iran. In addition, horizontal proliferation includes second-tier proliferation, where developing countries trade and barter nuclear technology with each other. While vertical and horizontal proliferation are variants of the proliferation dynamic, it is entirely possible that a nuclear state (such as Pakistan) could make use of non-state networks in the pursuit of nuclear modernization. From the subcontinental perspective, one main question arises-given the lack of a comprehensive resolution of the disputes between India and Pakistan and India and China, how do nuclear doctrines in South Asia impact trends in the acquisition of nuclear and missile technology? The answer to this question links threat perceptions and nuclear doctrines with recent proliferation-related developments and requires a brief discussion of existing nuclear postures of India and Pakistan.

Subcontinental Rivalry

So what are the characteristics of the sub-continental rivalry that make nuclear proliferation in South Asia such a crucial security issue? Threat perceptions based on long-standing security disputes shape nuclear doctrines and proliferation dynamics. The intensity of disputes brings in security dilemmas that ensure continued dependence on nuclear weapons in South Asia. South Asia is one of the most populated regions of the world, with India and Pakistan alone accounting for about 1.35 billion people. Both countries have been bitter rivals since partition of the subcontinent in 1947 that led to the creation of independent Pakistan and independence for India. The two countries have fought two wars over Kashmir (1947, 1965), one over East Pakistan/Bangladesh (1971), one limited war (Kargil, 1999) and the ongoing insurgency in Kashmir (since 1989). The 2001-2002 crisis further highlighted the dangers of terrorist violence provoking a conventional conflict that could lead to a nuclear crisis. Kashmir, which lies at the heart of the dispute, is more than a simple territorial problem. The province has a Muslim majority, and for India it is a symbol of its secular credentials as well as a repudiation of the partition, which was based on religion. For Pakistan, Kashmir is crucial because it is seen as an unfinished agenda of partition, which was supposed to provide a homeland for the subcontinent's Muslim community. Thus, Kashmir is an integral part of both countries' perceived self-identities. Since the 2001-2002 crisis, Islamabad and New Delhi have conducted several rounds of peace talks aimed at bringing a lasting settlement to the Kashmir issue. This peace process has involved several confidence-building measures such as strengthening of transport links between the two countries. The two sides also signed a crucial agreement on reducing the risk of nuclear accidents in February 2007. Nevertheless, the key dispute, Kashmir, is nowhere near resolution. This implies that both New Delhi and Islamabad are more inclined toward strengthening existing military capabilities, both conventional and non-conventional, to prevent an unfavourably scenario in a future standoff.

Apart from notions of sovereignty and nationhood, Kashmir is also of considerable strategic importance. Rivers originating in the Kashmir region provide crucial water supplies for food producing areas in the heartland. Furthermore, the Siachen glacier is also a region of military significance. The glacier, to the north of Kashmir, commands a strategic overlook of the small border between Pakistan and China and can potentially be used as a point of attack on India from northwest Kashmir. The glacier became a battle ground between the two armies in April 1984 and despite repeated talks, there has been no movement toward demilitarization. The complex rivalry between India and Pakistan involves territorial disputes based on notions of national identity as well as terrorist violence. Another integral element of the subcontinental security dyad is the role of China.

The China Factor

The role of China in South Asian security issues as well as in future conflict scenarios is crucial when considering two realities- (a) the historical animosity between India and China, and (b) the long standing 'all-weather' political and military alliance between Pakistan and China. Indian analysts often cite transfer of nuclear and missile technology from Beijing to Islamabad as evidence of an encircled threat to India. Through nuclear and missile technology transfers to Pakistan, Beijing restricts India to the South Asian strategic framework, and this constrains New Delhi's stated desire to seek a more global presence.

From the Chinese political establishment's perspective, the concern is over India's defence expansion, its desire and movement toward a stronger regional and global role, and its increasing strategic connections with Washington.

Thus, any examination of the South Asian proliferation framework takes into account the Sino-Indian rivalry and dispute, the lowest point of which was the 1962 border war. In recent years, Indian and Chinese leaders and special representatives have met for regular talks on the border dispute issue; the most recent session (the 10th such round), took place in April 2007.

In early rounds of these talks, China granted de facto recognition of Sikkim as a province of India, while India accepted Tibet as part of China. However, serious differences remain, and strategically important areas such as the state of Arunachal Pradesh have been claimed by China, while India has claimed Aksai Chin and certain parts of Kashmir handed over by Pakistan to China.

Despite periodic meetings, little progress has been made on these issues, and from time to time, controversial statements by each side threaten to derail talks. Whether a hardening of positions or a negotiating strategy, it demonstrates that the potential for friction is ever-present.

Furthermore, there is also some dispute over an earlier agreement between the two sides to not insist on territorial exchanges of areas with settled populations, reflected in Beijing's recent demands that India cede Arunachal Pradesh, especially the Tawang tract. Therefore, in the absence of a permanent settlement, both India and China have adopted a hedging strategy to guard against any future strategic disadvantages.

A hedging strategy involves bolstering military-related capabilities in an ambiguous way that is not directly threatening to the adversary.

At the same time, cooperative ties are encouraged without necessarily making any major concessions. In part, such an approach is chosen due to uncertainty over the adversary's future intentions and capabilities and as a way to safeguard against a downturn in future ties or in the regional or global strategic environment. Therefore, modernization of nuclear arsenals in South Asia has to be considered in this context.

Similarly, in the case of India and Pakistan, despite sustained peace talks and CBMs, the two sides continue a hedging strategy to guard against future uncertainty, such as another crisis situation like Operation Parakram in 2001-2002. This is done by developing more reliable nuclear delivery systems (especially longer range ballistic missiles), perfecting and increasing fissile material stock, and acquiring conventional weaponry in line with contemporary war-fighting doctrines.

Thus, in South Asia, underlying security disputes, based on territorial rivalry and terrorist violence, combined with a need to expand the nation's global and regional position encourages future uncertainties that shape the actors' nuclear policy decision-making. As mentioned earlier, apart from the Indo-Pakistan rivalry, strategic uncertainty, and suspicion in New Delhi is also generated by Pakistan's close military links with China. With China in the picture as a rival of India and a strategic ally of Pakistan, even if Delhi and Islamabad move towards a peaceful resolution of the Kashmir dispute, Beijing is likely to be the biggest factor in Indian threat calculations.

At the same time, the present threat perceptions between India and China are not the same as between India and Pakistan, which are more immediate and based on a 'hot' territorial dispute and state-sponsored terrorism.

Nevertheless, analysts in New Delhi have long pointed to Chinese military modernization as a coercive threat to India. This modernization includes missile development, such as the current deployment of the DF-21 and DF-3 missiles in Qinghai and Yunnan provinces.

Furthermore, there is some suspicion among Indian analysts that though Beijing's stated policy is that of minimum deterrence, the stationing of missiles such as DF-3 and DF-21 reflects a posture of nuclear coercion, and under some conditions, does not preclude a first strike against its neighbours. It is also possible that since 1998, Beijing may have deployed nuclear weapons on the Tibetan plateau in response to a perceived Indian conventional military advantage and the May 1998 nuclear tests.

Thus, despite growing trade between the two sides, there is some degree of unease in India over China's long-term intentions, more so in light of predictions of increased competition between the two countries for global energy resources. The concern in New

Delhi is that if bilateral relations take a negative turn at some point in the future, China's current military modernization will give Beijing a significant advantage.

The Sino-Indian security dilemma is also a function of China's desire to establish close relationships with other countries in the Indian Ocean region (most notably Myanmar), a policy that is seen as a potential threat by India and termed as "strategic containment." For India and China, the security dilemma also arises from threat perceptions based on consequences of future nationalistic tendencies. Both sides fear that a rise in nationalism in the other could lead to more hostile attitudes.

China's concerns over future expansions of the U.S. nuclear arsenal, missile defence and space dominance plans also lessen the possibility of any immediate restraint with respect to Beijing's nuclear plans. Therefore a chain reaction exists in South Asia where New Delhi, at the very least, wants to maintain its current relative capabilities vis-à-vis Beijing, if not actually improve them. The interconnected security dilemmas in the Asia-Pacific region shape defence policies and impact stability.

6

Conflict of South China Sea and ASEAN

The summit meeting of the heads of government of the Association of Southeast Asian Nations (ASEAN) issued a major statement that declared, "[a]n ASEAN Community shall be established comprising three pillars, namely political and security cooperation, economic cooperation, and socio-cultural cooperation..." Each successive ASEAN Summit and Annual Ministerial Meeting (AMM) of foreign ministers has advanced this goal. It was expected that the 45th AMM, held under the motto "ASEAN: One Community, One Destiny," would follow its predecessors by adopting further measures to make the ASEAN Community a reality. As events transpired, differences among ASEAN states over how to manage territorial disputes in the South China Sea emerged as a litmus test of their ability to achieve an ASEAN Political-Security Community by 2015.

This article analyses internal ASEAN differences on the South China Sea by offering new insights provided by three documents: Philippine Working Draft, Philippines Draft Code of Conduct; ASEAN's Proposed Elements of a Regional Code of Conduct in the South China Sea (COC) between ASEAN Member States and the People's Republic of China; and Summary of Cambodia Chair's intervention at the AMM Retreat, 9 July 2012.

This chapter is divided into five parts. The first part briefly presents the historical background to the evolution of ASEAN's policy on a Code of Conduct in the South China Sea. It then sharpens the discussion by comparing the Philippine Working Draft, Philippines Draft Code of Conduct drawn up in early 2012 with ASEAN's Proposed Elements of a Regional Code of Conduct in the South China Sea approved by the 45th AMM in July. Part two examines internal discussions by ASEAN foreign ministers at their 45th AMM Retreat. These discussions reveal the issues that prevented the foreign ministers from reaching consensus on the wording of a single paragraph on the South China Sea and the unprecedented decision by the ASEAN Chair to withhold issuing the customary joint communiqué. Part three details the public recriminations that followed, while part four discusses Indonesia's shuttle diplomacy to restore ASEAN unity. Part five offers an evaluation of the implications of these developments for ASEAN unity, the prospects for an ASEAN-China COC, and an ASEAN Political-Security Community.

CHINA'S TERRITORIAL WATERS CLAIMS IN THE SOUTH CHINA SEA

Del Rosario then provided examples of Chinese "expansion and aggression" since the 1990s, including its occupation of Mischief Reef, and numerous intrusions in the Philippines' EEZ all before the confrontation at Scarborough Shoal. China's expansion was premised on ownership of the whole of the South China Sea, he argued. China employed overwhelming force thus preventing "the Philippines from enforcing its laws and forcing the Philippines to retreat from its own EEZ."

Del Rosario stated that the Philippines responded to Chinese actions by exercising patience and restraint under the terms of the DOC. The Philippines entered into negotiations to peacefully resolve the situation at Scarborough Shoal. But China acted in bad faith when it failed to honour its commitment to withdraw its vessels. Del Rosario argued that China's actions challenged ASEAN centrality, leadership and solidarity. The Philippines, as the aggrieved party and one of the founding members of ASEAN, failed to understand the lack of concern by some other members and their "seeming silence" on their commitment to the principles of the DOC, he concluded. Del Rosario then asked rhetorically, "what would be the real value of the COC if we could not uphold the DOC; in Scarborough Shoal the DOC is violated?" He stated that it was "important that ASEAN [make a] collective commitment to uphold the DOC [and this] be reflected in the joint communiqué of the AMM."

Del Rosario then quoted the remarks by Prime Minister Hun Sen at the opening of the AMM: "ASEAN should further demonstrate its ability and role as a driving force for the promotion of dialogue and cooperation on the political and security issues for the cause of peace, stability and prosperity in the region." Del Rosario asserted, "[t]o operationalize this principle [it is] necessary for the joint communiqué to acknowledge the problem rather than ignore [it]. We strongly recommend the [inclusion] of Scarborough Shoal, EEZ and continental shelf in the joint communiqué draft. [There must be] concerted action to address the threat to peace and stability in he region."

Del Rosario thanked ASEAN member states that supported the ASEAN Foreign Ministers' Statement on the Situation in Scarborough Shoal, and in particular he expressed great appreciation for the ASEAN founding fathers. With the creation of the ASEAN Community in 2015, ASEAN members would be "more conscious of our role to ensure peace and security." Finally, Del Rosario concluded his remarks by quoting from the German anti-Nazi theologian, Martin Neimöller:

- First they came for the communists, and I didn't speak out because I wasn't a communist.
- Then they came for the trade unionists, and I didn't speak out because I wasn't a trade unionist.
- Then they came for the Jews, ?and I didn't speak out because I wasn't a Jew.
- Then they came for me, and there was no one left to speak out for me.

The Thai Foreign Minister Surapong Tovichakchaikul spoke next. He observed that the South China Sea had attracted a lot of attention. Surapong stated that after discussions with Chinese officials he concluded that they did not want this issue to affect the excellent relations between ASEAN and China. "What is important is for all parties concerned to scale down, calm things down," he said.

Surapong asserted that, "the issue of territorial claims will have to be resolved between the claimant states through negotiation. But we have to recognize the broader implications. Apart from that, there is room for greater dialogue between both sides. Rather than being seen as source of conflict, the South China Sea should be seen [as an opportunity] for cooperation. [ASEAN and China] should build trust and [a] win-win situation." Surapong noted that as the ASEAN Dialogue Coordinator for China (2012-15), "Thailand will try its best towards this end. We will push ahead with concrete implementation of the DOC, while ensuring the COC drafting process that is inclusive and comfortable for all sides. We must get it right from the start."

Surapong concluded, "Last and most important: ASEAN unity; the whole world is watching ASEAN with high expectations; major powers want to be part of this fast growing region; we must ensure that this competition is a healthy one." ASEAN should have a "positive influence on regional and international issues; ASEAN need[s] to speak more with one voice. Our collective voice does matter internationally. Bali Concord II: [ASEAN] unity would enhance credibility and [its] centrality in [the] regional architecture."

Pham Binh Minh, Vietnam's Foreign Minister spoke next. He began by noting, "[o]ver recent months the situation has [been] aggravated due to [a] series of Chin[ese] moves to impose their 9 dash claim. Apart from Scarborough Shoal, China announced the establishment of Sansha City [Hainan, to administer an area] which covers almost all the South China Sea... [The China National] Offshore [Oil] Company invited bidding for nine oil and gas blocks [lying] within Vietnam's EEZ and continental shelf with several points only sixteen miles off Vietnam's coast. [These are] serious violations of Vietnam's sovereignty and jurisdiction over its EEZ and continental shelf [under] UNCLOS. [China's actions] go against the spirit of the DOC, create a serious concern for the maintenance of peace and stability, bring[ing] about long term consequences and implications."

Binh noted, "we have discussed the South China Sea many times [and] agree that territorial disputes should be solved by the parties [directly] involved. But this issue has a much broader implication for maritime security, peace, stability and security in the region. [It is] important for ASEAN to show [a] central role in regional peace and security [and] promote dialogue and cooperation. [ASEAN should] speak with one voice, maintain unity… with agreed common points."

Foreign Minister Binh also quoted approvingly from Prime Minister Hun Sen's remarks at the opening of the 45th AMM on ASEAN's role as the "driving force for the promotion of dialogue and cooperation" in the region and Hun Sen's emphasis on the implementation of the DOC, including the eventual conclusion of a Code of Conduct. Binh then argued "that the joint communiqué should reaffirm further the importance of universally recognized principle[s] of international law, including respect of territorial integrity, sovereignty and sovereign rights and jurisdiction of coastal states in [their] EEZ and continental shelf as stipulated in UNCLOS." Binh noted that the incidents that took place earlier in the year occurred within the EEZs of ASEAN member states. Binh added that "all disputes should be settled through peaceful means through dialogue in accordance with international law, [including] UNCLOS and [the] DOC."

Binh concluded by noting that the ASEAN Senior Officials' Meeting had completed the ASEAN paper on key elements of the COC. He reiterated the COC was an "important legal document [that] contributed to peace, maritime security and safety in the South China Sea; ensuring that disputes will be settled by peaceful means. Based on [the] ASEAN paper, ASEAN should decide to initiate consultations with China on the COC through existing mechanisms, namely the ASEAN-China SOM on the DOC as it is quite appropriate." Binh ended his remarks by re-emphasizing "that during consultations ASEAN should maintain close coordination, unity and speak with one voice, based on the agreed paper."

Indonesia's Foreign Minister spoke next and observed that developments in the South China Sea had been discussed in the past, would likely be discussed in the future, and were unlikely to go away. Marty stated that, "we must have [an] ASEAN outlook... on the matter. It is self-evident whenever ASEAN speaks with one voice we are able to maintain our centrality [and] ensure that we deliver results." He gave as an example ASEAN's contribution to developing the Guidelines to Implement the DOC and the work of the ASEAN SOM in identifying the key elements of the COC. Marty further noted that while the diplomatic process of implementing the DOC was underway, "the situation on the ground at sea is showing signs of concern for all of us. We have been following what has been transpiring. All those developments reinforce the need to get the COC concluded as soon as possible." If there is no progress on the COC "the situation [will] become more destabilizing. [This is] not in our common interest."

Marty further noted that ASEAN's proposed key elements on the COC were "well crafted and well thought through." He asked rhetorically to what extent would the COC guide ASEAN when it faced the situation with China over Scarborough Shoal? Marty concluded: "We want to be sure that the COC is operational in nature, and not simply repeat statements and principles that are available in the DOC. [The] COC must be prescriptive, [provide] rule[s] to avoid incidents in the South China Sea, and provide [the] means whereby the conduct of countries can be better regulated..."

Malaysia's Foreign Minister Anifah Aman spoke on two issues, the DOC and the COC. With respect to the former he noted, "ASEAN and China should continue close consultation and coordination through existing mechanisms [to] fully implement [the] DOC." He proposed that ASEAN "should consider fully utilizing the ASEAN-China Maritime Cooperation Fund [and] look[ed] forward to seeing the details of the fund from China."

With respect to the COC, Anifah Aman noted that ASEAN had concluded a draft of the key elements of the COC. He thanked Cambodia for convening informal consultations with China on this draft. This would contribute to "build[ing] mutual trust and confidence towards peace and stability. As we embark on [the] intergovernmental process on [the] COC [ASEAN and China] should first discuss the [key] elements before discussing the text of the COC [because it was] more practical to do so before the actual drafting begins."

Anifah Aman then turned to a proposal by China, presented to the ASEAN Summit earlier in the year by Cambodia as ASEAN Chair, to establish an Eminent Persons and Expert Working Group. "We should not prevent [the ASEAN-China] SOM from seeking inputs from experts as the need arise[s] on certain technical and legal matters." Malaysia's Foreign Minister then argued that ASEAN should reiterate its position that the "COC aim[s] to create [a] rules based framework; it should not serve as an instrument to resolve territorial disputes. Existing disputes should be resolved between [the] parties concerned based on existing mechanism[s], including UNCLOS."

Next Anifah Aman focused on the proposed paragraph on the South China Sea in the draft joint communiqué. He agreed with Indonesia: "We must talk with a single voice; ASEAN must show [its] united voice; [otherwise] our credibility will be undermined. We must refer to the situation in the South China Sea, particularly any acts that contravene the international law on EEZ and continental shelves. It is totally unacceptable that we can't have it in the joint communiqué."

Brunei's Foreign Minister, Prince Mohamed Bolkiah, spoke briefly. He noted with approval ASEAN's engagement with China on the COS. He then indicated that the proposed key elements in the ASEAN draft COC were acceptable. As for the joint communiqué, Brunei would be "guided by your [ASEAN Chair] decision, [Brunei] can support the statement." It was important for ASEAN and China to have "mutual trust and confidence."

Thongloun Sisoulith, the Laotian Foreign Minister followed Brunei. He noted that there was no doubt the South China Sea was an important issue. "All efforts," he argued, "should be made in order to maintain and promote peace and stability in this part of the world." He was pleased that "ASEAN and China have been engaging in dialogue to contribute to further confidence building and mutual trust. The 5th ASEAN-China SOM on [the] DOC agreed on various activities to implement the DOC including the convening of the joint workshop. Laos fully supports these activities."

The Lao Foreign Minister noted that working toward the eventual adoption of the COC was part of the implementation of the DOC. Thongloun said he was pleased to take note of the proposed key elements in ASEAN's draft COC and these should be for internal ASEAN reference. The Lao Foreign Minister fully concurred "with the proposal that it is time to start the consultation with China on the COC and the upcoming Post-Ministerial Conference should task the ASEAN-China SOM to start talks. The convening of [the] informal ASEAN-China SOM on [the] COC demonstrated the readiness of ASEAN and China to work towards the eventual adoption of the COC." He concluded by noting that "[t]he implementation of the DOC has gained good impetus [and] we should maintain and further strengthen it and therefore contribute to making the South China Sea the sea of peace, cooperation and partnership and prosperity."

Myanmar's Foreign Minister Wunna Maung Lwin spoke briefly on the South China Sea. He reiterated his country's desire that territorial disputes be settled peacefully through dialogue and engagement. He noted the importance of the DOC and its aim to build confidence among the parties and to settle disputes by peaceful means. Myanmar fully supported the Guidelines to Implement the DOC and welcomed the proposal by ASEAN and China to undertake cooperative projects in the South China Sea.

Maung Lwin concluded that Myanmar would "[c]ontinue to support the full and effective implementation of the COC, and support all efforts that ensure [the] peaceful resolution of disputes." He also noted ASEAN's formal engagement with China on the COC and wished "to emphasize that we [ASEAN] have gained positive achievements with China and should keep the momentum of the achievements."

Foreign Minister K. Shanmugam opened his remarks by noting that Singapore was not a claimant state and that "specific claims have to be resolved among [the] parties concerned." Singapore, however, had an interest in seeing that the South China Sea "must be shared by all states, claimant and non claimant," and it was in the common interest to the maintain peace and stability in the region.

Shanmugam asserted that "freedom of navigation [is] very important to all of us. Freedom of navigation can not be respected if the rule of law is not observed." He noted that "recent developments were of special concern" because they "invoke novel interpretations of international law that could undermine the entire UNCLOS regime" and create uncertainty over the future of UNCLOS.

Shanmugam said that Singapore welcomed "the internal agreement of ASEAN on possible elements of [the] COC" and suggested empowering the SOM to begin discussions with China. These discussions should proceed in parallel with the implementation of the DOC. He also noted that negotiations on the COC would not be easy, but it was important that ASEAN begin a dialogue with China. Shanmugam concluded by asserting, "it is important that ASEAN has a clear expression of our concerns on the South China Sea in the joint communiqué," and he shared the points made by previous speakers. It would be "damaging to us if we don't say anything. If ASEAN is not united, our negotiations with China will be more difficult and protracted."

Cambodia's Foreign Minister Hor Namhong rounded off the discussion on the South China Sea by bluntly declaring, "[t]here is no consensus, [we should] bracket the entire paragraphs 14-17 for our decision. The most difficult is paragraph 16. It is a complex problem."

According to the Summary of the Cambodia Chair's intervention at the AMM Retreat, Hor Namhong made the following points:

On Scarborough Shoal, we all know it is situated in the South China Sea, and we are talking here about the South China Sea. So why should we specify the Scarborough Shoal precisely in the South China Sea. Up to now, we all know the disputes among the concerned parties [are] in Spratlys and Paracels, but we never mention these name[s] in our talks with China. We always mention only the South China Sea.

On the inclusion of the wording on EEZ and continental shelf, we believe that every one is perfectly aware that the 1982 UNCLOS have precisely defined the EEZ and continental shelf, and other issues related to the sea. Why should we repeat again? In case we [do] not find a way out, Cambodia as Chair has no more recourse to deal with this issue. So the problem we are facing now is either we have compromise text, [that will] not satisf[y] everyone. If we cannot agree on [the] text, there should be no text at all. For the Joint Communiqué, countries should not try to impose [their] national position, but the common view in spirit of compromise.

ASEAN-China met twice recently to discuss informally the drafting of COC. Cambodia [is] to host formal SOM on COC in near future. All the meetings are steps forward to de-escalate tension… in the South China Sea. We should not take position that may lead in creating or escalating tension in the SCS. What I propose now is in line with what my Prime Minister has proposed, that we have to work for peace, security and stability in the region.

The remarks by Cambodia as ASEAN Chair provoked an interchange with the foreign ministers of Indonesia, Malaysia, Vietnam, and the Philippines. Marty Natalegawa took the floor first and suggested it would be better if the foreign ministers could address paragraph 16 now so they could conclude the AMM Retreat. Malaysia immediately endorsed Indonesia's proposal. Hor Namhong responded by stating that Cambodia was not "talking against anybody or for anybody. We want to move forward the COC to de-escalate the tension. If we put strong wording in the joint communiqué it is not preferable for the solution."

Malaysia's Anifah Aman noted that the 2011 AMM joint communiqué did not reflect the decisions reached at that time. Malaysia was concerned over "how to settle our disputes [and] respect freedom of navigation." With respect to freedom of navigation Anifah Aman argued that the joint communiqué "does not specifically mention the settlement of disputes through international law and UNCLOS. I am concerned that we have left out the most important concern: all disputes must be settled in international law. We have to be mindful of the disputes. UNCLOS and international law should be the mechanism."

Hor Namhong interjected, "now or [in] the near future we can't expect to resolve the disputes. Not ASEAN." Anifah Aman responded: "[the] DOC and COC are the main frameworks. [They are] rules-based frameworks, [they] are not meant to settle the disputes, the mechanisms are based on UNCLOS. We are not happy..."

Vietnam's Pham Binh Minh broke in to raise a question of procedure. "We should discuss this issue right now. Every year the joint communiqué has a paragraph on the South China Sea, [some are] stronger and [other are] milder... There is no question that the joint communiqué does not have that one. Around the table here we have the discussion and [the] ministers already indicated that the joint communiqué must have a paragraph on the South China Sea. Every year we have to update the situation, the development over the South China Sea. This year what happened to the South China Sea? Those incidents occurred not only in the South China Sea but deeper in the EEZs, [these were] new developments. That is why in the draft we have to update the new developments in there. We put here [words] calling [for] the respect of EEZs and continental shelves, these [are] new developments in the South China Sea."

Hor Namhong responded. "We can never achieve [consensus] even though we stay here for the next four or five hours..." Indonesia's Foreign Minister broke in to ask "how detailed are we [going to be in our] references to Scarborough Shoal and EEZs and continental shelves?" Apparently referring to paragraph 16 in the draft joint communiqué Marty read out:

In this context, we discussed in-depth recent developments in the South China Sea, including the situation in the affected Shoal / disputed area, exclusive economic zones and continental shelves of coastal states, particularly those contrary to the provisions of the 1982 UNCLOS. In this connection, we call upon all parties to respect the universally recognized principles of international law including the 1982 UNCLOS. Further [we call] upon all the parties to resolve the disputes in accordance with universally recognized principles of international law.

Hor Namhong replied, "Up to now there have been disputes in the Paracels and Spratlys but we have never mentioned the names of these. But now why do we include these in the joint communiqué? Second if we need again paragraph 16..."

Del Rosario interjected, "There is no clarity that the disputes must be settled peacefully and in accordance with international law, especially UNCLOS. You refer to freedom of navigation and over flight, it [the joint communiqué] does not mention disputes. Right now there are two gross violations of the DOC. They are in [Scarborough] Shoal and in the oil service contract of the EEZ and continental shelf. These are very clear distinct violations of the DOC. If we are going to be protecting peace and stability and freedom of navigation in the South China Sea we should deal with the problem as it present[s] itself at this point in time. We are also ignoring the fact that there are gross violations of the DOC in the EEZs in the Philippines and Vietnam. It is a challenge to ASEAN's leadership, centrality and solidarity. Why are we ignoring these gross violations instead of identifying them so that we can deal with them?"

Hor Namhong responded: "We are not a tribunal, [we should] not escalate tension but diffuse tension. When we refer to shoal where is the shoal? Are the Spratlys or Paracels shoals? When you say violation of Scarborough Shoal, we have to know to whom it belongs. We are not a tribunal. Maybe it belongs to the Philippines, I don't know. I still don't understand, when we said disputed areas that covers all the areas [that are] disputed. Why should we add the shoal and EEZ and continental shelf? Before we go to [the] concluding session, I propose we delete the South China Sea in the joint communiqué, and [proceed] without paragraph 16. I have no other recourse. Or claimant states will deal directly with China."

Indonesia's Marty then asked the Chair to "read again the formulation." Hor Namhong responded, "[where] we refer to [the] shoal?" He then asked if the joint communiqué should include actions contrary to UNCLOS. "UNCLOS already defines the EEZs and continental shelves, should we repeat it again?" he asked.

Del Rosario took up the discussion. "With due respect," he stated, "the first sentence [reads:] 'in this context we discussed in depth the developments [in the South China Sea], including the situation in the Scarborough Shoal and expressed serious concern over such developments in the area, particularly those provisions in the UNCLOS related to Exclusive Economic Zones and continental shelves.' Nowhere in that sentence is ASEAN [taking a] position as to who owns the shoal. We are just calling attention that they are violating the DOC. We are not looking at the resolution of territorial claims here. There is no reference [to] who is owning what."

Malaysia's Anifah Aman declared, "It [violations] is happening. Nowhere did we mention that it [Scarborough Shoal] belongs [to one country or another]. Instead of 'affected shoal' we [should] put it as 'disputed area'." Del Rosario retorted, "There are many disputed areas in the South China Sea but not in the Scarborough Shoal. All we are saying [is] discussion in conflict areas." Anifah Aman replied, "We are trying to find... I don't think we can progress forward if we specifically mention an area... It reflects the united stand of ASEAN to encompass all disputed areas." Marty Natalegawa responded, "We [Indonesia] are not one of those claimant states. We suggested earlier to use the word 'affected shoal.' [We are] trying to be sensitive; affected shoal [is] without prejudice to national claims. Be we can agree to [use the term] disputed area. We don't think that this issue is impossible to resolve. We have discussed in depth the situation [in the South China Sea].

Hor Namhong stated, "I can support the disputed areas, disputed areas covers everything." Vietnam's Pham Binh Minh then interjected, "Disputed area, the EEZ is not a disputed area, certainly not. Some countries [try] to turn an undisputed are into a disputed area. That's for sure [an EEZ is not a disputed area] in accordance with international law." Minh then proposed a break for small group discussion. The notes on the discussions at the AMM Retreat end at this point.

Media and other reporting reveal that discussions on the wording of the South China Sea paragraphs continued until the morning of July 13 without breaking the impasse. Ernest Bower, who spoke to diplomats in Phnom Penh, wrote that after the four-member ministerial committee came up with a draft communiqué, "[r]epeatedly, however, after taking the draft under consideration, Hor Namhong consulted with advisers outside of the meeting room and came back rejecting language referring to Scarborough Shoal and the EEZs, even after multiple attempts to find compromise. He said Cambodia's view was that those were bilateral issues and therefore could not be mentioned in the joint statement." By one account, the original AMM joint communiqué went through a total of eighteen drafts.

Over the four days following the AMM Retreat, the Indonesian and Singaporean foreign ministers made a last-ditch effort to broker a compromise. They persuaded Vietnam and the Philippines to agree to a compromise on the wording. But repeated attempts to persuade Cambodia's Hor Namhong failed. At their last meeting Foreign Minister Hor Namhong "picked up his papers, and stormed out of the room" arguing it was a matter of principle for ASEAN not to take sides in bilateral disputes. Finally, according to an account by a Philippine official who attended the meetings in Phnom Penh: "[t]he text of the proposed Joint Communiqué's item/subhead on the "South China Sea" was drafted by the ASEAN foreign ministers and several revisions were made to make the text acceptable to all. However, the Cambodian Chair consistently rejected any proposed text that mentions Scarborough Shoal.

Blame Game

The failure of ASEAN foreign ministers to issue a joint communiqué at the conclusion of the 45th AMM led to immediate public recriminations. On the morning of the last day, immediately after a special meeting failed to reach an eleventh hour compromise, the Philippines issued a statement taking "strong exception" to the decision by the ASEAN Chair not to issue a joint communiqué. Foreign Minister Hor Namhong hit back accusing the Philippines of attempting to "hijack" the AMM and declaring that the "joint communiqué has become hostage to a bilateral issue." The Philippine Undersecretary for Foreign Affairs, Erlinda Basilio, penned a personal account entitled, "Why There Was No ASEAN Joint Communiqué" that provoked a Cambodian diplomatic response.

Unnamed diplomatic sources leaked information to the press suggesting collusion between China and Cambodia. One senior diplomat was quoted as stating, "China bought the chair, simple as that" and pointed to comments by Foreign Minister Yang thanking Prime Minister Hun Sen for supporting China's "core interests." A veteran journalist reported that when the first draft of the joint communiqué was submitted to the ASEAN Chair "the Cambodians, in a breach of ASEAN protocol, showed it to the Chinese, who said it was unacceptable unless the South China Sea reference was removed. So the Cambodians sent it back for amendment."

ASEAN's failure to issue a joint communiqué attracted widespread media coverage and critical commentary by academics and other observers. On July 26-27 Cambodia hit back with a barrage of three letters to the editors. The first was written by Kou Kuong, spokesperson for Cambodia's Ministry of Foreign Affairs and International Cooperation. This letter was addressed to the Editor-in-Chief of *The Cambodia Daily* in response to a story that quoted critical comments on Cambodia's role as ASEAN Chair by the International Crisis Group. Kou Kuong argued that "two countries…tried to sabotage and hijack our meetings" and held the 45th ASEAN Foreign Ministers' Joint Communiqué "hostage to its [sic] national interests."

The second letter was written by the Cambodian Ambassador to Thailand in response to an opinion piece by Thitinan Pongsudhirak, a well-known academic, published in the *Bangkok Post*. Ambassador You Ay first corrected a common media misperception that the Peace Palace, where the 45th AMM was held, was funded by China. She then targeted her remarks on comments that were critical of Cambodia's relations with China. Ambassador You pointed out that "China provided assistance only for the construction of the adjacent building and not the Peace Palace. Next, the Ambassador rejected Thitinan's assertion that China was an "open patron state" of Cambodia as a result of providing U.S. $10 billion in aid and investment. Finally, the Ambassador dismissed (but did not directly deny) as "extremely disparaging and slanderous" Thitinan's claim that Cambodia "shared the draft version of the joint statement with the Chinese, who then vetoed it."

The third letter was written by Cambodia's Ambassador to the Philippines to the editor-in-chief of *The Philippines Star*. Ambassador Hos' letter took direct issue with Undersecretary Basilio's article mentioned above. Ambassador Hos reiterated Cambodia's argument that the failure to achieve consensus at the 45th AMM was due to the "inflexible and non-negotiable position" of "two countries" [the Philippines and Vietnam]. Cambodia's Ambassador further argued that the "two countries wanted to sabotage and hijack the JC [joint communiqué]" in retaliation for Cambodia's refusal to issue an ASEAN Statement on the Situation in the South China Sea." The Ambassador's parting shot - accusing "the two countries" of "dirty politics" - resulted in two summons by the Philippine Department of Foreign Affairs. The Ambassador failed to appear for either reportedly on the ground of ill health. Shortly after it was announced that Ambassador Hos was being recalled.

Analysts are divided on the details of and extent to which China influenced Cambodia's decision to block the AMM joint communiqué, but few analysts argue that Cambodia's acted independently. Kishore Mahbubani, a former senior Singaporean diplomat, wrote "the whole world, including most ASEAN countries, perceived Cambodia's stance as the result of enormous Chinese pressure." Amitav Acharya wrote, "[t]here is little question that Hun Sen's refusal to accommodate Philippines and Vietnam resulted at least partly from Chinese pressure. According to a highly placed source, the Chinese specifically reminded the Cambodians that [Norodom] Sihanouk... had accepted the Chinese claims to the South China Sea." A Chinese scholar close to the Ministry of State Security revealed, "[w]e co-ordinated very well with Cambodia in that case [blocking objectionable wording in the 45th AMM joint communiqué] and... prevented an incident which would have been detrimental to China."

Shuttle Diplomacy

In the midst of the above recriminations, Indonesia's Foreign Minister initiated consultations with the nine other members of ASEAN in an effort to restore unity in ASEAN ranks and commit ASEAN to a common position. Foreign Minister Marty conducted an intense round of shuttle diplomacy flying to five capitals (Manila,

Hanoi, Bangkok, Phnom Penh and Singapore) over a two-day period (July 18-19). Marty and del Rosario agreed to a six-point proposal that Marty put to his other ASEAN counterparts. When he obtained their agreement Marty left it to Cambodia's Hor Namhong, as ASEAN Chair, to complete the diplomatic formalities.

On July 20, Hor Namhong, acting in his capacity as ASEAN Chair, officially released ASEAN's Six Principles on the South China Sea. Under the terms of this statement all ASEAN Foreign Ministers reaffirmed their commitment to: the full implementation of the DOC; Guidelines for the Implementation of the DOC; the early conclusion of a Regional COC in the South China Sea; full respect of the universally recognized principles of international law including the 1982 UNCLOS; continued exercise of self-restraint and non-use of force by all parties; and peaceful resolution of disputes in accordance with the universally recognized principles of international law including the 1982 UNCLOS. The ASEAN statement concluded: "The ASEAN Foreign Ministers resolve to intensify ASEAN consultations in the advancement of the above principles, consistent with the Treaty of Amity and Cooperation in Southeast Asia (1976) and the ASEAN Charter (2008)."

A Chinese Foreign Ministry spokesperson, Qin Gang, responded to these developments by introducing a pre-condition linking compliance with the DOC and discussions on the COC. Qin Gang stated:

> What concerns people now is that some individual countries, showing no respect for or compliance with the DOC, have time and again resorted to provocative means, which undermined the basic principles and spirit of the DOC and created difficulties for discussing a code of conduct (COC) in the South China Sea. Therefore, while being open to discussing a COC with ASEAN countries, China believes that all parties concerned must act in strict accordance with the DOC to create the necessary conditions and atmosphere of a COC.

China then dispatched its foreign minister for a fence-mending visit to Indonesia and Malaysia for talks with his counterparts. Foreign Minister Yang Jiechi stated at a joint press conference that China was willing to work with ASEAN to implement the DOC and "on the basis of consensus" to work toward the eventual adoption of the COC. Foreign Minister Yang held discussions with Malaysian Foreign Minister Anifah Aman in Kuala Lumpur. There was no joint press conference. Anifah Aman stated he was "confident we can resolve this matter [disputes in the South China Sea]... through peaceful means." He then observed, [t]here are overlapping claims by member countries. Let us discuss these among ASEAN countries first before we talk to China. We can only achieve this objective in the South China Sea if all parties agree. Then China can appreciate this and realise it is ASEAN's wish." This statement seemed to imply that ASEAN-China discussions on the COC, if and when they take place, would be a protracted process.

Conclusion

ASEAN's objective of creating an ASEAN Political-Security Community by 2015 is predicated on the assumption that ASEAN members share a common identity and a common responsibility for contributing to "peace, stability and security" in Southeast Asia. The *ASEAN Political-Security Community Blueprint* states that one of its goals is to "[e]nsure full implementation of the DOC for peace and stability in the South China Sea." In order to achieve this objective the *Blueprint* calls for a continuation of "ASEAN's current practice of close consultation among Member States to achieve full implementation of the DOC... and [w]ork towards the adoption of a regional Code of Conduct in the South China Sea." The *ASEAN Charter* calls for "[e]nhanced consultations on matters seriously affecting the common interest of ASEAN." ASEAN's failure to issue a joint communiqué after its 45th AMM poses procedural questions about the fate of 128 paragraphs in the draft that recorded decisions on a range of issues other than the South China Sea, including ASEAN community-building and the appointment of a new Secretary General. It also raises questions about the status of ASEAN's agreement on key principles in its draft COC.

The analysis presented in part one clearly shows that the Philippines has made major concessions in its discussions with fellow ASEAN members in order to reach consensus on the key principles in the COC. The Philippines has been diplomatically circumspect about this. There were no public recriminations when the Philippines proposals for a ZOPFF/C and a joint development area were stripped from its draft COC. As a result, ASEAN was able to reach agreement on the key principles of its COC and approach China informally to discuss the way ahead. ASEAN still has to fine-tune its draft by considering inputs from Indonesia in the form of a "non-paper."

Part two provided a detailed insight into internal ASEAN dynamics as its foreign ministers discussed and debated the South China Sea question and how to word its members' concerns in a joint communiqué. The analysis clearly demonstrates that the Philippines, as a founding member of ASEAN, expected support on an issue that touched not only on its national sovereignty but regional security as well. The analysis also demonstrates that there was a "majority consensus" to include reference to disputes concerning Scarborough Shoal and oil leasing in Vietnam's Exclusive Economic Zone.

The record indicates that the failure to achieve consensus was the result of Cambodia's handling of its role as ASEAN Chair. Foreign Minister Hor Namhong was not conciliatory at the AMM Retreat and his subsequent actions in rejecting repeated attempts at compromise appear obstinate. At the same time, it is revealing that ASEAN foreign ministers acquiesced to Cambodia's high-handedness in vetoing the draft joint communiqué drawn up by four of their colleagues. No minister directly challenged Hor Namhong's handling of the discussion/debate at the AMM Retreat.

Part three dealt with the recriminations that followed the failure of ASEAN to issue a joint communiqué. It is clear that Chinese influence played a major role in influencing Cambodia to play an obstructionist role. Cambodia's actions indicate that the idea of an ASEAN Community played second fiddle to its relations with China. In the short run the Philippines (and Vietnam) will be hyper sensitive to Cambodia's role as ASEAN Chair in any discussions with China on the South China Sea. In the longer term some ASEAN members will be concerned about China's ability to influence Laos and Myanmar who will assume the ASEAN Chair in 2014 and 2015, respectively. In this respect the events at the 45th AMM may serve as a wake up call and result in amended decision-making procedures.

Part four dealt with Indonesia's decision to engage in a round of shuttle diplomacy in order to obtain unanimous agreement on ASEAN's Six-Point Principles on the South China Sea. Foreign Minister Marty Natalegawa's diplomatic initiative provided a much-needed boost to ASEAN morale. His efforts also helped to dispel the perception outside of Southeast Asia that there was disunity among ASEAN members on how to deal with the South China Sea issue.

More importantly, Indonesia's intervention served notice to Cambodia that as ASEAN's chair for 2012 it could not unilaterally control ASEAN's agenda. Natalegawa's intervention was unprecedented in assuming a leadership role that normally would fall to the ASEAN chair and signalled that Indonesia is willing to play a more proactive role in regional affairs.

Current indications are that ASEAN will pursue the implementation of the DOC and discussions on the COC with China in tandem. ASEAN will seek to obtain agreement with China on the key principles and then move on to drafting the final text. China will have to take Indonesia's new role into account and this may prove a positive factor in addressing current tensions in the South China Sea.

ASEAN'S CODE OF CONDUCT IN SEA

The genesis of ASEAN's 2012 draft COC may be traced back to 1995 when China occupied Mischief Reef, a maritime feature claimed by the Philippines. The Mischief Reef incident marked a turning point. ASEAN foreign ministers issued a statement expressing their "serious concern" and urged the concerned parties "to refrain from taking actions that de-stabilize the situation." The Philippines, as the aggrieved party, sought the backing from its fellow ASEAN members for a Code of Conduct in the South China Sea that would constrain China from further encroachments on Philippines sovereignty. In late 1999 ASEAN members finally reached agreement on a COC.

In March 2000, ASEAN and China exchanged their respective drafts and agreed to consolidate them into one document. Four major areas of disagreement were identified: the geographic scope, restrictions on construction on occupied and unoccupied features, military activities in waters adjacent to the Spratly islands, and whether or not fishermen found in disputed waters could be detained and arrested. A formal ASEAN-China COC proved a bridge too far. In November 2002, ASEAN member states and China signed a non-binding political statement known as the Declaration on Conduct of Parties in the South China Sea (DOC). This document set out four trust and confidence building measures and five voluntary cooperative activities. The parties to the DOC reaffirmed "that the adoption of a code of conduct in the South China Sea would further promote peace and stability in the region and agree to work, on the basis of consensus, towards the eventual attainment of this objective."

The DOC was stillborn. It took a further twenty-five months before senior officials reached agreement on the terms of reference for the ASEAN-China Joint Working Group (JWC) to implement the DOC. In August 2005, ASEAN tabled draft Guidelines to Implement the DOC at the first meeting of the JWC. Point two called for ASEAN consultations prior to meeting with China. China objected and repeated its long-held position that the relevant parties should resolve sovereignty and jurisdictional disputes bilaterally. This proved such a sticking point that another six years of intermittent discussions and twenty-one successive drafts were exchanged before final agreement was reached.

In July 2011, the Guidelines to Implement the DOC were adopted after ASEAN dropped its insistence on prior consultation and agreed instead to promote dialogue and consultation among the parties. A new point was added to the Guidelines specifying that activities and projects carried out under the DOC should be reported to the ASEAN-China Ministerial Meeting. All the other points in the 2011 Guidelines remained unchanged from the original ASEAN draft tabled in 2005.

ASEAN and Chinese senior officials commenced discussions on the implementation of the Guidelines. At a meeting held in

Beijing from January 13-15, 2012, agreement was reached to set up four expert committees on maritime scientific research, environmental protection, search and rescue, and transnational crime. These committees were derived from the five cooperative activities mentioned in the 2002 DOC. Significantly no expert committee on safety of navigation and communication at sea was established due to its contentious nature.

The agreement on DOC Guidelines led to the revival of the long-standing proposal by the Philippines for a COC that was included in the 2002 DOC. ASEAN senior officials began drafting the COC with the intention of reaching a common ASEAN position before presenting it to China for discussion. China initially took the position that the implementation of the DOC Guidelines should be given priority over the COC. China stated it would discuss the COC with ASEAN at an "appropriate timing" or when "appropriate conditions" were met.

In January 2012, the Philippines circulated an informal working draft simply titled, Philippines Draft Code of Conduct. The document was eight pages in length and comprised ten articles. In line with official Philippine foreign policy promoting the South China Sea as a Zone of Peace, Freedom, Friendship and Cooperation (ZOPFF/C), the draft COC proposed a Joint Cooperation Area in the South China Sea (Article III), a Joint Permanent Working Committee to implement the ZOPFF/C (Article IV), the Application of Part IX of the 1982 United Nations Convention on Law of the Sea in the South China Sea (Article V), and Dispute Settlement Mechanisms (Article VI). The remaining articles contained standard provisions such as principles (Article I), objectives (Article II), reservations (Article VII), signature and ratification (Article VIII), entry into force (Article IX) and review and amendments to the code (Article X). In discussions held by ASEAN senior officials during the first quarter of 2012 it became apparent that ASEAN members were divided on Articles III-VI in the Philippines draft. Some ASEAN members also shared reservations about being too prescriptive concerning dispute settlement mechanisms.

It was at this point that China changed tack and sought a seat at the ASEAN discussions. The timing of China's involvement with ASEAN in drafting a COC quickly became a contentious issue within ASEAN. These tensions surfaced at the 20th ASEAN Summit held in Phnom Penh from April 3-4. Cambodia, the ASEAN Chair, pushed for China's inclusion in ASEAN discussions. The Philippines and Vietnam objected strongly and a compromise was reached. ASEAN would proceed on its own to draft a COC, while communication with China would take place through the ASEAN Chair at the same time.

The ASEAN Senior Officials Meeting (SOM) Working Group on the COC concluded its discussions on June 13, 2012 at its seventh meeting. According to an official statement, "The meeting agreed to submit the draft ASEAN proposed key elements of the regional Code of Conduct in the South China Sea to the ASEAN SOM for consideration." The ASEAN SOM met in Phnom Penh from July 6-7 and forwarded the agreed draft to the ASEAN foreign ministers for deliberation at their 45th AMM on July 9. At the end of the AMM formal discussions Kao Kim Hourn, Secretary of State in the Cambodian Ministry of Foreign Affairs, told reporters that the ASEAN foreign ministers had adopted the "key elements" of the COC and "agreed to have the ASEAN senior officials meet with the senior official from China to discuss the (code of conduct) from now on."

According to the document ASEAN's Proposed Elements of a Regional Code of Conduct in the South China Sea, the original Philippine Working Draft was heavily pruned. Articles III-VI were dropped entirely. The ASEAN "key elements" were reduced to a preamble and two articles. A comparison of the Philippine draft preamble with the agreed ASEAN preamble reveals that two items contained in the former were dropped. The first was a reference to "the principles and norms of international law applicable to maritime space, in particular the principles on the peaceful uses and cooperative management of the oceans." The second and more sensitive reference that was deleted referred to "the need to preserve the region from any form of increased militarization and intimidation."

Both preambles began by referencing the 1997 Joint Statement of the meeting of heads of government/state of ASEAN members and China. Next, the Philippines inclusion of the 2003 declaration of the ASEAN-China Strategic Partnership for Peace and Prosperity was replaced with a reference to the more recent 2006 Joint Declaration on Strategic Partnership for Peace and Towards an Enhanced ASEAN-China Strategic Partnership. Both preambles included a reference to the 2002 DOC and its commitment to develop a COC. Both preambles also referred to protection of the environment and biodiversity. The ASEAN draft altered the formulation in the Philippine draft from "advance a lasting and durable solution of disputes" to read "comprehensive and durable solution of disputes." The Philippines original proposal for a "zone of peace, freedom, friendship and cooperation" was modified to read "an area of peace, stability, friendship and cooperation."

Article I of the ASEAN draft COC contained its operative provisions and called on the parties to "respect and adhere to the United Nations Charter, 1982 UNCLOS, Treaty of Amity and Cooperation in Southeast Asia, DOC and the Five Principles of Peaceful Co-existence. However, five of the principles contained in the Philippine draft were deleted in their entirety: respect for freedom of navigation and over flight; the need to define, clarify and segregate disputed areas from the non-disputed areas; full resolution of the territorial and jurisdictional disputes; refrain from undertaking activities that may disrupt the peace and endanger the environment; and build trust and confidence on the basis of equality and mutual respect.

The ASEAN draft contained four principles: (1) to "develop modalities and arrangements for the promotion of settlement by peaceful means of disputes and prevent their escalation...;" (2) to respect the provisions of and take actions consistent with the COC; (3) to encourage other countries to respect the purposes and principles contained in the COC; and (4) to establish an effective mechanism to monitor the implementation of the COC.

Article II of the ASEAN draft enumerated eight obligations: a ministerial level mechanism to monitor the implementation of the COC; prohibition on reservations to the COC; provisions of entry into force; mechanism for settling disputes; amendment of the COC; provisions for other countries to respect the COC;

indefinite duration of the COC; and registration of the COC with the ASEAN Secretary General and Secretariat of the United Nations

Article III(4) required signatories to "establish a mechanism for settling disputes relating to the interpretation and application of the Code of Conduct." The ASEAN draft, following deletion of any mention of the joint cooperation area, also dropped reference to a dispute settlement mechanism in the joint cooperation area.

Two dispute settlement mechanisms were included that closely reflected the wording in the Philippine Working Draft on disputes arising from a breach or violation of the COC. The first mechanism is the dispute settlement mechanism included in the ASEAN Treaty of Amity and Cooperation in Southeast Asia (TAC). The TAC provides for a ministerial-level ASEAN High Council and empowers it to recommend to parties in dispute, subject to their prior agreement, such measures as good offices, mediation, inquiry or conciliation. The High Council also is given the authority to "recommend appropriate measures for the prevention of a deterioration of the dispute..." The People's Republic of China acceded to the TAC in 2003 and undertook in writing "faithfully to perform and carry out all the stipulations therein contained."

In the event that parties are unable to resolve their dispute within the ASEAN framework, the ASEAN COC sets out a second mechanism: the disputants "may resort to dispute settlement mechanism provided under international law, including UNCLOS." This could include taking their case to an international court for adjudication. UNCLOS, however, does not contain any provisions for the settlement of sovereignty disputes over islands and rocks. It does provide for an International Tribunal for the Law of the Sea (ITLOS) to adjudicate disputes over maritime jurisdiction. Under international law "the land dominates the sea" and before disputants can take their case to ITLOS they would first have to determine sovereignty over disputed islands and rocks on which their maritime claims are based.

At the 45th AMM Retreat, the Cambodian foreign minister reported that, "ASEAN-China met twice recently to discuss informally the drafting of [the] COC" and that "Cambodia will host another formal ASEAN China SOM on the COC in the near future." An informal senior-level working meeting was held on July 8 and Japanese media sources reported "ASEAN and China had agreed to start talks on a legally-binding maritime code of conduct to manage the disputes."

A day later the Cambodian Foreign Minister told his ASEAN counterparts that Vice Foreign Minister Fu Ying stated that China was willing to commence talks on the COC in September. Also on July 9, Foreign Minister Yang Jiechi met with Secretary of State Hillary Clinton to discus the South China Sea. After these talks, U.S. officials revealed that "foreign minister Yang gave Secretary Clinton 'a careful indication' that Beijing is willing to join a dialogue on the code as soon as September, ahead of November's ASEAN summit." On July 10, ASEAN Secretary General Surin Pitsuwan also confirmed that the first formal meeting between ASEAN and Chinese senior officials on the COC would take place in Phnom Penh in September. China's commitment to meet in September to discuss the COC may be in doubt. According to Japanese sources, "on July 11, China's attitude suddenly shifted and it refused to begin talks." Ian Storey argues that Vice Foreign Minister Fu Ying's agreement with ASEAN to begin talks on a COC in September "was overruled by Foreign Minister Yang... At present there is no timetable to discuss a CoC though both sides will meet in September or October to talk about implementing cooperative projects in areas outlined in the DoC."

The document, ASEAN's Proposed Elements of a Regional Code of Conduct in the South China Sea (COC) between ASEAN Member States and the People's Republic of China, has not been officially released and remains an internal draft ASEAN document. At the 45th AMM Retreat Marty Natalegawa promised that "Indonesia will circulate a non paper [on] possible and additional elements of [the] COC. It is meant to be more prescriptive and operational." In other words, ASEAN members will have to meet to approve any further additions to their draft COC before meeting with Chinese senior officials.

Why Was There No Joint Communiqué?

Cambodia, as the ASEAN Chair for 2012, hosted the 45th AMM and related meetings in Phnom Penh from July 8-13. In his opening address Prime Minister Hun Sen stated that "realising the ASEAN Community by 2015 is the top priority for ASEAN." With respect to the ASEAN Political-Security Community, Hun Sen declared, "we should give emphasis to the implementation of the DOC [Declaration on Conduct of Parties in the South China Sea], including the eventual conclusion of *'Code of Conduct (COC) in the South China Sea'* emphasis in original]."

The AMM has a busy agenda that extends well beyond South China Sea issues. In 2011, for example, the joint communiqué issued at the end of the 44th AMM listed 120 items and ran to twenty-nine pages. At the 45th AMM Cambodia's Foreign Minister, Hor Namhong, assigned responsibility for drafting the joint communiqué summarizing the AMM deliberations to a working party of four foreign ministers: Marty Natalegawa (Indonesia), Anifah Aman (Malaysia), Albert del Rosario (Philippines) and Pham Binh Minh (Vietnam). Their 132-paragraph draft summarized the wide range of issues taken up by the AMM including the terms of reference for the ASEAN Institute of Peace and Reconciliation, the ASEAN Human Rights Declaration and the nomination of Mr. Le Luong Minh as the next Secretary.General. The draft communiqué also summarized discussions on the South China Sea including the stand off at Scarborough Shoal between China and the Philippines and Vietnam's concerns about the award of oil exploration leases by the China National Offshore Oil Company within Vietnam's Exclusive Economic Zone (EEZ).

The wording of one paragraph in the South China Sea section of the joint communiqué became such a sticking point between Cambodia and the drafters of the joint communiqué that no communiqué was issued. This was unprecedented. Since ASEAN was founded in 1967 all forty-four previous AMMs had issued joint communiqués. Indeed, a media advisory announcing the 45th AMM, released by Cambodia on July 6, 2002, concluded, "[a] Joint Communiqué will be adopted at the end of the Meeting."

Cambodia argues that the failure of the AMM to adopt a joint communiqué rests squarely with the Philippines and Vietnam and their insistence on including a reference to Scarborough Shoal and EEZs in the final text. According to Cambodia, the actions by the

Philippines and Vietnam prevented a consensus from being reached and Cambodia had no recourse but to withhold the joint communiqué. The leaked record of the foreign ministers' retreat held after the AMM reveals a different story.

Discussion on the South China Sea took place in the plenary session under the agenda item "preparation for the upcoming ministerial meetings." All ten foreign ministers spoke in turn with Cambodia speaking last. The Philippines opened the discussion. Foreign Secretary del Rosario stated that ASEAN should adopt a rules-based approach in resolving maritime disputes and territorial claims and adhere to international law to ensure maritime safety and maritime cooperation mechanisms. He noted that under the DOC the signatories were committed to promote a peaceful, friendly and harmonious environment in the South China Sea. He argued that recent events involved repeated intrusions into Scarborough Shoal, violating the principles of the DOC and universally recognized principles of international law, including the United Nations Convention on Law of the Sea (UNCLOS).

ASEAN IN RESOLVE P'ROVINCIAL DISPUTES IN SOUTH CHINA SEA

The territorial disputes revolving around the South China Sea came into focus in the 1990s as China began to claim almost the entire South China Sea region on the basis of historical records. China's claim has since been challenged by smaller Southeast Asian countries like Vietnam, the Philippines, Brunei and Malaysia. Indonesia too has few issues especially regarding the Nansha Islands.

As the major disputant, China, while emphasising its sovereign rights on specific islands, wants to deal with the issues bilaterally. China has been building artificial islands on the Spratlys to purportedly protect its national interests. On the other hand, most of the members of the Association of Southeast Asian Nations (ASEAN) want to settle the issues multilaterally and want ASEAN to play a central role in it.

Few ASEAN members even tried to involve extra-regional powers to balance China's growing assertiveness in the region.

However, the situation takes more twists and turns as the Southeast Asian disputants have conflicting claims even between them.

China clearly has a dual-track approach towards the region. Beijing prefers to deal with regional countries through bilateral frameworks and mechanisms on the South China Sea issue, but recognises ASEAN as a collective entity when it comes to the question of economic cooperation and integration of the region.

In addition, China's investments in the region are too overwhelming for any country in the region to ignore. This has also caused differences amongst the Southeast Asian countries which tend to have varied perceptions about China's economic engagements in the region. Countries like Malaysia and Cambodia tend to adopt softer approach towards China as they do not share any territorial dispute with China. Similarly, Myanmar too has a softer attitude given China's huge investments in the country.

China's success in dividing the Southeast Asian countries first became evident when Cambodia that hosted and chaired the 2012 ASEAN Summit refused to issue the ASEAN communiqué to avoid condemning China's assertion in the South China Sea. Member countries again failed to agree on issuing a joint statement specifying China's growing stakes in the South China Sea at the end of the 2014 ASEAN Summit held in Myanmar. In the latest ASEAN Summit, held in Malaysia in November 2015, the member countries once again failed to come up with a joint statement referring to China's assertiveness as a threat to regional peace and stability. It is clear that countries in the region have different perceptions and attitudes towards China and certainly do not share unanimity in their approach towards ASEAN. The failure of multilateralism to craft a unified approach on resolving regional disputes is as much a reality for ASEAN as is the fact that it gives China ample space and opportunity to vigorously nurture and pursue its proclaimed national interests in the region.

DECLARATION ON THE CONDUCT OF PARTIES IN THE SOUTH CHINA SEA

The Government of the People's Republic of China and the Governments of the Member States of ASEAN,

REAFFIRMING their determination to consolidate and develop the friendship and cooperation existing between their people and governments with the view to promoting a 21st century-oriented partnership of good neighbourliness and mutual trust;

COGNIZANT of the need to promote a peaceful, friendly and harmonious environment in the South China Sea between China and ASEAN for the enhancement of peace, stability, economic growth and prosperity in the region;

COMMITTED to enhancing the principles and objectives of the 1997 Joint Statement of the Meeting of President of the People's Republic of Chinaand the Heads of State/Government of the Member States of ASEAN;

DESIRING to enhance favourable conditions for a peaceful and durable solution of differences and disputes among countries concerned;

HEREBY DECLARE the following:

1. The Parties reaffirm their commitment to the purposes and principles of the Charter of the United Nations, the 1982 UN Convention on the Law of the Sea, the Treaty of Amity and Cooperation in Southeast Asia, the Five Principles of Peaceful Coexistence and other universally recognized principles of international law which shall serve as the basic norms governing state-to-state relations;
2. The Parties are committed to exploring ways for building trust and confidence in accordance with the above-mentioned principles and on the basis of equality and mutual respect;
3. The Parties reaffirm their respect for and commitment to the freedom of navigation in and overflight above the South China Sea as provided for by the universally recognized principles of international law, including the 1982 UN Convention on the Law of the Sea;
4. The Parties concerned undertake to resolve their territorial and jurisdictional disputes by peaceful means, without resorting to the threat or use of force, through friendly consultations and negotiations by sovereign states directly concerned, in accordance with universally recognized

principles of international law, including the 1982 UN Convention on the Law of the Sea;

5. The Parties undertake of exercise self-restraint in the conduct of activities that would complicate or escalate disputes and affect peace and stability including, among others, refraining from action of inhabiting on the presently uninhabited islands, reefs, shoals, cays, and other features and to handle their differences in a constructive manner.

   Pending the peaceful settlement of territorial and jurisdictional disputes, the Parties concerned undertake to intensify efforts to seek ways, in the spirit of cooperation and understanding, to build trust and confidence between and among them, including:

   a. holding dialogues and exchange of views as appropriate between their defense and military officials;
   b. ensuring just and humane treatment of all persons who are either in danger or in distress;
   c. notifying, on a voluntary basis, other Parties concerned of any impending joint/combined military exercise; and
   d. exchanging, on a voluntary basis, relevant information.

6. Pending a comprehensive and durable settlement of the disputes, the Parties concerned may explore or undertake cooperative activities. These may include the following:

   a. marine environmental protection;
   b. marine scientific research;
   c. safety of navigation and communication at sea;
   d. search and rescue operation; and
   e. combating transnational crime, including but not limited to trafficking in illicit drugs, piracy and armed robbery at sea, and illegal traffic in arms.

   The modalities, scope and locations, in respect of bilateral and multilateral cooperation should be agreed upon by the Parties concerned prior to-their actual implementation.

7. The Parties concerned stand ready to continue their consultations and dialogues concerning relevant issues, through modalities to be agreed by them, including regular consultations on the observance of this Declaration, for the purpose of promoting good neighbourliness and transparency, establishing harmony, mutual understanding and cooperation, and facilitating peaceful resolution of disputes among them;
8. The Parties undertake to respect the provisions of this Declaration and take actions consistent therewith;
9. The Parties encourage other countries to respect the principles contained in this Declaration;
10. The Parties concerned reaffirm that the adoption of a code of conduct in the South China Seawould further promote peace and stability in the region and agree to work, on the basis of consensus, towards the eventual attainment of this objective.

Done on the Fourth Day of November in the Year Two Thousand and Two in Phnom Penh, the Kingdom of Cambodia.

CHINA'S POWER SECURITY AND SOUTH ASIAN SEA LANES OF STATEMENT

China's spiraling demand for energy, plus its growing dependence on imported petroleum, have made Beijing increasingly concerned with ensuring the uninterrupted flow of oil at reasonable prices. The Middle East plus North and East Africa provide well over half of China imported oil. Virtually all of that oil moves to China by tanker across the Indian Ocean. Beijing confronts several potential threats to its trans-Indian Ocean oil supply. A confrontation between Iran and the United States could lead – either via sanctions or by military actions – to the restriction of oil shipments through the Strait of Hormuz. An Indian-China conflict might escalate into the naval dimension. India might respond to defeats by the PLA in the Himalayas, or to Chinese support for Pakistan in the context of a "fourth round" between India and Pakistan, by using India's naval supremacy in the Indian Ocean to sever China's vital oil imports. Then there are scenarios of U.S.-PRC conflict over Taiwan that escalated into U.S. naval blockade of China. None of these contingencies is a high probability, yet military institutions everywhere devote attention to remote but potentially dire scenarios.

In any of these contingencies the ability of PLA-N warships to escort vessels carrying oil from Middle Eastern ports to China might be part of an effort to prevent hostile powers from interfering with delivery of China's oil supply. Development of robust overland transportation systems between Yunnan and the Bay of Bengal, and between western Xinjiang and Gwadar could substantially strengthen the PLA's ability to sustain intense military operations in the eastern and western Indian Oceans. As a neutral power in a possible U.S.-Iran confrontation, China would enjoy the right under international law to continue trading with both belligerents. But historically neutral powers have often found protection by military force essential to upholding those legal rights. Were China's leaders to conclude PLA-N escort of China's oil commerce across the Indian Ocean necessary, the newly created transport lines via Myanmar and Pakistan could become quite useful. In terms of possible Sino-Indian conflict, the PLA-Navy is substantially superior to the Indian Navy in terms of overall tonnage and ship numbers, but the latter enjoys overwhelming geographical advantages when operating in the Indian Ocean. If the PLA-N could obtain bases on the Indian Ocean littoral (perhaps at Gwadar and Kyaukpyu), and link those forward bases to China by robust road and rail lines, India's geographic advantages would be substantially diminished to the PLA-N's advantage.

Termination

China's omni-directional friendship policy in South Asia is not cant, but serves Chinese interests well. Chinese relations with other South Asia nations will be more robust and stable if India views those ties as non-threatening. A friendly and cooperative relation with India will give China a stronger position in South Asia than would a conflictual Sino-Indian relationship. An economic, diplomatic, and even military partnership between China and India, surrounded by similar partnerships between China and the other South Asian countries — a sort of Asian zone of friendship and cooperation – would maximize Chinese influence in South Asia, and ensure that threats to China did not emanate from that region. China's omni-directional friendship diplomacy toward South Asia is working relatively well. China's broad strategic objective is to persuade India to look benevolently on an open-ended and expanding Chinese economic, political, and military presence in South Asia and the Indian Ocean, to eliminate suspicion in Sino-Indian relations, and to transform India into China's partner. In this way the rise of China in Asia will not lead to Indian efforts to countervail China in coalition with the United States. But the conversion of India to friendship with China is to be done without making concessions to India on the status of Tibet, the Sino-Pakistan strategic link, or by restricting China's expanding military, security, and transportation ties with other South Asian nations.

China's optimal outcome would be open-ended, growing political, economic, and military cooperation between China and all the South Asian countries, with India accepting an open-ended expansion of Chinese influence in that region and learning to live comfortably under China's benevolent protection. India would gradually evolve into a key Chinese partner in South Asia. China's intention, its objective, in South Asia is most definitely not to establish dominance over that region, or draw it into some sort of Chinese sphere of influence. That, however, might be the outcome over a period of twenty or thirty years.

China and the South Asian Equilibrium of Power

China has an interest in maintaining the existing balance of power between India and Pakistan. The existence of a strong and confident Pakistan able and willing to challenge India confers important advantages on China. Politically it hobbles India's efforts to act on the global stage as China's equal. Militarily, it forces India to confront the possibility of a two front war, thereby compelling it to divide its military forces. This is the geopolitical rationale for China's large and long-standing economic and military assistance to Pakistan. It is *possible* that one reason why Beijing is not in a hurry about resolving the boundary dispute with India is that it would fundamentally ease India's two-front problem, intensifying Indian pressure on Pakistan. China's interest in keeping Pakistan strong was one reason why Beijing endorsed Islamabad's re-engagement with the United States after 9-11. While that re-engagement diminished somewhat the potential utility of Pakistan and Gwadar as a logistics "back door" for China in the event of confrontation with the United States or India, it also brought Pakistan in from a situation of increasingly dangerous isolation. Pakistan's close ties with the Taliban in Afghanistan plus the growing Islamisization of Pakistani politics and the steady deterioration of Pakistan-Western relations since the mid-1990s, posed an increasing danger of Pakistan's isolation, perhaps even designation by the international community as a "rogue state." This would have been a serious blow to China's interests, and to the extent that U.S. re-engagement with Pakistan could move Pakistan in a different direction, it served China's strategic interest in a strong Pakistan that constrains India. U.S. engagement with Pakistan also made development of India-US strategic partnership more difficult, and diffused Indian anger over China's own strong military and nuclear links to Pakistan.

This is not to say that Beijing's interests are served by confrontation between Pakistan and India. Beijing's objective, as noted earlier, is to develop cooperative ties with all the countries of South Asia. Confrontation between Pakistan and India would put Beijing in the unfortunate position of having to choose between Islamabad and New Delhi. Failure to support Pakistan could endanger China's fundamental interest in keeping Pakistan strong and independent of Indian domination, and threaten China's strategic partnership with Pakistan. Alignment with Pakistan, on the other hand, would spoil China's ties with the most important south Asian power, India, and possibly push that power further into alignment with the United States. In this sense, peace between India and Pakistan is in China's interests.

In the event of Pakistan-Indian confrontation, China will piggy-back on the peace diplomacy of the United States and other powers, adding its voice to efforts to restore peace and the status quo ante as quickly as possible. A Chinese tilt toward Pakistan but well below the level of threatened belligerency on Pakistan's behalf, would be virtually certain, but only in the event that India roused itself and threatened to decisively subordinate Pakistan (perhaps in the aftermath of a nuclear exchange) would Beijing move toward actual co-belligerency on Pakistan's behalf.

CHINA'S SOUTH ASIAN INTERESTS AND POLICIES

China's broad objective in South Asia is to expand multi-dimensional cooperative relations with all the countries of that region. "Multi-dimensional" signifies military ties as well as more innocuous political and economic cooperation. "All" means both India and India's smaller neighbours: Pakistan, Myanmar, Nepal, Sri Lanka, Bangladesh, Bhutan, and the Maldives. India has sometimes objected to China's relations — especially military-security ties — with these countries. Beijing views South Asian countries as "neighbours" with whom it is especially important to have friendly, cooperative ties both to increase China's own economic and political influence and to lessen the ability of potentially hostile powers (currently the U.S.) to injure China's interests.

Economically, China seeks to draw South Asia's resources into China's development drive. India with its fast-growing, industrialized, and relatively affluent economy has become China's strongest economic partner in South Asia. Two-way Sino-Indian trade in 2003 was $7.6 billion, compared to $2.4 billion for Sino-Pakistan, $1.4 billion for Sino-Bangladesh, and $1.1 billion for Sino-Myanmar trade. During their April 2005 meeting, Wen Jiabao and Manmohan Singh agreed to increase trade to $20 billion by 2008. While that amount is paltry compared to China's trade with countries like Japan, Germany, South Korea, or the United States, it leads China's South Asian trade by far.

The simple fact is that India produces much more that Chinese firms want to purchase than do Pakistan, Bangladesh, or Myanmar — let alone the small countries like Nepal, Bhutan, or the Maldives. In 2003, China imported $1 billion more from India than it exported to it, while Chinese exports to Pakistan were three times the value of China's imports, exports to Bangladesh were forty times the value of China's imports, and exports to Myanmar were over five times the volume of imports. While these figures are based on official statistics and do not reflect smuggling (which is substantial in the case of Myanmar), the broader point is that India simply has more to offer China. From India China imports a wide array of mining and industrial products: steel and iron ore, zinc, aluminum and aluminum products, copper and copper products, acids and alkalines, dyes, colouring, alcohol and other chemical products, rubber, plastics, cotton, wool, thread and yarn, leather, and machinery and machine parts. From Pakistan, in contrast, China buys largely cotton, yarn, and leather.

China also recognizes that in key economic-technological areas it has much to learn from India. Chinese analysts recognize India's world-leadership position in computer software creation and aspire to learn from India in this area, meshing these strengths with China's existing strengths in computer hardware production to help catapult China to world-class-economy status. There are no comparable inducements in the case of the other South Asian countries. Pakistan and Bangladesh offer attractive markets for Chinese consumer goods and machine tools. But the ability of these poor countries to purchase Chinese goods, and to produce things useful to China's booming industry, is limited compared to India's. China has not been able to forge with the South Asian countries a robust foreign energy-for-Chinese-capital-goods swap such as it has engineered with Iran. The exploitation of Bangladesh's natural gas deposits could conceivably overcome this structural imbalance, with Bangladesh entering into an energy for Chinese capital goods swap similar to that characterizing the Sino-Iranian relation. Politically, there are interrupted visits between China and the larger South Asian countries at the minister and vice minister level to "exchange views" on various bilateral, regional, and international subjects. Beijing seeks to engage South Asian governments in dialogue and cooperation on substantive subjects of mutual concern: countering narcotics traffic, smuggling, and terrorism; stabilizing the Karzai government in Afghanistan; or dealing with Tibetan presence and activities in various South Asian countries. Beijing also strives to line up South Asian support on the Taiwan subject: to counter Taiwan efforts to expand ties and to guarantee South Asian neutrality in the event of a U.S.-PRC clash over Taiwan.

Friendship with China is often attractive to smaller South Asian countries living in India's shadow. People in those countries often see ties with China as affirming their independence from India and as a way of gaining bargaining leverage with New Delhi. China's voice in the U.N. Security Council is valued by South Asian governments because of Beijing's occasional willingness to say a few words on behalf of smaller South Asian countries, or even to criticize Washington on behalf of those smaller countries. China has expressed a desire for observer status in the South Asian Association for Regional Cooperation (SAARC) where its ability to offset India will be valued by the other South Asian states.

China views military links as part of the normal repertoire of international cooperation and seeks to expand military ties with South Asian countries. Every year China exchanges with Pakistan, India, Bangladesh, and Myanmar two or three delegations at the deputy chief of staff through defence minister level, or from military regions, military academies, or defence industrial agencies. China has recently attempted to institutionalize exchange of views with the larger South Asian countries in the security / military areas. At the political level, there are periodic discussions of regional security subjects of common concern. Bangladesh, Pakistan, and Myanmar have been preferred and heavy customers for Chinese military equipment. Chinese training, maintenance, and parts have come with equipment purchases. Exchange of intelligence between China and Pakistan and Myanmar is routine, with Yangong providing important electronic listening posts at several points in the Bay of Bengal / Strait of Malacca area. Chinese naval squadrons have made friendly port calls to Pakistani (1985, 1993, 2001), Bangladeshi (1986, 1995), Myanmar (2001), and Indian (1993, 2001) ports. In October 2003, the PLA-Navy conducted its first-ever joint exercises with the Pakistani navy in the East China Sea. The next month it conducted joint exercises in the same region with the Indian Navy. China assists Pakistan's missile development and its nuclear energy efforts. Although China's involvement in the latter is under IAEA supervision, the intrinsic fungibility of nuclear materials and know-how makes it likely there is some spill over to Pakistan's nuclear weapons capabilities.

In the past India, has objected to China's military links with South Asian nations. In 1989, for example, a Nepalese attempt to purchase Chinese weapons and initiate an intelligence exchange agreement with China precipitated severe Indian economic sanctions that forced Kathmandu to abandon the objectionable policies. Given New Dehli's opposition to Sino-South Asian military cooperation, Beijing's insistence on forging such links is testament to its determination to become a multi-dimensional power in the region, and its refusal to cede South Asia to an Indian sphere of influence.

China's response to Indian concerns over China-South Asian military cooperation has been to assert that since China does not have aggressive or malevolent intentions, China's military cooperation with India's neighbours does not threaten India.

If India is concerned about China's military ties with the smaller South Asian nations, Beijing argues, the proper course is to increase mutual trust between China and India via security dialogues and other such venues. Or if New Delhi is unhappy with Chinese military cooperation with India's South Asian neighbours, China is quite willing to expand such cooperation with India itself. There is no valid reason to object to these friendly, cooperative relations, Beijing argues. In fact, such objections manifest "anti-China" sentiments and hostility toward China, which will be answer in kind by China.

The sort of punishment contained in this implied threat was demonstrated during the eighteen months after India's May 1998 nuclear tests that New Delhi had justified as a response to threat from China. After the Indian tests with their China threat justification, Beijing cancelled scheduled sessions of the Joint Working Group on the boundary. Chinese media rhetoric became harsher, even resurrecting charges of Indian "hegemony." Beijing urged Washington and the U.N. Security Council to adopt tough measures against India, and to target mainly India, not Pakistan's "response" to India's tests. Beijing hinted it might shift to a more pro-Pakistan position on Kashmir. Beijing's carrot and stick approach seems to have been fairly successful. India has agreed to open-ended cooperation with China, even while China expands military ties with India's neighbours.

RISK OF CONFLICT AND SOUTH CHINA SEA DISPUTES

The South China Sea has been the focus of several conflicting maritime claims by the littoral countries. The most prominent of these has concerned the Spratly Islands in the southern reaches of the South China Sea. It is one of the most complicated territorial disputes in Asia, involving approximately 100 small islands, reefs, submerged banks, and rocks that total only a few square kilometres in an ocean area of several hundred thousand square kilometres. Five countries (China, Malaysia, the Philippines, Taiwan, and Vietnam) have standing claims to various portions of the South China Sea. These countries have occupied some of the Spratly locations with military outposts or civilian facilities over the past six decades. (Brunei is another claimant even though it does not physically occupy any of the disputed locations.)

Other potential South China Sea flashpoints include the Paracel Islands, which are occupied by China and also claimed by Vietnam. In addition, Scarborough Shoal, a desolate rock formation located north of the Spratlys in the Philippines' exclusive economic zone (EEZ), was the scene of a non-violent maritime showdown between China and the Philippines in April 2012. More recently, Manila declared that it has aerial images of concrete blocks on the shoal that indicate China is laying the foundations for building a facility.

Multiple factors drive the competing countries to aggressively defend their interests in the South China Sea. The sovereignty issue alone (i.e. states claiming ownership of various parts of the waters and island territories therein) accounts for the willingness to press their claims to the point of crisis and even armed clashes on occasion. Growing nationalism only complicates the situation by limiting diplomatic flexibility when these disputes periodically flare up. Security interests and regional competition for natural resources (fishing grounds and potential hydrocarbon resources) are also important complicating factors. Both fishing vessels and energy exploration ships have become pawns as the competing countries jockey for advantage to support their competing interests. Finally, the scramble for limited maritime resources is exacerbated by how some claimant countries choose to interpret the United Nations Convention on the Law of the Sea (UNCLOS). Most claimants use their continuous occupation of key locations among the Spratly Islands to support their national claims for an EEZ covering large portions of the South China Sea, although China relies on expansive claims concerning much of the South China Sea based on historical sovereignty considerations.

The competition among the claimant countries for sovereign control of the Spratlys appears to present less risk than a corresponding dispute between China and Japan in the East China Sea centered on the Diaoyu/Senkaku Islands, which flared up again in September 2012. However, the risk of unintended armed conflict from the persistent South China Sea disputes with wider international implications should not be underestimated, particularly given the interests of the claimant countries and several outside countries with strategic interests in the South China Sea, such as freedom of navigation. The complexity of the South China Sea disputes is increased by China's greater willingness to engage in coercive diplomacy to protect its interests along with the assertive role of the Philippines and Vietnam in confronting what they regard as Chinese encroachments on their maritime interests. The unexpected escalation of the protracted sovereignty disputes between Argentina and the United Kingdom over the Falkland Islands (or Malvinas) in 1982 is a prudent reminder that persistent territorial disputes sometimes erupt into unintended armed conflict with broader implications despite general expectations.

Although these disputes largely involve a war of words, they occasionally become violent. When the disputes move beyond diplomatic protests and charges, they can involve more provocative actions, sometimes resulting in the loss of lives, exacerbating regional tensions. About four decades ago, China forcibly displaced Vietnam from the Paracel Islands, which are located north of the

Spratly Islands. In 1988, China and Vietnam fought over the Fiery Cross Reef in the Spratlys with the resulting loss of three Vietnamese ships and an estimated 70 Vietnamese sailors killed or missing. In the mid-1990s, the Chinese substantially increased their presence by building "sea bastions" manned by troops at Mischief Reef, which is located in the heart of waters claimed by the Philippines. More recently, the South China Sea rivalry has taken the traditional form of sporadic incidents at sea as the claimant countries jockey to protect their interests. Sometimes these incidents turn deadly, usually when fishing boats are seized or sunk.

Along with the continuing skirmishes among the competing claimants, such incidents suggest the potential for such confrontations to escalate into deadly incident and military conflict. The persistent risk of armed conflict arising over the Spratly Islands is all the more dangerous because of its seemingly routine nature, which serves to conceal an underlying unpredictability. These territorial disputes, which mostly involve minor incidents and diplomatic exchanges, have the potential to escalate into armed conflict. Efforts to develop a Code of Conduct for the South China Sea have generally stalled within the Association of Southeast Asian Nations (ASEAN) forums. In at least one instance, however, a legal route is being undertaken: the Philippines has initiated an international arbitration process as part of UNCLOS, challenging Chinese claims to disputed South China Sea areas.

The risk of military conflict among the competing claimants has broader security implications even for non-claimant countries, including the United States, Japan, South Korea, Indonesia, Singapore, and Australia. One reason is the sheer volume of trade shipments that use the important maritime routes. For example, a substantial amount of Japan's energy resources are shipped along sea lanes that transit the South China Sea. The United States and other countries also have strong interests in maintaining the principle of freedom of navigation and overflight through the strategically located waters. Such activities occasionally result in confrontations. For example, an incident occurred on April 2001 when a Chinese interceptor collided with a U.S. EP-3 reconnaissance aircraft operating in the South China Sea. The

Chinese fighter crashed, killing the pilot, and the damaged U.S. aircraft made an emergency landing on China's Hainan Island. The crew and aircraft were held for several days before finally being released. The unexpected incident caused a short-lived but intense diplomatic showdown between Beijing and Washington.

The competing claims to the Spratly Islands might elicit relatively little concern among most non-claimant countries. But an armed conflict in the South China Sea, whether large or small, will create significant problems for certain neighbouring countries, particularly Japan, South Korea, Singapore, and Australia. Fighting in the South China Sea could threaten critical sea lanes and disrupt maritime trade flows, including energy supplies. The United States is likely to be placed in a difficult position of wanting to support American allies and friends while avoiding irreparable damage to U.S.-Chinese political and economic relations. It is preferable to mitigate the chances of armed conflict in the South China Sea than to deal with the consequences of a crisis or conflict being driven by actions of other countries.

WHY COOPERATIVE MONITORING VIA SATELLITE IMAGERY

A better alternative to recurring maritime confrontations in the South China Sea is to explore new opportunities for cooperative monitoring that take advantage of growing global access to high-resolution satellite imagery. Cooperative monitoring provides a practical initial step to moving the competing parties in the South China Sea, along with other concerned parties, toward an approach to help manage these territorial disputes while focusing greater attention on common interests, such as information sharing for regional disaster response and monitoring shared environmental problems.

Thanks to the rapidly evolving information technology age, new instruments to support conflict prevention and management are more widely available, bolstering global transparency. One of these technologies is a new generation of high-resolution commercial and civilian observation satellites (e.g., GeoEye 1, IKONOS, Pleiades-1, QuickBird, WorldView-2) that can produce imagery data for monitoring developments in the South China Sea, including the Spratly disputes. These imaging satellites can generate images that are available for purchase by government agencies, businesses, nongovernment organizations, and even individuals.

Compared with earlier non-military imaging satellites, the new commercial and civilian systems collect higher-resolution images (e.g. the ability to resolve objects less than 1 meter in size), and most can produce somewhat less precise multispectral images that capture data not readily discernible by the naked eye. Unlike the earlier low-resolution civilian observation satellites, these satellites produce imagery data that enable experienced imagery analysts to detect and identify buildings, piers and runways, aircraft, naval and civilian vessels, and other objects that often are issues of contention in the Spratly Islands disputes. (Imagery analysis indicates that images of one-meter resolution are sufficiently detailed to allow analysts to judge whether new outposts are being built or substantially expanded among the Spratly Islands.) Satellite images possess several advantages compared to aerial overflights and naval patrols that the claimant countries now use to keep watch on their rivals' activities. Satellites are much less provocative than low-altitude overflights and close-in patrols by armed vessels, which sometimes are subjected to gunfire. And because commercial satellite images typically come from disinterested commercial firms, they are likely to be viewed as relatively impartial compared with the aerial photographs taken by any of the Spratly claimants. Finally, unclassified satellite imagery can be widely shared among claimant states, with other countries not involved in the disputes, and even with regional or non-government organizations with interests in South China Sea issues.

The risk of armed conflict over the disputed Spratly Islands could be mitigated if the claimant countries agreed to "freeze-in-place" their Spratly occupations and to rely mainly on cooperative satellite monitoring and imagery data sharing to monitor compliance with such a confidence-building measure. Other countries, including the United States, Australia, Canada, Singapore, and Thailand, are in good positions to serve as facilitators by assisting with acquisition, processing, analysis, and periodic dissemination of satellite images of any significant location in the Spratly Island or larger South China Sea.

The practicalities of developing a cooperative monitoring regime have been previously explored and will be left to the countries most interested in enhancing transparency of the South China Sea disputes. Most likely, a cooperative arrangement would involve developing an impartial approach to collecting high-resolution satellite images of all disputed locations in the South China Sea on an annual (or more frequent) basis. Our previous work has estimated that some two to three hundred high-resolution satellite images should be collected annually to provide a robust basis for monitoring activities in the South China Sea. The aim would be to focus regional and international attention on what actions are occurring in the disputed areas, but in a way that limits the military utility of such monitoring. The purpose would be to make public the actions of the claimant countries. New outposts would draw international attention, as would substantial upgrades to existing outputs and facilities. More transient activities, such as ship deployments, would be captured in the imagery data. In some cases, the claimant country may have a good reason for upgrading a facility, and the legitimacy can be affirmed by access to international scrutiny. The discussion and debate over such actions is a better alternative to the provocative actions and reactions that continue to occur in the South China Sea.

Concerned countries, including Australia, Singapore, and Thailand possess substantial capabilities in satellite remote sensing, and could serve as natural facilitators to a cooperative monitoring regime for the South China Sea. Similarly, other outside countries (e.g., Canada, the European Union, Japan, the United States) and their associated remote sensing enterprises are well positioned to provide commercial and civilian satellite imagery and needed resources to encourage movement away from persistent conflict.

ENCOURAGING PARTICIPATION

A cooperative satellite monitoring regime for the South China Sea should involve more than helping countries keep a close watch on the Spratlys and other disputed features. A complementary purpose should be to address the common remote-sensing needs of the countries bordering the South China Sea. These needs include having a shared capability for natural disaster warning and response, as well as monitoring of environmental challenges.

Despite their reservations, most of the countries along the South China Sea have faced various types of major natural disasters and have a need for timely and accurate information to deal with these events. Satellite imagery data of various types is often used for disaster warning, response, and recovery purposes.

These disasters include major earthquakes in China, volcanoes and typhoons affecting the Philippines, major flooding in Vietnam, and the tsunamis that devastated substantial parts of Thailand and Indonesia. They can result in the loss of lives as well as displaced populations, substantial property damage, and economic loss. Having access to timely satellite imagery is important for countries with populations suffering in a disaster. It also provides an opportunity for unaffected countries to share their imagery analysis capabilities to help address the urgent needs of the affected countries.

More generally, satellite images are well-suited for environmental monitoring, particularly in maritime areas. Satellite imagery data can be used to assist in preserving the vital resources of the South China Sea by monitoring coastal pollution (e.g., red tides) and the health of coral reefs, as well as detecting and tracking major oil spills from ship accidents or illegal discharges from maritime vessels. The littoral countries of the South China Sea have a common interest in sustaining its viability as a vital food source and for tourism purposes.

A precedent for cooperative monitoring for scientific purposes exists for the South China Sea. In 1998, nearly a dozen countries, including several Spratly Islands claimant countries (i.e., China, Malaysia, the Philippines, Taiwan, Vietnam), and other countries (i.e., Australia, Indonesia, Japan, Singapore, Thailand, and the United States) cooperated in undertaking the South China Sea Monsoon Experiment (SCSMEX). This collaborative activity undertook extensive meteorological and oceanographic observations using satellite, aerial, or surface data to better understand the dynamics of summer monsoon patterns, partly for greater preparedness against major flooding to minimize the loss of life and property.

The willingness of the claimant countries is likely to be varied, although the support of concerned external countries could greatly influence their choices to participate. Some countries, such as the Philippines and Vietnam, potentially have strong interests in fostering regional arrangements that focus international attention on the South China Sea disputes. They also have practical interests in having access to satellite imagery of the disputed areas, as well as for disaster response purposes.

While China prefers to manage its interest in the South China Sea on a bilateral basis, Beijing may be reluctant to be left out of a regional activity involving what it considers to be vital interests in the South China Sea. China may be more receptive to participating in confidence-building activities that are distinct from other diplomatic or legal efforts seeking to resolve the competing sovereignty claims in the South China Sea. No matter which countries choose to be active participants, no country should be excluded, nor should any country be permitted to hinder the rest of the participating countries from finding ways to use cooperative monitoring to reduce the risk of conflict in the South China Sea while improving opportunities for meaningful cooperation related to disaster response and environmental challenges.

The enduring nature of the South China Sea disputes, particularly those concerning the Spratly Islands, discourages both formal and informal Track 2 diplomacy efforts to manage the risk of conflict. Developing cooperative satellite monitoring in a way that involves the Spratly claimant countries and other countries interested in preventing a military conflict will not solve the underlying sovereignty disputes, but it does provide a way to increase regional transparency and foster collaboration among countries with common concerns, such as environmental monitoring and disaster preparedness. Cooperative monitoring offers a solution while constructive formal and informal ways to enhance stability in the South China Sea continue to be sought, despite the competing interests of the claimant countries.

THREE DISPUTE AND OBJECTIVES OF THE SOUTH CHINA SEA

There are three severable categories of disputes, each with its own parties, rule sets, and politics. Unfortunately, the region's states are currently pursuing win-lose solutions to these three disputes based on competing claims of exclusive sovereignty and jurisdiction. A careful analysis of the nature of each dispute reveals opportunities for more productive pathways to dispute resolution based on a return to Asia's history of win-win problem solving based on mutual interests.

The recent heightening of the competition between China and its neighbours over sovereignty, resources, and security in the South China Sea has drawn the attention of U.S. diplomatic and military leaders who seek to promote stability and security in these globally important waters. As American leaders discuss policies and strategies in support of regional stability, some have described the complex disputes in the South China Sea as essentially a single tangled knot of intractable challenges. In fact there are three severable categories of disputes, each with its own parties, rule sets, and politics. Unfortunately, the region's states are currently pursuing win-lose solutions to these three disputes based on competing claims of exclusive sovereignty and jurisdiction. A careful analysis of the nature of each dispute reveals opportunities for more productive pathways to dispute resolution based on a return to Asia's history of win-win problem solving based on mutual interests.

THREE DISPUTES

There are three basic categories of disputes in the South China Sea, each with its own parties, rule sets, politics, and security concerns. These disputes have resulted in recurring flashes of tension and conflict for approximately forty years. Notable incidents over sovereignty include the Chinese attack on the forces of the Republic of Vietnam in the Paracel Islands in 1974, China's attack on Vietnamese forces near Fiery Cross Reef in 1988, and China's military ouster of Philippines forces from Mischief Reef in 1995. The result of this series of incidents was the coalescence of a unified ASEAN political position in opposition to China's behaviour and, to decrease tensions with its neighbours, to China's acceptance of the 2002 ASEAN Declaration on the Conduct of Parties in the South China Sea, which included the agreement to "resolve their territorial and jurisdictional disputes by peaceful means, without resorting to the threat or use of force...." What followed was more than 15 years of relative regional calm as China pursued a policy of regional integration with its Southeast Asian neighbours with generous economic, commercial, infrastructure, and cultural programs. The United States repeatedly professed neutrality over the outcome of the sovereignty and jurisdictional disagreements as long as all parties continued to pursue peaceful means of dispute resolution.

This stability was shattered by a series of antagonistic Chinese actions. Recent flare-up in tensions in the South China Sea began when China pressured Vietnam and several oil companies over oil exploration and drilling off the Vietnamese coasts. As U.S. Deputy Assistant Secretary of State Scot Marciel testified before the Senate Foreign Relations Committee in July 2009, "Starting in the summer of 2007, China told a number of U.S. and foreign oil and gas firms to stop exploration work with Vietnamese partners in the South China Sea or face unspecified consequences in their business dealings with China." The Senate hearing was held in the wake of the March 2009 "Impeccable Incident," in which an American naval research vessel was aggressively harassed approximately 70 nautical miles off Hainan Island by Chinese 'fishermen' with the support of Chinese civilian and military vessels.

These Chinese actions resulted in a return to tensions in the region. In response to China's new strategy, U.S. Secretary of State Hilary Clinton stated at the ASEAN Regional Forum in July 2010,

The United States supports a collaborative, diplomatic process by all claimants for resolving the various territorial disputes without coercion. We encourage the parties to reach agreement on a full code of conduct. The United States, like every nation, has a national interest in freedom of navigation, open access to Asia's maritime commons and respect for international law in the South China Sea."

Until this time, the only common attribute of all South China Sea disputes was that they involved China as a party. However, China's turn in 2009 toward an assertive, even aggressive approach—especially in its efforts to control American naval activities in the South China Sea—resulted in new American attention to and interest in all three categories of disputes. In order to find a pathway to return to the desired state of regional stability, it is helpful to examine the attributes of each type of dispute.

Sovereignty. Disputes over sovereignty involve the question of which coastal state has the right to exercise sovereignty over the physical territory of the islands in the South China Sea. It involves China, Vietnam, Malaysia, the Philippines, Taiwan and perhaps Brunei. In 1992, China established its Law on the Territorial Sea and Contiguous Zone, which specifically claims sovereignty over each of the island groups in the South China Sea—the Pratas Islands (Dongsha), Paracel Islands (Xisha), Macclesfield Bank (Zhongsha), and the Spratly Islands (Nansha). In 1947 the government of the Republic of China began to publish maps with a U-shaped series of lines in the South China Sea to delineate its maritime boundaries. The Chinese government repeated this cartographic feature after the Communist party came to power on the mainland in 1949 and today remains depicted on maps published in China or Taiwan. However, the nature of China's claim over the expanse of water and the numerous islands, shoals, rocks and islets contained within the nine dashes of the U-shaped line has never been specified. Among Chinese scholars and officials, there appear to be four dominant schools of thought as to the line's meaning, but the Chinese government maintains a studied policy of ambiguity about the meaning of the nine-dashed line

Sovereign Waters. Some Chinese policy analysts maintain that the waters within the U-shaped line should be considered sovereign Chinese waters, subject to the full measure of the government's authority, presumably as either internal waters or territorial seas.

One group of senior Chinese defence analysts, for instance, describes Chinese offshore interests as "the area extending out from the Chinese mainland coastline between 200 nautical miles (to the east) and 1600 nautical miles (to the south)" or roughly to the 4 degrees northern latitude claimed in the 1935 report. They consider these "sea domains under Chinese jurisdiction ... [as] the overlaying area of China's national sovereignty."

Historic Waters. Some Chinese have suggested that the concept of 'historic waters' enables the government to legitimately claim broad control over the South China Sea. The concept is a variation on China's claim of sovereignty in the South China Sea and reflects the perspective held by many Chinese academics and policy-makers that the nine-dashed line represents a claim to historic waters, historic 'title,' or at least some kind of exclusive historic rights to administer the waters and territory within the line's boundaries. Perhaps the most authoritative statement of international law on the point was issued in 1951 by the International Couth of Justice in the *Fisheries Case,* in which the United Kingdom challenged before the International Court of Justice Norway's claim to sovereignty over waters along its craggy coast line beyond the traditional three-mile territorial sea limit at the time.

The Court considered three relevant factors: 1) the close geographical dependence of the territorial sea upon the land domain—the relevant portions of the Norwegian coastline are deeply indented with complex geographic features and an estimated 120,000 minor islands, islets, rocks and shoals; 2) sufficiently close links between the land formations and the sea space to make the region susceptible to a fully-sovereign regime of governance; and 3) unique economic interests belonging to the coastal state based on clear evidence of long usage. Based on its assessment of these factors, the court approved Norway's extension of sovereignty over the sea areas and the features contained within them based on its historic claims.

The requirements laid out in the Fisheries Case for an extension of sovereignty over water space by a coastal state do not lend support to China's claim. In particular, there is no close geographical dependence between the sea and the land in this region. Indeed, the land features are so insignificant that they have long been seen more as navigational hazards than as productive territory. Additionally, the islets themselves are relatively widely dispersed in comparison with the features along the Norwegian coastline. As such, the lack of sustainable land available to support an indigenous population and the sporadic presence of fishermen and traders strongly suggests that the region is not susceptible to a fully sovereign regime of governance. Accordingly, China's claim of historic waters has weak support on these bases.

Concerning the question of unique economic interests, China has had well-documented contacts with the islands of the South China Sea for many centuries by fishermen, traders and the occasional government official, but the historical record also reflects that Vietnam has had similar well-documented contacts with the islands and neither country has a record of sustained, exclusive use and reliance upon the resources of the South China Sea. The people of the Philippines, Malaysia and Indonesia also maintained contacts with these islands in support of traditional fishing activities and in support of local trade. Thus, there is no evidence supporting any unique economic interests of China, or any single country, in and around the islands of the South China Sea. Rather the evidence suggests the contrary—that the waters of the South China Sea and the sparse islands, islets, rocks, and reefs among them have for many centuries been the common fishing grounds and trading routes of all regional peoples. Indeed, this long-standing common usage suggests that rather than having been supervised as a zone of sovereignty, the South China Sea developed as a sort of commonly held regional zone in which all parties pursued their interests without fear of molestation by the authorities of other coastal states.

Island Claims. Some Chinese academics and policy-makers view the U-shaped line as asserting a claim of sovereignty over all the islands, rocks, sand bars, coral heads and other land features that pierce the waters of the South China Sea, and to whatever jurisdiction international law of the sea allows coastal states to claim based on sovereignty over these small bits of land. On their face at least, China's claim to sovereignty over the islands and jurisdiction that is lawfully derived from it are legitimate in that the claims comply with the general provisions of UNCLOS and other aspects of law of the sea. However, a series of fundamental problems undermine China's claims, including the fact that Vietnam, Malaysia, the Philippines, and Taiwan all maintain claims to sovereignty over some or all of the islands in the South China Sea. Since the 1995 Mischief Reef Incident between China and the Philippines there has been a static situation in which each of the claimants occupies some of the features.

China, of course, occupies and administers all of the Paracels, though Vietnam still maintains its claim to sovereignty over them. The Spratlys present a mixed case. Since 1996, Vietnam has occupied or controlled approximately 22 features, China 10 features, the Philippines 8 features, Malaysia 4 features, and Taiwan 1 feature. In order to support a claim of sovereignty over an island, international law requires that a coastal state must demonstrate effective occupation or continuous administration and control. On this basis, China's claim to those of the Spratly Islands that it does not occupy or effectively administer and control is unsupported by international law. The same is true of the claims of any other parties that do not actually occupy a feature over which they claim sovereignty. Some observers wrongly conclude that the non-Chinese claims are based solely on European claims from the colonial era. In fact, the claims of Southeast Asian states are at least in part an expression of the contacts all coastal peoples had with the South China Sea's islands and waters for many centuries and the national consciousness that international law should protect those interests.

Security Interests. Finally, a fourth Chinese perspective is that the U-shaped line reflects China's longstanding maritime security interests in the South China Sea and that these security interests should have legal protection. The Chinese have long viewed the Bohai Gulf, the Yellow Sea, the East China Sea, and the South China Sea—the so-called 'near seas'—as regions of core geostrategic interest and part of a great defensive perimeter established on land and at sea to protect China's major population and economic centres along the coasts. As one PLA Major General recently put it, the South China Sea comprises part of China's maritime "strategic stability belt."

China's assertiveness about its claims in the waters of its 'near seas' has grown in tandem with the size of its navy and maritime services, and from these forces. As one Chinese analyst put it, "The Navy is just one of the means of protecting our maritime rights and interests ... the primary means should be to rely on the law, on international law and internal legislation." To enforce these laws and our sovereign interests at sea, "in recent years we have started to carry out periodic patrols to safeguard our rights in the East and South China Seas." Thus, some Chinese see international law in conjunction with their developing maritime power as a means to establish the long-desired maritime security buffer throughout the 'near seas,' including the South China Sea. That international law does not provide protection for a coastal state's security interests beyond the narrow territorial sea has not deterred Chinese proponents from seeking to change those norms.

Jurisdiction. A second category of disputes involves the delimitation of jurisdictional boundaries between neighbouring sea zones, including exclusive economic zones (EEZ) and continental shelves. China complicates these disputes through its ambiguous claims of authority over the water space within a nine-dashed line, but it is clear that the claim encompasses aspects of jurisdiction as well as aspects of sovereignty. Jurisdiction under international law is something less than full sovereignty in that it does not include the same degree of absolute and exclusive authority to govern all matters of interest to the state. Like sovereignty, jurisdiction is a reflection of *state power* within *specified boundaries*, but the concept of jurisdiction connotes the application of state authority only over *a limited, specified set of subject matters.* All of the disputants involved in the question of sovereignty are also involved in the jurisdictional disputes, plus Indonesia, which has an EEZ claim extending from Natuna Island that overlaps with China's nine-dashed line.

The two main sources of jurisdictional disputes in the South China Sea are the boundaries of the various national EEZ and continental shelf zones over which each state may exercise its authority. Within the geographic limits outlined in Article 76 (specified boundaries), coastal states are afforded exclusive authority (state power) to regulate the exploration and exploitation of the resources of the seabed, although the legal character of the water space above the continental shelf remains unchanged (a limited, specified set of subject matters). Thus, international law provides for limited coastal state jurisdiction within a specified zone known as the continental shelf.

Similarly, one of the key innovations of UNCLOS was that it specified coastal state authority in the water space beyond the territorial sea, a concept that had been steadily developing over the course of the 20th century. UNCLOS Part V established coastal state jurisdiction over a vast littoral swath of water space known as the EEZ, which may extend to 200 nautical miles from the coastal state's baselines (specified boundaries), in which the coastal state has "sovereign rights" to the resources plus related jurisdictional authorities (exclusive state power), for the purpose of managing those resources and (a limited, specified set of subject matters). Thus, UNCLOS completed the creation of jurisdictional regimes over resources in littoral waters. Accordingly, this second category of disputes is at its core disagreement over jurisdictional authority in the South China Sea to explore and exploit the resources on and under the Sea's continental shelf and in its water column.

China's Ambiguous Jurisdictional Claims. All states with a coastline that borders the South China Sea claim a continental shelf and an EEZ, however very little actual delimitation of the boundaries between coastal state zones has occurred. China's nine-dashed line claim in particular presents a major problem for resolving these disputes because in addition to relying on the line as a source of sovereignty, Chinese policymakers also refer to it as the basis for China's South China Sea jurisdictional claims. Some Chinese scholars and policymakers assert that the concept of historic rights (as an alternative to, or in addition to, China's claim to historic waters in the South China Sea) applies as a basis for Chinese jurisdictional control over water space within the nine-dashed line. The concept of historic waters has only the briefest mention in UNCLOS, but exists in customary international law related to bays. It allows coastal states to claim extended jurisdiction over water space or islands when the coastal state's claim has been open and long-standing, exclusive, and widely accepted by other states.

China's claim to a historic right to jurisdiction over the waters of South China Sea is seriously undermined by similar, overlapping claims maintained by the Philippines, Vietnam, Malaysia, Brunei and Indonesia, not to mention parallel claims made separately by Taiwan. This demonstrates that however long-standing China's claims of jurisdiction in the South China Sea might be, clearly they are not exclusive or widely accepted by other states. Nonetheless, Chinese law asserts historic rights as a basis for jurisdiction over the South China Sea. The 1998 Law of the People's Republic of China on the Exclusive Economic Zone and Continental Shelf claims an exclusive economic zone emanating from all Chinese territory, which would logically include all relevant Chinese territory as specified in the 1992 Territorial Sea Law, which, specifically includes each of the island groups in the South China Sea. Thus, in combination, these two Chinese laws assert an EEZ and therefore jurisdictional control over nearly the entire South China Sea area within the U-shaped line.

In addition to its ambiguity and lack of specificity, there are many problems with China's approach to jurisdiction in the South China Sea. For instance, only a very few of the South China Sea's islands qualify under UNCLOS for more than the mere twelve nautical mile territorial sea. Another weakness of China's claim of jurisdiction over the South China Sea based on its assertion of sovereignty over the sea's rocks and sandbars is that China has objected to similar claims made by Japan to an exclusive economic zone and continental shelf rights around Okinotorishima, a small coral feature in the Pacific Ocean about 1,050 nautical miles south of Tokyo. International law prevents a state from claiming legal rights if it objects to the same type of claims by other states. As such, neither the provisions of UNCLOS nor historic rights are especially persuasive sources of law on which China can base its claims.

Jurisdictional Claims by Other States. In stark contrast to China's, the jurisdictional claims of Vietnam and Malaysia conform much more closely to international law. Vietnam, for instance, claims an exclusive economic zone that "is adjacent to the Vietnamese territorial sea and forms with it a 200-nautical-mile zone from the baseline used to measure the breadth of Viet Nam's territorial sea." In addition to clarity about the boundaries of its claim, Vietnam also specifies the extent of its national jurisdiction. Vietnam's jurisdictional claims track nearly word-for-word with the requirements of UNCLOS articles 57 and 56 respectively, although it should be noted that Vietnam's baselines are considered to be excessive.

Malaysia's Exclusive Economic Zone Act 1984 make similarly normative EEZ and continental shelf claims. Additionally, the Joint Submission of Malaysia and Vietnam to the Commission on the Limits of the Continental Shelf makes a reasonable claim to an extended continental shelf beyond the 200-nautical-mile EEZ in accordance with UNCLOS article 76. The submission uses each coastal state's baselines as the starting point and measures 200 nautical miles without regard to any island features. Concerning the Spratly Islands, the legal approach taken by Vietnam and Malaysia, in contrast with the various Chinese approaches, complies with UNCLOS article 121 concerning the regime of islands and with recent case law. Specifically, the Malaysia-Vietnam approach recognizes that the various islets, reefs and shoals in the southern part of the South China Sea are too small to form the basis of a claim to an EEZ or a continental shelf (or any other form of jurisdiction other than a territorial sea) of their own right.

Another important aspect of Malaysia and Vietnam's claims is that they are specific and public. They represent a choice made by each government concerning how international law should be interpreted in regard to their jurisdiction over offshore zones. They provide a basis for discussion, negotiation, and even potentially litigation by other states that may have different perspectives. They do not rely on power—military or economic—to decide the issue. In these ways, the Malaysia-Vietnam approaches provide a basis for a stable resolution to any disputes.

The government of the Philippines established archipelagic baselines for its main islands in legislation completed in 2009 and filed on deposit with the UN. This legislation also claims a separate, non-specific regime of islands for its claims among the Spratly Islands, known as Kalayaan Islands, and its claim to the Scarborough Shoals. The Philippines also maintains an EEZ claim based on a 1978 Presidential Proclamation. The Philippines EEZ extends 200 nautical miles from its baselines, which were publicly established by the 2009 legislation. Thus, with regard to its main islands, the Philippines made a specific and public claim concerning the extent of its EEZ.

Concerning its continental shelf claim, the Philippines retains on file with the UN its Presidential Proclamation of 1968, which claims a continental shelf "to where the depth of the [Philippines] superjacent waters admits of the exploitation of such resources, including living organisms belonging to sedentary species." This outdated expression of the jurisdictional limits of the Philippines continental shelf claim stems from the definition that appeared in the 1958 Continental Shelf Convention, the provisions of which were updated by UNCLOS article 76. Additionally, the Philippines made a claim to an extended continental shelf in the Philippines Sea, but not in the South China Sea. The Philippines could improve the clarity of its jurisdictional claims to a continental shelf by bringing its proclamation into alignment with UNCLOS. Additionally, the government of the Philippines should publicly state what, if any, claims to jurisdiction over maritime zones it maintains, based on its claim of sovereignty over some of the Spratly Islands and Scarborough Reef. These steps would promote stability by removing sources of ambiguity and allowing for negotiations or arbitration in concert with international law.

In sum, the jurisdictional claims of Malaysia and Vietnam are fully public and stated with specificity. The claims of the Philippines are improving in clarity, but there continues to be room for improvement in that regard. The claims of Brunei should be made more publicly accessible by placing them on deposit with the UN. The jurisdictional claims of China in the South China Sea, however, remain ambiguous and non-public and therefore contribute to regional instability and present problems for all states whose vessels navigate the sea lanes of the South China Sea.

Control.The third category of disputes relates to control over the water space itself, and is fundamentally about the correct interpretation of international law concerning the balance of coastal state and international rights and obligations in the EEZ and other coastal state waters. This dispute primarily involves only China and the United States, but many other countries around the globe have an interest and a stake in its outcome since they involve China's attempts to alter international norms concerning freedom of navigation for military purposes and to roll back the balance of coastal state and international rights in coastal zones that were negotiated in the development of the provisions of UNCLOS. This resulted in a series of confrontations between American and Chinese government vessels in the South China Sea between 2001 and 2009 that, although tension-producing, were manageable from a political and military perspective. China ended this mutual policy of 'managed friction' however on March 8, 2009 when it confronted the USNS *Impeccable* (T-AGOS 23) with five vessels—a PLA Navy intelligence ship, a government fisheries patrol vessel, a Maritime Surveillance Service Vessel of the State Oceanographic Administration, and two small fishing trawlers

Under the observation of all three Chinese government vessels, the fishing trawlers maneuvered dangerously to a within 8 meters ahead of *Impeccable* and then abruptly stopped. This forced*Impeccable* to take emergency action to avoid a collision. Additionally, the Chinese aboard the fishing trawlers used a grappling hook to try to snag the Impeccable's towed cable. These Chinese actions violated international norms related to the duty to exercise due regard in navigation of vessels at sea and also constituted unlawful interference with the sovereign vessel of another state. The Impeccable left the scene in order to reduce immediate tensions, but returned to the exact location several days later in the company of an American warship, the USS *Chung Hoon* (DDG). Thus, the Chinese escalation from past patterns raised the dispute over navigation issues from 'managed friction' to 'near conflict,' thereby initiating renewed American strategic attention to the waters of the South China Sea and to the international norms governing freedom of navigation for military purposes in the EEZ. The creation of the exclusive economic zone in 1982 by UNCLOS as a region extending beyond the territorial sea to a maximum of 200 nautical miles from a coastal state's shores was a carefully balanced compromise between the interests of coastal states in managing and protecting ocean resources and of maritime user states in ensuring high seas freedoms of navigation and over-flight, including for military purposes. Thus, while in the exclusive economic zone the coastal state was granted sovereign rights to the resources and jurisdiction to make laws related to those resources, to ensure the participation of maritime powers high seas freedoms of navigation were specifically preserved for all states.

Nonetheless, China has persistently attempted to shift this carefully balanced compromise by making more expansive claims of legal protection for its security interests, especially in the South China Sea. For instance, one statement by a Chinese military spokesman concerning international freedoms of navigation in the South China Sea is typical. Chinese Defence Ministry Spokesman, Senior Colonel Geng Yansheng, stated "We will, in accordance with the demands of international law, respect the freedom of the *passage* of ships or aircraft from relevant countries which are in compliance with international law." When pressed to explain the distinction between 'passage' and 'navigation', other senior Chinese officials have stated that the Chinese government has not objected to U.S. Navy vessels that pass through the Chinese EEZ en route to another destination. However, when such vessels conduct exercises, gather intelligence or other militarily useful data, or undertake activities other than mere passage, these officials argue that the vessels are in violation of international law and Chinese domestic law. U.S. Secretary of State Hilary Clinton, however, made clear at the ASEAN regional Forum in July 2010 that in the South China Sea, the United States will not accept China's limitations on freedoms of navigation for military purposes. She stated that the U.S., like all states, has "a national interest in freedom of navigation, open access to Asia's maritime commons, and respect for international law in the South China Sea."

7

ASEAN and Free Trade Area Cover China, Japan, India

The Eighth Asean Summit concluded last week on a high note with the region committing to long term plans for free trade areas (FTAs) with China, Japan and India. At the Asia Pacific Economic Cooperation (APEC) Summit in Los Cabos last month, the US announced the Enterprise for Asean Initiative which also provides for FTAs with Asean countries.

Asean signed a framework agreement for economic cooperation with China at the Asean Summit which would result in the creation of a FTA by 2010. Under the accord, tariff negotiations are to be completed by 2004 and implementation would commence by 2005. An "early harvest" package to liberalise trade, mainly in agricultural products, will be implemented by 1 January 2004 to show commitment to the accord and to bring early benefits. With Japan, Asean signed a declaration on a comprehensive economic partnership which contains elements for an FTA in 10 years' time. India too offered Asean an FTA with the sub-continent that could take shape in 10 years.

The FTAs are expected to have a positive impact on the region as summed up by Prime Minister Goh Chok Tong who compared the flurry of FTAs to that of an airplane that would help the region to take off on a new economic flight path. When the FTAs are implemented in a decade or more, the region would witness the making of the first Asian FTA with Asean being the driving force. An economy worth USD 8 trillion would be created representing a quarter of world's gross domestic product and about 40 per cent of its reserves. This would rival Asean's major trading partners such as the EU and provide Asia with the bargaining power in multilateral economic fora. It will also give the developing world a voice through Asia so that their aspirations could be realised in a more globalised world.

Economic liberalisation under the FTAs would help to integrate the region more quickly and generate more and new economic activities. Specialisation and economies of scale would also set in with the removal of barriers to trade in goods and services, and investments. Investment flows will be less discriminatory with a more harmonised region and cost of services will fall due to efficient allocation of resources. Asean would be seen by investors as complementary within the overall production and distribution networks in the FTAs.

Besides, more efficient infrastructural and transport networks would be an inevitable outcome of the FTAs aimed at cutting the cost of distribution crucial for pricing of goods and services. The newer Asean countries will certainly benefit from such linkages since they are at the crossroads of economic activities between the Asean-6 (Brunei, Indonesia, Malaysia, the Philippines, Singapore and Thailand) and its partners in Northeast Asia and India. The Singapore-Kunming railway line and the Bangkok-Singapore highway will play important roles in the FTAs as well as the transport routes being developed by China and India with the CLMV (Cambodia, Laos, Myanmar and Viet Nam). With the likely surge in energy requirements in China and India due their forecasted economic growth, Asean may be in a position to support their needs, including the possibility of extending its energy grid to these countries in the longer term with the financial backing of the private sector.

The political consequence of the FTAs would be the ensuring of regional peace and stability important for economic development. The consumers will be the biggest beneficiary in terms of high quality and cheaper goods and services with wider choices. While the FTAs look promising, many issues will have to be first addressed. Asean may have to advance the implementation of the Asean Free Trade Area (AFTA) to gain a fair deal out of the FTAs. Asean will have to improve its economic competitiveness and regional integration to better deal with its FTA partners. Customs procedures and nomenclatures will have to be simplified, product standards harmonised, transport and communication networks strengthened, rule of law, transparency and governance improved, and labour productivity raised.

While the Asean-6 launched AFTA in January 2002, the CLMV would be phased in by 2010. The CLMV countries may have to look at other ways of financing government spending instead of relying on custom tariffs. Some Asean countries may also face severe competition in the shorter term from cheaper Chinese goods, especially electronics, footwear, apparels and textiles.

Removing protection for selected industries in Asean countries would be inevitable with the FTAs but it is expected to be a painful process. Besides, services and investment liberalisation have to be quickened if Asean is to implement the FTAs in a decade's time. Asean would also have to tackle the sensitive issue of freer flow of labour. While Asean countries may be willing to accept freer movement of professional and skilled labour, many would not be comfortable with opening up completely their labour markets since the wealthier countries in Asean have considerably smaller labour markets, and due to possible social problems with foreign labour.

There are also issues in the FTA arrangements that need to be tackled. While Asean and China are committed to an early harvest package, their export structures are similar in many respects and therefore competition is expected to increase with the FTA. However, Asean is fortunate in that its technological progress has been the key to its international competitiveness while China's advantage has been its low wages and huge market potential. Besides with the growing middle class population in China's coastal cities, Asean exports of food and agricultural products could increase. In investments too, they are competitors but Asean would become an important market of China for raw materials and industrial components as China develops rapidly.

The FTA with India can gain momentum when India reduces its very high tariff rates to that of Asean level. India is committed to bringing them down to East Asian rates in three years. Also, India would have to keep to its economic reform plans if it wishes to see the FTA taking off in 10 years.

Asean FTAs with Japan and the US may need the fulfilment of more stringent requirements. Japan wants to sign FTAs with Asean modelled after its FTA with Singapore despite Asean's preference to negotiate a pact similar to that of China. Besides, agriculture will be a issue in the negotiations since unlike Singapore many of the Asean countries have larger agricultural sectors.

As for the US, signing bilateral trade and investment framework agreements (TIFAs) would be a precursor to FTA negotiations. The US has signed TIFAs with Indonesia, the Philippines and Thailand. The US is expected to complete its FTA with Singapore by the year's end. It expects to sign similar high quality FTAs with other Asean countries which would certainly take time. Besides, the US has other economic interests such as negotiating FTAs with Australia, Central America, and the South Africa Customs Union. Human rights issues and the terrorism situation in the region may also have an impact on the negotiations of the FTAs.

Asean intentions to forge FTAs with its partners are commendable and show Asean's commitment to revitalise its economies to put them on a wining flight path. However, the viability of the FTAs will be dependent on the commitment of Asean countries and its partners to remove the tariff and non tariff barriers as quickly as possible. At the same time, Asean would have to work on its economic competitiveness and regional integration to be in a better bargaining position when negotiating the FTAs and to reach a cruising height of its new economic flight path.

CHINESE PERSPECTIVES ON INDIA'S "LOOK-EAST" STRATEGY

In what's referred to as New Delhi's "Look-East" policy, India is also seeking an expanded role in Southeast Asia and East Asia as it attempts to mirror China's successful effort to woo Southeast Asia. This policy has several objectives: to build more ties and create more diplomatic space as India extends its naval power in the Indian Ocean, to tap into Southeast Asia's dynamic economic growth, and to secure energy supplies. In the eyes of an American scholar, India develops its relationships with Southeast Asian countries "at the least to avoid Southeast Asia from becoming China's exclusive influential area; at the best to make Southeast Asia become a force containing China, just like China makes Pakistan a force containing India." While in the eyes of Chinese scholars, "geopolitics, strategic needs, domestic economic reforms, and traditional links with Southeast Asian countries made this strategic adjustment possible and feasible". Southeast Asia has been of special importance to China and the shift in New Delhi's stance has thus generated a sense of rivalry between the two for the affectations of Southeast Asia. Politically, China has worked hard to maintain a peaceful and stable environment on its periphery for its domestic economic construction and it has placed special value on having good-neighborly with Southeast Asia. Economically, Southeast Asia is an important source of raw materials and capital for China as well as a great potential export market. In terms of security, the sovereignty of some islands in the South China Sea is still a sensitive issue in Sino-ASEAN relations but has been put aside for now. Southeast Asia is also a source of oil and gas supplies for China. Especially worth mentioning is the fact China's primary energy supply routes from the Middle East and Africa pass through Southeast Asian chokepoints. In its various dimensions energy is likely to assume an increasingly prominent role in Beijing's diplomacy with its southern neighbours.

Given ASEAN's significance and importance to both China and India, and the potential for rivalry between the two rising powers for ASEAN's favours, it is useful to examine these complex relationships along the three dimensions of economics, politics and security.

Economic Interactions

China's trade relations with ASEAN have grown rapidly, overshadowing India's trade with ASEAN. In 2005, ASEAN-China trade volume reached US$113.4 billion, or 9.3% of ASEAN's total trade volume (US$1224.9 billion). In contrast, the amount of ASEAN-India trade volume was US$23 billion, or merely 1.9% of

ASEAN's total trade volume. ASEAN's trade relations with China and India thus reflect China's emphasis on and prowess in manufacturing. The share of electronic products in China's exports to ASEAN increased from 43.1 per cent in 2001 to 50.2 per cent in 2004, while that of India's decreased from 21.3 to 1.9 per cent. Although India's IT sector is more competitive than China's – in 2001, India's IT exports reached US$7.8 billion, while China's was only US$0.72 billion – the IT sector accounts for only 3 per cent of India's GDP.

In order to eradicate domestic poverty and realize industrialization, India will be making be efforts to develop its industrial sector. While China will greatly develop its service sector so as to absorb more labour forces and maintain social stability. As India's manufacture sectors develop and China's service sectors become more competitive, it is possible that these two countries' trade competition in Southeast Asia will become more serious. This competition is the logical extension of their search for potential markets and political influence, and will continue in the near future.

The same pattern holds for FDI as well. By the end of 2003, ASEAN's accumulated FDI in China was US$64.6 billion, or 6.5 per cent of the total FDI inflows to China. In contrast, ASEAN's accumulated FDI in India was US$4 billion, or 6.1 per cent of total. Going in the other direction, China's FDI in ASEAN amounted to US$1 billion or 0.4 percent of the total FDI inflows into ASEAN for 1995-2004; the comparable figures for India were US$0.7 billion (0.3 percent).

Political Engagements

With regard to political cooperation with ASEAN, China was ahead of India in making political relations tilt in its favor. Starting from 2000, China has held an annual summit meeting with ASEAN under the framework of "10+1" and "10+3". Both China and the ASEAN have concentrated on constructive engagement, not simply creating economic interdependence, with the overall aim of creating cooperative relations in international and regional affairs. In multilateral forums such as the Asia-Pacific Economic Cooperation (APEC) and the ASEAN Regional Forum (ARF), China and ASEAN have behaved almost as de facto allies, articulating an "Asian way" in organizing regional interactions.

India began participating in the ASEAN Post-Ministerial Conferences and the ASEAN Regional Forum (ARF) in 1996. After intensive efforts to achieve parity with China, Japan, and South Korea in the ASEAN scheme of partnerships, India became a summit-level partner in 2002. In April 2005, with the strong advocacy of Singapore, Indonesia, and Thailand for India's inclusion in the East Asia Summit (EAS), the ASEAN Foreign Ministers endorsed India's participation in the EAS, indicating India's Look-East strategy had reached an important milestone.

China initially viewed India's growing involvement in East Asia with a measure of apprehension. Beijing feared that this would enable New Delhi to win recognition as a political and military power in Asia, thus complicating the political situation there. China was also concerned that the United States might manipulate India's evolving relations with ASEAN to contain China or "smother" China's attempt to exert its influence in the region. As East Asian regional cooperation develops and China-ASEAN relations become more matured, however, China has shifted its stance toward multilateralism, moving away from the initial caution to being more confident.

China believes multilateralism is a safer way to expand its international influence and protect its national interests. The ASEAN-sponsored multilateralism in East Asian security and economic affairs, for example, has offered China the opportunity to develop a counterweight to the U.S.'s dominant role in the Asia-Pacific region, and to argue against Japan's EAC (East Asian Community) design based on the creation of Japan-ASEAN axis and Tokyo's more prominent regional political-military role. Chinese scholars believed that India's involvement will not challenge China's role in the process of East Asian Community, because "China at present has neither intention, nor precondition to become a leadership country in this process." Many Chinese hold that India's comparative advantages and potential in its economic development will make East Asian economy more open and inclusive. In this context, China has also become more optimistic and comfortable with India's Look-East Strategy in providing new momentum for East Asian cooperation, and thereby strengthening the trend towards multi-polarity in Asia and the Asia-Pacific.

Security

Overlapping territorial claims in the South China Sea, whose seabed contains oil and substantial natural gas deposits, is the most sensitive traditional security issue between China and ASEAN countries. The core of ASEAN's security policy in this region is to maintain its autonomy as an independent regional group, and avoid any big power from dominating the security situation there. From its strategy of "balance of powers", ASEAN hopes that big powers from outside this region could play some role on the South China Sea issue. This policy provided India with a good opportunity to take part in the security mechanism in Asia Pacific region. The Indian navy currently ranks seventh in the world and India is the only country in South Asia that boasts aircraft carriers. The Indian navy force began holding military exercises with some ASEAN countries in the early 1990s, and formally expanded the sphere of its navy activities to the South China Sea in 2000 when conducting joint exercises with its South Korean and Vietnamese counterparts. It is declared that the strategic goal of the Indian navy force in the South China Sea is to "secure the peace and stability in Southeast Asia, ensuring that this region will not be under the influence and control of any big power".

Some Chinese strategic analysts believed that India has now developed a strategy of regional deterrence and sought to play a greater role beyond South Asia. "One of the main motives for Indian navy force entering into Southeast Asia and South China Sea is to curb China's growing military influence in this region, containing China in terms of security, so as to raise its own international status and strengthen the negotiating position in its competition with China". But Chinese scholars also believe that it is important for these two sides to cooperate further and exchange more information, so as to reduce misunderstanding and know the real situation, and thus enhance mutual trust. In reality, "even though India has intention to curb China, considering its present capability and the goals of its foreign policy, it is infeasible and unrealistic for it to take China as an 'enemy'". While ASEAN welcomes India coming into this region, but it does not want to see any big conflicts and clashes in this region, because this does not cohere with its interests. Hence, from the perspectives of developing China-ASEAN relationships, it is to the interests of all parts to hold a positive and cooperative attitude to India's military existence in this region.

The Malacca Strait is another locus of China's security concerns in Southeast Asia. The strait is the quickest passage between the Indian and Pacific Oceans. China has become increasingly dependent on the Malacca Strait as a conduit for its manufactured goods to reach European and other markets, as well as for commodity and energy supplies. It is estimated that approximately 65 per cent of China's energy imports, primary crude oil from the Middle East and Africa, passes through the Malacca Strait, and this figure is set to increase over the next decade.

India has clearly recognized the strategic importance of its naval influence. It has built a navy base on the Andaman and Nicobar islands in the Bay of Bengal, declaring that these islands are India's door to the East, "to the Malacca Strait which is a 'throat channel' for our neighboring Southeast Asia as well as Far East Asia". For their part, Chinese scholars note that "India has repeatedly declared that it has security interests in the Malacca Strait, and its navy strategy stresses on maintaining its 'legitimate interests' from the Persian Gulf to the Malacca Strait".

In view of these sentiments, it appears likely that both sides would give substantial attention to the Malacca Strait as a strategic point for controlling and containing each other should Sino-Indian relations become tense. In sum, while India has expanded its role in Southeast Asia, Chinese scholars believe these Indian activities are mainly for expanding Indian regional influence and are part of its general strategy of becoming a world power, rather than targeted at China. On this account, China and India have no strategic conflicts in Southeast Asia, and that opportunities for Sino-Indian cooperation and competition in Southeast Asia are equal, although the expressions are different in economic, political and security areas, and this competition could hopefully become a sort of healthy one. Thus far, Beijing has adopted a relaxed attitude and response to the India's Look-East policy, and does not appear to view India as an impediment to the implementation of its strategic goals in Southeast Asia, which are mainly to maintain a stable environment on its periphery and encourage economic ties that contribute to China's economic modernization and thus to regime stability.

For decades China and India had looked at each other with a mixture of apathy and suspicion. As India's economy opened up in the early 1990s and exchanges between these two countries have increased, Chinese perspectives on India's development have become more positive. India's improved economic performance in recent years, combined with its growing importance in international affairs, has led Beijing to reassess India's role. China now sees India as a "comprehensive national power", acknowledging that its rise cannot be contained and is beneficial to Asia and the world. An article in *Beijing Review* notes that "with its 1.1 billion population, seventh largest land mass and strategic location on the Indian Ocean rim, India has everything necessary to become a major power." Nevertheless, divergent perceptions and interests do exist between these two rising powers. Like any other established status quo power, China wants to ensure that its position remains strong vis-à-vis India for strategic, economic and geopolitical reasons. Meanwhile India feels the need to take some counter-balancing measures with respect to China. China's recent tougher stance on the territorial disputes with India, its high concerns over the U.S.-India nuclear deal and related agreements, and its opposition to the possible "alliance of values" among the U.S., Japan, Australia, and India have served to reinforce the views of those pessimistic analysts to some extent. They believed that "the relationship between the two rising Asian giants with overlapping spheres of influence and disputed frontiers will be characterized more by competition and rivalry than cooperation".

ASEAN-CHINA FREE TRADE AREA

The ASEAN–China Free Trade Area (ACFTA), also known as China–ASEAN Free Trade Area is a free trade area among the ten member states of the Association of Southeast Asian Nations (ASEAN) and the People's Republic of China. The initial framework agreement was signed on 4 November 2002 in Phnom Penh, Cambodia, with the intention to establish a free trade area among the eleven nations by 2010. The free trade area came into effect on 1 January 2010. The ASEAN–China Free Trade Area is the largest free trade area in terms of population and third largest in terms of nominal GDP.

Signatories

ASEAN members and the People's Republic of China had a combined nominal gross domestic product of approximately US$6 trillion in 2008. The free trade area had the third largest trade volume after the European Economic Area and the North American Free Trade Area.

ASEAN

Members of ASEAN have a combined population of more than 580 million. Indonesia accounts for more than 40 percent of the region's population, and its people have voiced the greatest amount of opposition to the agreement. Several days following the implementation of the free trade area, it announced plans to renegotiate tariffs on 228 product categories. In exchange, Indonesia would accelerate implementation of the agreement on 153 categories.

People's Republic of China

China first proposed the idea of a free trade area in November 2000. It had overtaken the United States as the third largest trading partner of ASEAN, after Japan and the European Union, when the free trade area came into effect. Between 2003 and 2008, trade with ASEAN grew from US$59.6 billion to US$192.5 billion. China's transformation into a major economic power in the 21st century has led to an increase of foreign investments in the bamboo network, a network of overseas Chinese businesses operating in the markets of Southeast Asia that share common family and cultural ties. China is also the world's largest exporter.

Framework agreement

Leaders of ASEAN and China, during a meeting in Singapore in November 2000, decided to explore measures aimed at economic integration within the region. In Brunei the following year, they endorsed the establishment of an ASEAN–China Free Trade Area.

The framework agreement was signed on 4 November 2002 in Phnom Penh by eleven heads of government.

- Hassanal Bolkiah, Sultan of Brunei Darussalam
- Hun Sen, Prime Minister of Cambodia
- Megawati Soekarnoputri, President of Indonesia
- Bounnhang Vorachith, Prime Minister of Laos
- Mahathir bin Mohamad, Prime Minister of Malaysia
- Than Shwe, Prime Minister of Myanmar
- Gloria Macapagal-Arroyo, President of the Philippines
- Goh Chok Tong, Prime Minister of Singapore
- Thaksin Shinawatra, Prime Minister of Thailand
- Phan Văn Kh£i, Prime Minister of Vietnam
- Zhu Rongji, Premier of the State Council of the People's Republic of China

Amendments

Amendments for the framework of the free trade area mostly concerned Vietnam. These amendments were designed to assist Vietnam lower tariffs and put forth dates as guidelines.

Upgrade

Negotiations on upgrading the Free Trade Area are expected to conclude in 2015. The upgrade will allow more goods to be traded tariff free and normalize procedures for services, investment, and customs.

Tariffs

The free trade agreement reduced tariffs on 7,881 product categories, or 90 percent of imported goods, to zero. This reduction took effect in China and the six original members of ASEAN: Brunei, Indonesia, Malaysia, the Philippines, Singapore and

Thailand. The remaining four countries will follow suit in 2015. The average tariff rate on Chinese goods sold in ASEAN countries decreased from 12.8 to 0.6 percent on 1 January 2010 pending implementation of the free trade area by the remaining ASEAN members. Meanwhile, the average tariff rate on ASEAN goods sold in China decreased from 9.8 to 0.1 percent.

The six original ASEAN members also reduced tariffs on 99.11 percent of goods traded among them to zero.

ASEAN FREE TRADE AREA

The ASEAN Free Trade Area (AFTA) is a trade bloc agreement by the Association of Southeast Asian Nations supporting local manufacturing in all ASEAN countries.

The AFTA agreement was signed on 28 January 1992 in Singapore. When the AFTA agreement was originally signed, ASEAN had six members, namely, Brunei, Indonesia, Malaysia, Philippines, Singapore and Thailand. Vietnam joined in 1995, Laos and Myanmar in 1997 and Cambodia in 1999. AFTA now comprises the ten countries of ASEAN. All the four latecomers were required to sign the AFTA agreement to join ASEAN, but were given longer time frames in which to meet AFTA's tariff reduction obligations.

The primary goals of AFTA seek to:

- Increase ASEAN's competitive edge as a production base in the world market through the elimination, within ASEAN, of tariffs and non-tariff barriers; and
- Attract more foreign direct investment to ASEAN.

The primary mechanism for achieving such goals is the Common Effective Preferential Tariff scheme, which established a phased schedule in 1992 with the goal to increase the *region's competitive advantage as a production base geared for the world market.*

The Common Effective Preferential Tariff (CEPT) scheme

Unlike the EU, AFTA does not apply a common external tariff on imported goods. Each ASEAN member may impose tariffs on goods entering from outside ASEAN based on its national schedules. However, for goods originating within ASEAN, ASEAN members are to apply a tariff rate of 0-5 %(the more recent members of Cambodia, Laos, Myanmar and Vietnam, also known as CMLV countries, were given additional time to implement the reduced tariff rates). This is known as the Common Effective Preferential Tariff (CEPT) scheme.

ASEAN members have the option of excluding products from the CEPT in three cases: 1.) Temporary exclusions; 2.) Sensitive agricultural products; 3.) General exceptions. Temporary exclusions refer to products for which tariffs will ultimately be lowered to 0-5 %, but which are being protected temporarily by a delay in tariff reductions.

For sensitive agricultural products include commodities such as rice, ASEAN members have until 2010 to reduce the tariff levels to 0-5 %.

General exceptions refer to products which an ASEAN member deems necessary for the protection of national security, public morals, the protection of human, animal or plant life and health, and protection of articles of artistic, historic, or archaeological value. ASEAN members have agreed to enact zero tariff rates on virtually all imports by 2010 for the original signatories, and 2015 for the CMLV countries.

Rule of Origin

The CEPT only applies to goods originating within ASEAN. The general rule is that local ASEAN content must be at least 40% of the FOBvalue of the good. The local ASEAN content can be cumulative, that is, the value of inputs from various ASEAN members can be combined to meet the 40% requirement. The following formula is applied:

(Raw material cost

+ Direct labour cost

+ Direct overhead cost

+ Profit

+ Inland transport cost)

x 100 % FOB value

However, for certain products, special rules apply:

- Change in Chapter Rule for Wheat Flour;
- Change of Tariff Sub-Heading for Wood-Based Products;
- Change in Tariff Classification for Certain Aluminum and Articles thereof.

The exporter must obtain a "Form D" certification from its national government attesting that the good has met the 40% requirement. The Form D must be presented to the customs authority of the importing government to qualify for the CEPT rate. Difficulties have sometimes arisen regarding the evidentiary proof to support the claim, as well as how ASEAN national customs authorities can verify Form D submissions. These difficulties arise because each ASEAN national customs authority interprets and implements the Form D requirements without much co-ordination.

Administration

Administration of AFTA is handled by the national customs and trade authorities in each ASEAN member. The ASEAN Secretariat has authority to monitor and ensure compliance with AFTA measures, but has no legal authority to enforce compliance. This has led to inconsistent rulings by ASEAN national authorities. The ASEAN Charter is intended to bolster the ASEAN Secretariat's ability to ensure consistent application of AFTA measures.

ASEAN national authorities have also been traditionally reluctant to share or cede sovereignty to authorities from other ASEAN members (although ASEAN trade ministries routinely make cross-border visits to conduct on-site inspections in anti-dumping investigations). Unlike the EU or NAFTA, joint teams to ensure compliance and investigate non-compliance have not been widely used. Instead, ASEAN national authorities must rely on the review and analysis of other ASEAN national authorities to determine if AFTA measures such as rule of origin are being followed. Disagreements may result between the national authorities. Again, the ASEAN Secretariat may help mediate a dispute but has no legal authority to resolve it.

ASEAN has attempted to improve customs co-ordination through the implementation of the ASEAN Single Window project.

The ASEAN Single Window would allow importers to submit all information related to the transaction to be entered electronically once. This information would then be shared with all other ASEAN national customs authorities.

Dispute resolution

Although these ASEAN national customs and trade authorities co-ordinate among themselves, disputes can arise. The ASEAN Secretariat has no legal authority to resolve such disputes, so disputes are resolved bilaterally through informal means or through dispute resolution.

An ASEAN Protocol on Enhanced Dispute Settlement Mechanism governs formal dispute resolution in AFTA and other aspects of ASEAN. ASEAN members may seek mediation and good offices consultations. If these efforts are ineffective, they may ask SEOM (Senior Economic Officials Meetings) to establish panel of independent arbitrators to review the dispute. Panel decisions can be appealed to an appellate body formed by the ASEAN Economic Community Council.

The Protocol has almost never been invoked because of the role of SEOM in the dispute resolution process. SEOM decisions require consensus among all ASEAN members, and since both the aggrieved party and the alleged transgressor are both participating in SEOM, such consensus cannot be achieved. This discourages ASEAN members from invoking the Protocol, and often they seek dispute resolution in other fora such as the WTO or even the International Court of Justice.

This can also be frustrating for companies affected by an AFTA dispute, as they have no rights to invoke dispute resolution yet their home ASEAN government may not be willing to invoke the Protocol. The ASEAN Secretary General has listed dispute resolution as requiring necessary reform for proper administration of AFTA and the AEC.

Further trade facilitation efforts

Efforts to close the development gap and expand trade among members of ASEAN are key points of policy discussion. According to a 2008 research brief published by the World Bank as part of its Trade Costs and Facilitation Project, ASEAN members have the potential to reap significant benefits from investments in further trade facilitation reform, due to the comprehensive tariff reform already realised through the ASEAN Free Trade Agreement.

This new analysis suggests examining two key areas, among others: port facilities and competitiveness in the Internet services sector. Reform in these areas, the report states, could expand ASEAN trade by up to 7.5% ($22 billion) and 5.7% ($17 billion), respectively. By contrast, cutting applied tariffs in all ASEAN members to the regional average in Southeast Asia would increase intra-regional trade by about 2% ($6.3 billion).

Membership

Countries that agree to eliminate tariffs among themselves:

- Brunei
- Indonesia
- Malaysia
- Philippines
- Singapore
- Thailand
- Myanmar
- Cambodia
- Laos
- Vietnam

Regular Observers

- Papua New Guinea
- Timor-Leste

The most recent ASEAN meeting was observed also by:

- China
- Japan
- South Korea
- India
- Australia
- New Zealand

ASEAN Plus Three

ASEAN Plus Three (APT) is a forum that functions as a coordinator of co-operation between theAssociation of Southeast Asian Nations and the three East Asia nations of China, Japan, and South Korea. Government leaders, ministers, and senior officials from the 10 members of the ASEAN and the three Northeast Asian states consult on an increasing range of issues. The APT is the latest development of East Asian regional co-operation. In the past, proposals, such as ROK's call for an Asian Common Market in 1970 and Japan's 1988 suggestion for an Asian Network, have been made to bring closer regional co-operation.

The first leaders' meetings were held in 1996 and 1997 to deal with Asia–Europe Meeting issues, and China and Japan each wanted regular summit meetings with ASEAN members afterwards. The group's significance and importance was strengthened by the Asian Financial Crisis. In response to the crisis, ASEAN closely cooperated with China, Japan, and ROK. Since the implementation of the Joint Statement on East Asia Cooperation in 1999 at the Manila Summit, APT finance ministers have been holding periodic consultations.

ASEAN Plus Three, in establishing the Chiang Mai Initiative, has been credited as forming the basis for financial stability in Asia, the lack of such stability having contributed to the Asian Financial Crisis. The Asian Currency Unit (ACU) is a proposed weighted index of currencies for ASEAN+3. The ACU was inspired by the now defunct European Currency Unit, replaced by the Euro. The Asian Currency Unit's purpose is to help stabilise the region's financial markets. The ACU as it is proposed is a currency basket and not a real currency, i.e., a weighted index of East Asian currencies that will function as a benchmark for regional currency movements.

The Asian Development Bank is currently reviewing different options concerning the technical aspects related to the ACU calculation, including the nature of the basket, the choice of fixed weights vs. fixed units, the selection of currencies to be included in the basket, the choice of weights, the criteria for their periodical revision, and other aspects as well. The Asian Development Bank was to announce the details of the ACU in March 2006 or later. However external pressures delayed this announcement although the concept was still being studied in detail. A panel discussion in February 2007 cited technical and political obstacles as having prevented the project from advancing. The unit, limited to ASEAN+3, was said to be still moving forward by mid-July 2007.

Since the process began in 1997, ASEAN Plus Three (APT) co-operation has broadened and deepened to also focus on subjects other than finance too in the discussion such as the areas of food and energy security, financial co-operation, trade facilitation, disaster management, people-to-people contacts, narrowing the development gap, rural development and poverty alleviation, human trafficking, labour movement, communicable diseases, environment and sustainable development, and transnational crime, including counter-terrorism. APT co-operation in the area of political and security co-operation has been deepened by regular dialogue and exchange of views through existing APT mechanisms, such as the APT Summit, APT Foreign Ministers' Meeting, APT Senior Officials' Meeting (SOM) and as well as through track 1.5 and track two dialogue, including East Asia Forum and Network of East Asia Think-tanks.In combating transnational crime in the region, the APT Work Plan on Cooperation in Combating Transnational Crime was adopted in 2006. With the aim to further strengthening APT co-operation, East Asia Vision Group (EAVG) II was established by the Leaders of APT at the 13th APT Summit on 29 October 2010 in Ha Noi to stock-take, review and identify the future direction of APT co-operation.

COMPREHENSIVE ECONOMIC PARTNERSHIP FOR EAST ASIA

The Comprehensive Economic Partnership for East Asia (CEPEA) is a Japanese led proposal for trade co-operation, free trade agreement, among the 16 present member countries of the East Asia Summit. All those movements and efforts were taken over by the following Regional Comprehensive Economic Partnership.

Countries involved

The 16 countries are:

1. the 10 members of ASEAN
   - Indonesia
   - Malaysia
   - Philippines
   - Singapore
   - Thailand
   - Brunei
   - Vietnam
   - Laos
   - Myanmar
   - Cambodia
2. plus the three additional members of ASEAN Plus Three
   - China
   - Japan
   - South Korea
3. plus
   - India
   - Australia
   - New Zealand

Background

The concept has been in discussion stages since 2006 but gained momentum in 2008 and 2009 when India and ASEAN; and Australia, New Zealand and ASEAN respectively concluded free trade agreements. The CEPEA proposal was advanced by Japan in conjunction with the establishment of the Economic Research Institute for ASEAN and East Asia (ERIA). The two mechanisms are designed to be mutually supporting liberalisation and co-operation. The details of the concept and its relationship with other proposals for the region, such as the East Asian Community, remain unclear. An alternative proposal based on the 13 members of the ASEAN Plus Three is called the East Asia Free Trade Agreement (EAFTA).

The Third East Asia Summit agreed that a final report on the CEPEA proposal was to be received at the Fourth East Asia Summit which was held in October 2009.

The Chairman's Report for the Fourth East Asia Summit (25 October 2009) stated: We noted the final Phase II Report of the Track Two Study Group on Comprehensive Economic Partnership in East Asia (CEPEA) and welcomed the decision of our Economic Ministers who met in Bangkok on 15 August 2009 to task the Senior Economic Officials to discuss and consider the recommendations in the Phase I and II reports. CEPEA and East Asia Free Trade Area (EAFTA) could be examined and considered in parallel.

The report for the ASEAN Plus Three meeting, held the day before with 13 of 16 of the same members, also stated: We noted the final report of the Phase II feasibility study of the East Asia Free Trade Area (EAFTA) and welcomed the decision of 12th AEM Plus Three Consultations in Bangkok on 15 August 2009 to task the Senior Economic Officials to discuss and consider the recommendations in the Phase I and II reports. EAFTA and Comprehensive Economic Partnership in East Asia (CEPEA) could be examined and considered in parallel.

The Chairman's Statement of the 16th ASEAN Summit (9 April 2010) stated: We noted the initiatives being undertaken to take forward broader regional integration by considering the recommendations of both East Asia Free Trade Agreement (EAFTA) and the Comprehensive Economic Partnership for East Asia (CEPEA) studies together. We looked forward to receiving the progress report at the 17th ASEAN Summit in October 2010 and to discussing with our Dialogue Partners the future direction of regional architecture with ASEAN at its core.

By August 2010 working groups involving the 16 nations to study Economic Cooperation, Rules of Origin, Customs Procedures and Tariff Nomenclature had been formed.

East Asia Free Trade Agreement

13 of the 16 nations (excluding India, Australia and New Zealand) are also simultaneously negotiating an East Asia Free

Trade Area. The two processes are not alternatives and both are being pursued simultaneously

Current arrangements

The 16 members are presently involved in a series of separate arrangements among the members of the grouping. The 10 members ASEAN have established the ASEAN Free Trade Area. Australia and New Zealand have the long established Closer Economic Relations. Between the 16 members bilateral and multilateral arrangements are in place or under negotiation.

ASEAN has the following arrangements in place:

- the ASEAN–China Free Trade Area came into force on 1 January 2010;
- a comprehensive economic partnership agreement with Japan came into force on 1 December 2008;
- the ASEAN Korea Free Trade Agreement, the trade in goods provisions came into effect on 1 June 2007, an agreement for trade in services was signed in 2007 and the trade in investments provisions were signed in 2009;
- a free trade agreement with Australian and New Zealand (jointly) AANZFTA that came into force on 1 January 2010;
- the ASEAN-India Trade in Goods (TIG) Agreement came into effect on 1 January 2010 and the ASEAN-India Trade in Services and Investment Agreements are still under negotiation;

plus China, Japan and South Korea are researching (as at October 2009) a joint arrangement between the three countries (China–Japan–South Korea Free Trade Agreement) with talks hoped to commence in 2012;

China has the following additional arrangements in place:

- China–South Korea Free Trade Agreement - negotiations are said to be announced to commence shortly (as at April 2010) with South Korea on an arrangement;
- China–Australia Free Trade Agreement - negotiations with Australia on an arrangement;
- the New Zealand – China Free Trade Agreement came into force 1 October 2008;

- a feasibility study on an arrangement with India was positively concluded in 2007;

Japan has the following additional arrangements in place:

- negotiations with South Korea on an arrangement but which have been suspended since 2004;
- Japan–Australia Economic Partnership Agreement - negotiations with Australia on an arrangement;
- negotiations with India on an arrangement;
- conducting a feasibility study with New Zealand as of (14 May 2008)

South Korea has the following additional arrangements in place:

- Australia–Korea Free Trade Agreement - negotiations with Australia on an arrangement;
- negotiations with New Zealand on an arrangement;
- India and South Korea signed a comprehensive economic partnership agreement in August 2009;

Australia has the following additional arrangements in place:

- as noted above Closer Economic Relations with New Zealand;
- a feasibility study with India about entry into an arrangement;

India has the following additional arrangements in place:

- a feasibility study with New Zealand about entry into an arrangement;

multiple additional bilateral arrangements between one or more ASEAN members separately.

In addition individual members of ASEAN may also have other arrangements in place beyond the arrangements negotiated by ASEAN as a bloc i.e., Singapore by itself outside of ASEAN has a series of FTAs.

CHINA-ASEAN FREE TRADE AREA

A major development in China-ASEAN relations since the end of the Cold War is perhaps the growing economic interdependence between the two. Indeed, two-way trade has been growing at a rate of 20 percent for the last decade and reached over U.S. $100 billion in 2004, a year ahead of a previously set target. It further registered a 23 percent increase in 2005, reaching $130.4 billion. ASEAN member states have benefted from China's spectacular economic growth as the Asian giant's growing demands also generate economic benefits for the region as a whole. For instance, in 2004, ASEAN had a roughly $20 billion trade surplus with China, while China's other major trading partners all sustained sizable defcits. Chinese analysts have divided the evolution of China-ASEAN economic relations into two phases. The first one, from 1991, when Chinese Foreign Minister Qian Qichen was invited to attend the 24th ASEAN Foreign Ministers meeting, to 2001 when Chinese Premier Zhu Rongji proposed a China-ASEAN free trade area, saw the two sides expand and deepen bilateral trade ties. The second phase began in November 2002, with the signing of the China-ASEAN Framework Agreement on Comprehensive Economic Cooperation moving toward regional economic integration. Over the years, China and ASEAN have institutionalized 48 regular mechanisms to facilitate closer economic cooperation. Prominent among them is the highest political mechanism—ASEAN+1, launched in 1997. In addition, there are five working groups: the China-ASEAN Senior Officials meeting, the China-ASEAN Joint Cooperation Committee, ASEAN-China Joint Committee on Economic and Trade Cooperation, ASEAN-China Joint Committee on Science and Technology (July 1994), and the ASEAN Beijing Committee. The two sides also have identified five key areas for cooperation—agriculture, information and communication technologies, human resource development, the Mekong River Development, and mutual investment.

At the eighth ASEAN summit in Phnom Penh, Cambodia, in November 2002, China and ASEAN signed the Framework Agreement on Comprehensive Economic Cooperation. If and when implemented, it would constitute a common market of 1.7 billion people, with a combined gross domestic product (GDP) of U.S.$1.5-2 trillion. The two sides sought to establish a free trade area (FTA) within 10 years, first with the original ASEAN-6 by 2010, followed by the entire ASEAN-10 by 2015. The initiative largely came from

China, as it recognized ASEAN member states' concerns over China's growing economy and its crowding-out effect on investment fows into Southeast Asia and increasing economic competition. After Premier Zhu proposed the FTA idea, an ASEAN-China Expert Group on Economic Cooperation was established to study Zhu's proposal, as well as the impact of China's World Trade Organization (WTO) entry in 2001. It also is a response to the 1997 Asian financial crisis and hence the need for a more regional approach to future economic challenges. Cooperation also includes the Mekong River Basin development project that has been supported by the Asian Development Bank and the endorsement by ASEAN of a U.S.$2.5 billion Trans-Asian railway joining Kunming and Singapore.

While there are many economic reasons for greater integration, some analysts also point to the strategic rationale for developing an FTA, especially from China's perspective. To begin with, such an arrangement could facilitate a more peaceful regional security environment critical to China's continued economic rise. Second, it addresses concerns in the region over China's growing power by more closely integrating itself with ASEAN, hence increasing the costs of conflicts. Chinese analysts suggest that the CAFTA should be viewed from a strategic perspective and as part of its peaceful rise. Geo-economics and greater economic interactions with ASEAN would support these objectives. To preempt Taiwan's strategy to buy its way into Southeast Asia, China should pay greater attention to the development of its southwestern region (Yunnan and Guangxi in particular) to develop and strengthen economic ties with the ASEAN countries.

Third, by taking the lead in forming an FTA, China also hopes to play a more prominent role as the region's centre of economic growth. Fourth, by investing more in the region and allowing a certain degree of self-discrimination—as in the form of the so-called "Early Harvest Program," giving ASEAN states preferential treatment on agricultural products in terms of tariff reduction and market access—Beijing seeks to address the perceived "China threat," not in the security area but in the context of economic competition. And fnally, by entering a rules-based free trade arrangement, China also wants to demonstrate its acceptance of multilateralism and respect for norms and rules. ASEAN member states for their own reasons sought to partake in China's dynamic economic growth; at least not to be left behind. An FTA also could energize other external powers to seek similar arrangements, therefore opening up more opportunities in the areas of trade and foreign direct investment (FDI).

While China-ASEAN trade has registered rapid growth over the last decade, both rank fifth as each other's trading partners, after intra-ASEAN, Japan, the United States, and the European Union (EU). Future developments will depend on how both could complement, rather than compete, in labour-intensive manufacturing sectors and increase investment in each other. ASEAN countries recognize the opportunities that a growing China provides, but they also are worried over the long-term impact of a stronger China competing with them for foreign direct investment and replacing them as the manufacturer of labour-intensive consumer products. There remain serious concerns that China may compete and crowd out ASEAN in terms of foreign direct investment, replace ASEAN states as a manufacturing base, and hence cause severe economic downturn in the ASEAN countries less capable of competition and with little room for adjustment.

To address these concerns, China in particular needs to make a greater investment in ASEAN, potentially in the energy and resource-based sectors, to raise two-way trade volumes further, as well as to generate a larger market as is supposed to be provided by the CAFTA. However, investment negotiations between the two still face major hurdles. For instance, during 1995-2004, Chinese investment ($1 billion) in ASEAN amounted to only 0.4 percent of the total. This compares poorly with EU-15 ($68.5 billion, 28.3 percent), the United States ($42.3 billion, 17.5 percent), and Japan ($32 billion, 13.3 percent). It even is lower significantly than Taiwan's investment in the region ($8.9 billion, 3.6 percent). At the same time, China has replaced Southeast Asia as the destination of FDI. Beijing also needs to manage potentially contentious issues such as the Mekong River project that has economic, ecological, and environmental impacts on downstream Southeast Asian countries.

The CAFTA has generated much interest in other extra-regional powers that seek FTAs with ASEAN. The United States proposed the Enterprise for ASEAN Initiative (EAI) that would enable member states to establish FTAs along the line of the U.S.-Singapore FTA. Japan also issued the "Joint Declaration of the Leaders of ASEAN and Japan on the Comprehensive Economic Partnership" on November 5, 2002, in Phnom Penh. At the 2003 ASEAN+1 summit held in Tokyo, Japanese Prime Minister Junichiro Koizumi pledged $3 billion in new aid. With CAFTA, ASEAN+1, and other regional forums, including the East Asia Summit in December 2005, there is what some would call the trend toward regionalism with shared markets, growing economic interdependence, and even shared ideas on what a regional security architecture should look like.

China-ASEAN relations have evolved from enmity and suspicion to amity and greater cooperation on a broad range of issues. Having established a strategic partnership for peace and prosperity, the two sides are working toward building a stable, long-term relationship for the future. In addition to the state-to-state security and economic ties since reform started in the late 1970s, the Chinese Communist Party (CCP) has sought to establish and expand ties with political parties in Southeast Asia. Today, the CCP has official relations with 39 political parties in the region, and the rationale and objectives are to promote mutual understanding, learning, economic success, and governance, regardless of ideologies. This is a far cry from the 1960s and 1970s when the CCP supported indigenous communist parties as part of a strategy to fan revolution in the region to topple ruling governments.

Beijing's efforts to assure its neighbours through the so-called new diplomacy have paid off in winning confidence from its Southeast Asian neighbours, if not completely erasing disputes between them. The 1997 Asian financial crisis was a turning point. Chinese responses to the crisis, including its pledges of $1 billion to help Thailand and not to devaluate the Renminbi, won good will in ASEAN. Beijing also emerged more confdent of its own potential leadership role in the region, although it remains deferential to ASEAN. China began to publish a defence white paper in 1998. Now published every 2 years, the document also has moved from mere exposition of general principles to some elementary explanations of defence budgets, modernization programs, and doctrinal issues. While still far from ideal, at least some modest steps have been made to enhance transparency. China also put forward the "New Security Concept" (NSC) at the ARF Inter-Sessional Support Group (ISG) on Confidence-Building Measures that it co-hosted with the Philippines in Beijing, March 1997. The NSC emphasizes cooperative security, confidence-building, peaceful resolution of disputes, and multilateral dialogue. In November 2004, China hosted the first ARF Security Policy Conference in Beijing. Within a decade, growing interdependence and skillful Chinese diplomacy have sustained a steady improvement and rising comfort level between China and ASEAN, allowing Beijing to exercise greater influence in the region.

China and ASEAN also are expanding areas of cooperation, in particular in the nontraditional security areas, including securing SLOCs, antiterrorism, and antipiracy; ecological issues related to the Greater Mekong River project and other environmental issues; responses to the severe acute respiratory syndrome (SARS) outbreak, for instance, the first China-ASEAN summit on SARS; transnational organized crimes; and money laundering. Chinese Premier Wen Jiabao has proposed *mulin, anlin, fulin* to ASEAN ["friendly neighbours—peaceful coexistence, regional stability, and harmony"; "secure neighbours—regional peace and stability through dialogue, negotiation to resolve disputes," and "rich neighbours"—develop, deepen regional and subregional economic cooperation, and promote regional integration].

8

India and ASEAN: Beyond 'Looking East'

As expected, the South China Sea issue once again grabbed the headlines in the latest round of Asian regional summitry held in Myanmar earlier this month. Less in the limelight, but no less consequential, was India's first engagement of the Association of Southeast Asian Nations (ASEAN) since its new Prime Minister Narendra Modi was electedlast month. Despite India's oft-cited cultural and civilizational links with Southeast Asia and some notable advances in its much-touted Look East Policy since 1991, both sides agree that ASEAN-India ties are far from reaching their full potential. Southeast Asia – with the exception of Myanmar – had also been conspicuously absent in Modi's foreign policy statements, which have largely focused on neighboring South Asian states and major powers like China and the United States.

The new Indian government's first foray into a formal ASEAN gathering produced some encouraging signs. At the India-ASEAN meeting, External Affairs Minister Sushma Swaraj focused her remarks on "connectivity," the reigning mantra in Modi's regional policies which refers to a host of infrastructure projects to speed up Asian integration. That suggests a strong economic bent in the relationship that would both help New Delhi to develop its Northeastern states and Southeast Asia to form a more united ASEAN Economic Community over the next few years. ASEAN, for its part, said both sides will likely sign a long-delayed free trade agreement in services and investments later this month and proposed strengthening cooperation in several areas, including agriculture, energy, and science and technology.

India's relationships with pivotal Southeast Asian countries are also gaining steam. New Delhi's ties with Singapore, its strongest in the region, are expected to grow even tighter as both sides agreed to step up their defense partnership on August 19. Relations with Vietnam are also on the uptick, with Hanoi renewing India's lease of two oil blocks in the South China Sea for another year before Swaraj's first visit there next week. And Myanmar, the only ASEAN country that shares a physical land border with India, is in a league of its own in Modi's eyes since it is New Delhi's gateway to Southeast Asia. Modi himself is expected to visit both Vietnam and Myanmar by the end of 2014.

But as is often the case with ASEAN-India relations, the problem is not the lack of ideas but the inability to follow through on them. Take India's relations with Myanmar. Earlier this month, India's former ambassador to Myanmar VS Seshadri warned in a report that two key infrastructure projects – the Trilateral Highway and the Kaladan Multi-modal Transit – need to be completed on time by 2016 in order to realize the full promise of bilateral ties. Judging from past experience, this is far from assured. For all the talk of India's Look East Policy, formal India-Myanmar land border trade is still a measly $35 million. At the sub-regional level, countless reports – including one I authored back in 2010 – have encouraged India to revitalize groupings like the Bay of Bengal Initiative for Multi-Sectoral Technical and Economic Cooperation (BIMSTEC) and the Mekong-Ganga Cooperation (MGC), but to no avail. Perhaps a Modi government, with its "neighborhood" focus, will finally take steps in this direction.

"Look East" has been the paradigm used to frame India's approach to ASEAN since the days of Narasimha Rao in the 1990s. But given the gap between rhetoric and reality in ASEAN-India relations in the past, I have preferred to say that New Delhi's strategy in the coming years should be to "Act East" more concertedly, following the remarks former U.S. Secretary of State Hillary Clinton delivered on a visit there back in 2011. As India prepares to draft the next five-year plan of action for ASEAN-

India relations beginning in 2016, it should keep in mind that it will be judged less on the platitudes in that document than on its ability to deliver on specific initiatives on the ground in Southeast Asia.

INDIA LOOKS EAST TO ASEAN WITH DELHI DIALOGUE

The India–ASEAN relationship received a shot in the arm with the conclusion of the 8th Delhi Dialogue on 17–19 February 2016. Since 1991 India has been aggressively pursuing increased trade and strategic relations with Southeast Asian Countries as a part of its 'Look East' policy. Now, ASEAN has grown to be India's fourth largest trading partner after China, the European Union and the United States.

The goal of courting ASEAN was to build historical and cultural ties, to expand markets, counter Chinese influence in the region and improve India's standing as a regional power. But India's relationship with its regional neighbours has not matured to the extent that it was originally envisaged. A stronger standing with ASEAN will give a major boost to India's stature as a growing global power. Since the conclusion of a free trade agreement (FTA) with ASEAN in 2009, trade has grown consistently and investment flows have been substantial, but the full potential of India–ASEAN relations is yet to be realised.

The Delhi Dialogue is an annual event for discussing political, security and economic issues between ASEAN and India. The dialogue focused on several issues and had a business, ministerial and an academic session. From a trade perspective, it is of the utmost significance. With the conclusion of the ASEAN Economic Community (AEC) in December 2015 and with the Regional Comprehensive Economic Cooperation agreement (RCEP) negotiations in full swing, ASEAN is poised to become the economic powerhouse of Asia. Realising this, the Indian government has made substantial efforts to boost relations with ASEAN.

The dialogue dwelt on the steps to be taken by both India and ASEAN to smooth the conclusion of the RCEP negotiations by the end of 2016 and the implications of the recently concluded Trans-Pacific Partnership (TPP) for the region.

Officials emphasised that a fast conclusion of the RCEP would deepen integration among the member countries, while promoting goods and services trade, investment, the IT sector, competition and dispute settlement. Given that the possibility of India joining the TPP is still a long way off, being a member of the RCEP will help India prepare itself to better engage with mega FTAs in the future. The RCEP itself will also benefit India. RCEP is an ambitious mega FTA that covers 16 countries, a third of the world's economy and 45 per cent of the global population.

The Delhi Dialogue provided an opportunity for India to assess how it would need to adjust to mega FTAs and other formal blocs, such as the One Belt, One Road initiative, emerging in the region. These blocs will be vital for both India's security and economic future. Also highlighted were the expected gains to India's services sectors from the conclusion of the India–ASEAN services agreement and the RCEP.

Another major issue for India is the need to link into global value chains. The discussion covered the steps already undertaken to better coordinate with ASEAN on industrial value chains, and how best to integrate small- and medium-sized enterprises (SMEs) into regional value chains, while ensuring that they have the required knowledge to navigate the complicated export procedures.

The Ministry of External Affairs seized the opportunity to explain the implications of its 5 billion rupee (about US$73 million) project development fund to encourage integration of Indian producers into ASEAN's regional value chains. This initiative plans to help create manufacturing hubs in Cambodia, Laos, Myanmar and Vietnam leading to the establishment of a new regional economic order within ASEAN.

The growing strategic partnership between India and ASEAN needs to be further strengthened by consistent engagement with the ASEAN member countries. Both ASEAN and India need each other. For ASEAN, India not only offers a huge domestic market with a growing aspirational middle class, but also a growing working population.

Given that India is a world leader in the IT sector and an attractive destination for foreign direct investment, there are huge opportunities for ASEAN to forge a deep relationship with India. Focusing on trade in services with ASEAN will give India an opportunity to use its competitive strength to become a services export hub for the ASEAN region. Being a part of the AEC, RCEP and having strong relations with ASEAN through its existing FTA will facilitate further economic reforms in India. And, more significantly, it will allow India to establish itself as a growing economic power in Asia.

ASEAN- INDIA RELATIONS

The Association of South-East Asian Nations (ASEAN) comprises of Indonesia, Singapore, Philippines, Malaysia, Brunei, Thailand, Cambodia, Lao PDR, Myanmar and Vietnam. India's focus on a strengthened and multi-faceted relationship with ASEAN is an outcome of the significant changes in the world's political and economic scenario since the early 1990s and India's own march towards economic liberalisation. India's search for economic space resulted in the 'Look East Policy'. The Look East Policy has today matured into a dynamic and action oriented 'Act East Policy. PM at the 12th ASEAN India Summit and the 9th East Asia Summit held in Nay Pyi Taw, Myanmar, in November, 2014, formally enunciated the Act East Policy.

Apart from ASEAN, India has taken other policy initiatives in the region that involve some members of ASEAN like BIMSTEC, MGC etc. India is also an active participant in several regional forums like the Asia-Europe Meeting, East Asia Summit, ASEAN Regional Forum, ASEAN Defence Ministers' Meeting + (ADMM+) and Expanded ASEAN Maritime Forum.

There has been steady progress in the ASEAN-India partnership since the Look East Policy was launched in 1991. India became sectoral dialogue partners in 1992 and full dialogue partners in 1996. Since 2002, India has annual Summits with ASEAN along with China, Japan and Republic of Korea. There are 30 Dialogue Mechanisms cutting across all the sectors including 7 ministerial level meetings.

Commemorative Summit: In 2012, ASEAN and India commemorated 20 years of dialogue partnership and 10 years of Summit level partnership with ASEAN with a Commemorative Summit in New Delhi under the theme 'ASEAN-India Partnership for Peace and Shared Prosperity' on 20-21 December 2012. The Commemorative Summit attended by the Leaders from all the 10 ASEAN countries endorsed elevating the partnership to a 'Strategic Partnership'. The Leaders also adopted the 'ASEAN-India Vision Statement', which charts the future of ASEAN-India cooperation. Two major events that were organized in 2012 in the run-up to the Commemorative Summit include the 2nd ASEAN-India Car Rally and Shipping Expedition of INS Sudarshini to ASEAN countries. During the Summit, the heads of the Government recommended establishment of ASEAN-India Centre (AIC) to undertake policy research, advocacy and networking activities with organizations and think-tanks in India and ASEAN, with the aim to promote the ASEAN-India Strategic Partnership. The AIC has been serving as a resource centre for ASEAN Member States and India since its establishment in 2013, for strengthening ASEAN-India strategic partnership and promoting India-ASEAN dialogue and cooperation in the areas of mutual interests. AIC has provided some very valuable inputs to policy makers in India and ASEAN on implementation of ASEAN-India connectivity by organising seminars, roundtables etc. AIC also organizes workshops, seminars and conferences on various cross-cutting issues relevant to ASEAN-India strategic partnership. It undertakes regular networking activities with relevant public/private agencies, organizations and think-tanks in India and ASEAN and EAS countries, with the aim of providing up-to-date information, data resources and sustained interaction, for promoting ASEAN-India Strategic Partnership

Plans of Action: As a reflection of the interest of ASEAN and India to intensify their engagement, the ASEAN-India Partnership for Peace, Progress and Shared Prosperity, which sets out the roadmap for long-term ASEAN-India engagement, was signed at the 3rd ASEAN-India Summit in 2004 in Vientiane. A Plan of Action (POA) for the period 2004-2010 was also developed to implement the Partnership. Most of the paras of the 2nd POA (2010-15) have been implemented. The 3rd POA (2016-20) was adopted by the ASEAN-India Foreign Ministers Meeting held in August 2015.

Security cooperation: The main forum for ASEAN security dialogue is the ASEAN Regional Forum (ARF). India has been attending annual meetings of this forum since 1996 and has actively participated in its various activities. The ASEAN Defence Ministers' Meeting (ADMM) is the highest defence consultative and cooperative mechanism in ASEAN. The ADMM+ brings together Defence Ministers from the 10 ASEAN nations plus Australia, China, India, Japan, New Zealand, Republic of Korea, Russia, and the United States. Defense Minister attended the 3rd ADMM Plus held from 4-5 November 2015 in Kuala Lumpur. Expanded ASEAN Maritime Forum (EAMF) is an avenue for track 1.5 diplomacy focusing on cross cutting maritime issues of common concern. India participated in the 4th EAMF held in Manado, Indonesia on 10-11 September 2015.

Trade and Investment: India-ASEAN trade and investment relations have been growing steadily, with ASEAN being India's fourth largest trading partner. The annual trade registered an average growth of 22% per annum in the decade upto 2011-12, but has stagnated thereafter. It stood at approximately US$ 76.53 billion in 2014-15.

Investment flows are also substantial both ways, with ASEAN accounting for approximately 12.5% of investment flows into India since 2000. FDI inflows into India from ASEAN between April 2007-March 2015 was about US$ 32.44 billion. Whereas FDI outflows from India to ASEAN countries, from April 2007 to March 2015, as per data maintained by DEA, was about US$ 38.672 billion.

The ASEAN-India Free Trade Area has been completed with the entering into force of the ASEAN-India Agreements on Trade in Service and Investments on 1 July 2015.

ASEAN and India have been also working on enhancing private sector engagement. ASEAN India-Business Council (AIBC) was set up in March 2003 in Kuala Lumpur as a forum to bring key private sector players from India and the ASEAN countries on a single platform for business networking and sharing of ideas.

Connectivity: ASEAN-India connectivity is a matter of strategic priority for India as also the ASEAN countries. In 2013, India became the third dialogue partner of ASEAN to initiate an ASEAN Connectivity Coordinating Committee-India Meeting. While India has made considerable progress in implementing the India-Myanmar-Thailand Trilateral Highway and the Kaladan Multimodal Project, issues related to increasing the maritime and air connectivity between ASEAN and India and transforming the corridors of connectivity into economic corridors are under discussion. A possible extension to India-Myanmar-Thailand Trilateral Highway to Cambodia, Lao PDR and Viet Nam is also under consideration. A consensus on signing and operationalizing the India-Myanmar-Thailand Motor Vehicle Agreement (IMT MVA) has been reached. This agreement will have a critical role in realizing seamless movement of passenger, personal and cargo vehicles along roads linking India, Myanmar and Thailand. PM announced a Line of Credit of US$ 1 billion to promote projects that support physical and digital connectivity between India and ASEAN and a Project Development Fund with a corpus of INR 500 crores to develop manufacturing hubs in CLMV countries.

Funds: ASEAN Multilateral Division offers project-based financial assistance to ASEAN countries. Financial assistance has been provided to ASEAN countries in following forms:

- ASEAN-India Cooperation Fund: At the 7th ASEAN-India Summit in 2009, India announced a contribution of US$ 50 million to the ASEAN-India Cooperation Fund, to support implementation of the ASEAN-India Plan of Action 2010-15. Till now 13 projects have been implemented, 17 projects are under implementation and 22 projects are in the planning stage. Projects and programmes worth US$ 35.68 million are under implementation, including the largest project under the ASEAN-India Cooperation, i.e., Space Project.
- ASEAN-India S&T Development Fund (AISTDF): At the 6th ASEAN-India Summit in November 2007 in Singapore, PM announced the setting up of an ASEAN-India Science & Technology Development Fund with a US$ 1 million

contribution from India to promote joint collaborative R&D research projects in Science & Technology sectors. An amount of US$ 373,352 has already been spent out of this Fund on various projects & activities. We have enhanced the ASEAN-India Science and Technology Fund from US$ 1 million to US$ 5 million w.e.f. 2016.

- ASEAN-India Green Fund: At the 6th ASEAN-India Summit on 21 November 2007 in Singapore, PM announced the setting up of an ASEAN-India Green Fund with an initial contribution of US$ 5 million from India to support collaboration activities relating to environment and climate change. Till July 2015, Projects worth US$ 2,079,287 covered under this Fund are at the implementation stage.

ASEAN-India Projects: India has been cooperating with ASEAN by way of implementation of various projects in the fields of Agriculture, Science & Technology, Space, Environment & Climate Change, Human Resource Development, Capacity Building, New and Renewable Energy, Tourism, People-to-People contacts and Connectivity etc.

Since 2011-12, while 13 projects have been completed, 17 projects are under implementation and 22 projects are in the planning stage, some of which are in the final stages of approval. Programmes and projects totalling over US$ 48.85 million have been proposed since September 2011 till date to ASEAN through the ASEAN Secretariat. Some of the prominent projects, which are either ongoing or in the final stages of approval are as follows:

Space Project envisaging establishment of a Tracking, Data Reception/Data Processing Station in Ho Chi Minh City, Vietnam and upgradation of Telemetry Tracking and Command Station in Biak, Indonesia; Setting up of Centres of Excellence in Software Development & Training in CLMV countries are some of the major projects under implementation.

Apart from the above projects, India has been supporting ASEAN specially CLMV countries under the Initiatives for ASEAN Integration, which include projects on Training of English Language for Law Enforcement Officers in CLMV countries and Training of professionals dealing with capital markets in CLMV by National

Institute of Securities Management Mumbai. To boost People-to-people Interaction with ASEAN, India has been organising various programme including Training Programme for ASEAN diplomats, Exchange of Parliamentarians, Participation of ASEAN students in the National Children's Science Congress, ASEAN-India Network of Think Tanks, ASEAN-India Eminent Persons Lecture Series etc.

In the field of agriculture, India and ASEAN have projects such as Exchange of Farmers, ASEAN-India Fellowships for Higher Agricultural Education in India and ASEAN, Exchange of Agriculture Scientists, Empowerment of ASEAN-Indian Women through Cooperatives etc. In the S&T field, there are projects such as ASEAN-India Collaborative Project on S&T for Combating Malaria, ASEAN-India Programme on Quality Systems in Manufacturing, ASEAN-India Collaborative R&D Project on Mariculture, Bio-mining and Bioremediation Technologies etc.

Delhi Dialogue: India has an annual Track 1.5 event Delhi Dialogue, for discussing politico-security and economic issues between ASEAN and India. Since 2009, India has had eight editions of this event. The 8th edition of Delhi Dialogue is being hosted by the MEA in partnership with IDSA, FICCI and other select Indian and ASEAN partners on 17-19 February 2016 in New Delhi. DD VIII has 'ASEAN-India Relations: A New Paradigm' as its theme and includes an Inaugural Business Session, a Ministerial Session, and an Academic Session.

Mission to ASEAN: India has set up a separate Mission to ASEAN and the EAS in Jakarta in April 2015 with a dedicated Ambassador to strengthen engagement with ASEAN and ASEAN-centric processes.

INDIA AND THE ASEAN: A PIVOTAL RELATIONSHIP

Prime Minister Manmohan Singh is scheduled to attend the 11th ASEAN-India Summit and 8th East Asia Summit (EAS) in the Bruneian capital of Bandar Seri Begawan on 10 October 2013. The Prime Minister's hosts, the 10-member ASEAN, would expect New Delhi to continue to play a role in the region that behoves India's economic size and strategic prowess.

The India-ASEAN relationship has entered its third decade. India became a sectoral partner of ASEAN in 1992, a dialogue partner in 1996 and a summit level partner at Phnom Penh in 2002. At the Bali Summit in 2003, India and the ASEAN signed the Instrument of Accession to the treaty of Amity and Cooperation in South East Asia, a framework agreement on Comprehensive Economic Cooperation and a joint declaration for cooperation to combat international terrorism.

The Vientiane summit of 2004 was a milestone in India-ASEAN relations. The ASEAN-India Partnership for Peace, Progress and Shared Prosperity and the Plan of Action to implement it were finalised. The first plan of action was implemented from 2004-10. The second plan of action for 2010-15 has been adopted and being implemented.

In December 2012, New Delhi hosted the India-ASEAN Commemorative Summit to mark 20-years of its association with the grouping and 10-years of its summit level partnership. It also marked the two decades of India's 'Look East Policy' and that of its economic liberalisation process. The India-ASEAN relationship was elevated to a strategic partnership at the 2012 meeting. The leaders also adopted a vision statement or a blueprint for the future India-ASEAN cooperation.

The last two decades of India-ASEAN dialogue has led to a deepening of cooperation across the three pillars of their relationship - politico-military, economic and socio-cultural. The India-ASEAN dialogue currently has 26 inter-governmental mechanisms that cover a wide spectrum of areas.

India's 20-year-old engagement of the ASEAN countries has made India's first PM Jawaharlal Nehru's words in the Discovery of India in 1944 prophetic. Nehru wrote: "The Pacific is likely to take the place of the Atlantic in the future as the nerve centre of the world. Though not directly a Pacific state, India will inevitably exercise an important influence there. India will also develop as the centre of economic and strategic importance in a part of the world which is going to develop in the future."

As if gazing at a crystal ball, Nehru further wrote that "India will have to play a very great part in security problems of Asia and the Indian Ocean, more especially of the Middle East and South East Asia" and that "India is the pivot around which these problems will have to be considered."

The developments of the last few years in the South East Asian and Far Eastern regions and the expectations that the ASEAN member countries have from India to provide leadership at a difficult period seem to confirm what Nehru saw clearly 70-years back. India has been a source of strength for most ASEAN countries for its unequivocal stand on maritime disputes. India supports unimpeded rights of passage and other maritime rights in accordance with the international law. New Delhi has welcomed the decision to implement the 2002 Declaration on the Conduct of Parties in the South China Sea and that countries in the region adopt a code of conduct on the basis of consensus.

Prime Minister Singh's talks with other ASEAN leaders at Bandar Seri Begawan are expected to take forward the various facets of the strategic partnership, particularly in the trade sector. India and the ASEAN members have concluded negotiations on a Free Trade Agreement in Services and Investments which is likely to be inked by this year-end. The negotiations on coming to a common ground on the Regional Comprehensive Economic Partnership or RCEP have begun. Its first round was held in Brisbane in September this year.

The above agreements are likely to increase the India-ASEAN trade. The total India-ASEAN trade increased by 37 percent in 2011-12 to reach US$ 79.3 billion, surpassing the trade target of US$ 70 billion by 2012. The target is to achieve trade worth $100 billon by 2015 and $200 billion by 2022. But to put this success into context, China-ASEAN trade was US $100 billion way back in 2005 and now exceeds $400 billion.

In the past year, New Delhi has tried to fulfil some of the agenda of the vision statement signed in December 2012. The ASEAN-India Centre was inaugurated in New Delhi on 21 June 2013. It will be a resource centre for India-ASEAN strategic partnership. The External Affairs Ministry is also setting up a separate ASEAN-India Trade and Investment Centre. Another area of focus is improving land, sea and air connectivity. New Delhi has started the annual ASEAN Connectivity Coordinating Committee with a meeting in June this year. The India-Myanmar-Thailand trilateral highway is expected to be completed by 2016 and is expected to boost growth in India's northeast region.

India is also supporting the ASEAN Community which is to take shape by 2015 and a Drug-Free ASEAN by 2015. India and the ASEAN have regular people to people exchanges as well through programmes for ASEAN students, farmers, diplomats, media and strategic communities.

The Prime Minister will also attend the 8th East Asia Summit (EAS). The EAS was set up in 2005 when the then president of the Philippines Gloria Arroyo called upon the ASEAN to "embrace China, Japan, South Korea and India" in a larger grouping that may be better able to "hold its own" in when negotiating with the US or the European Union.

The EAS, which later included Australia, New Zealand, the US and Russia as well, is a 'leaders led' forum for dialogue on broad strategic, geopolitical and economic issues of mutual interest and to engender peace, security, stability and economic prosperity in the region. This year US President Barack Obama will have to skip the EAS because of domestic compulsions.

Prime Minister Singh will meet his Australian counterpart the newly elected Tony Abbott on the sidelines of the EAS. It is likely that India and Australia take forward their negotiations to agree to a civilian nuclear cooperation agreement that would enable India to import Australian uranium. Australia has one third of the world's known reserves of uranium.

India will also table a Memorandum of Understanding on the creation of the Nalanda University at this year's EAS. The EAS has been supportive of the initiative. At Brunei India would begin the process of signing of the MoU with those countries which have completed their internal approvals. India is also working with EAS member countries to augment collective capacity for disaster relief and rescue. India will push for greater discussion on the EAS Declaration on Connectivity that it adopted at its sixth summit as New Delhi believes there is scope for greater cooperation among EAS members in this important area.

INDIA'S APPROACH TO ASIA PACIFIC

Several political, security, economic and socio-cultural factors are at play making Asia Pacific a highly dynamic region. India needs to have a long term strategy to make use of the opportunities arising in the Asia-Pacific while keeping in view the security challenges. The Asia-Pacific is marked by the following key trends: rise of China; the rebalancing strategy of the US; a regional architecture underpinned by centrality of ASEAN; the growing importance of the Indian Ocean region and maritime issues; the growing salience of non-traditional security threats.

This policy brief discusses some of the key trends in the Asia Pacific and sets out a long-term approach for India so as to maximise its security and developmental opportunities. The focus is on Indo-ASEAN relations while other countries are discussed in brief.

Rise of China

China's rise has created a flux. An economic giant, with a GDP of USD 7.3 trillion (2011-World Bank) & an annual military expenditure of Yuan 650 billion (approx USD 103 billion) in 2012, China has overtaken Japan in economic and military terms and may overtake the US' economy in the next 10-20 years depending upon the growth rate differential between the two countries.

China's rise is altering the balance of power globally & regionally. The confidence in China's peaceful rise and peaceful development has been seriously dented due to rising tensions in South China Sea and in East China Sea. The new leadership is nationalistic & sharply focused on China's 'core' interests.

China's rapid military modernisation and projection of its power beyond immediate neighbourhood and in the West Pacific, has raised apprehensions among its neighbours. It has developed a powerful navy – with aircraft carriers, submarines, anti-ship missiles – which is rivalling that of Japan and the US. China is following Anti Access Anti-Denial (A2D) strategy to deter the US from entering the island chain in the area of Chinese influence.

The rising tide of nationalism in China has caused anxieties among neighbours. China's formulations on 'core' interests with attendant focus on sovereignty, has created doubts in the minds of the neighbouring countries about China's intentions. China regards the South China Sea as its internal waters. This will have major impact not only in the neighbourhood but also for international shipping.

On the flip side, it must also be recognized that China's rise has also benefited the neighbours, particularly in the economic field. For most countries, China is number one trading partner. China-ASEAN trade is $ 380 billion. The ASEAN economies have got integrated with that of China. People-to-people contacts between China and its neighbours have also deepened with greater connectivity, openness and transparency.

China is getting integrated with the regional architectures. This has increased China's role in regional stability. For instance, China has an FTA with ASEAN. The ASEAN countries are part of a global supply chain which passes through China to global markets. Thus the economic and social interdependence has increased. China is participating in RCEP negotiations. RECP will bring about a higher level of economic integration between the ASEAN, China, Japan, Australia and India.

The future is uncertain. China's economic performance is suspect and riddled with many problems. How long will China maintain its growth and what will be the impact of the slow-down of Chinese economy in the region will be worth studying? China presents a complex picture. The talk of containment of China is problematic given the growing interdependence between China and most major economies of the region.

US rebalancing strategy

The US has been a key player in the security and economic architecture of the region. The biggest challenge before the US is to adjust to the rise of China. Having got entrapped in the highly expensive wars in Afghanistan and Iraq and having been affected by the economic slowdown, the US is in a perilous condition. The US has been compelled to reduce its defence budget due to lack of resources.

Many analysts believe that the US is declining vis-à-vis China although it will remain a military and economic power in the foreseeable future. The US also has the ability to bounce back due to its vast capabilities in innovation. Yet, according to some conjectures China will overtake the US as number one economy in the next two decades. That will be an important psychological moment for the world.

Beset by fundamental changes in the international order, the US has signalled a shift in its policies towards Asia. Doubts have arisen among the US allies in its ability to shore up its key military alliances in the region, for instance, with Japan, South Korea, the Philippines, Australia and Thailand. Faced with a rising China and a declining US, many countries are adopting hedging strategies vis-à-vis China. Essentially most of the countries are seeking greater engagement with China, while being on guard against its assertiveness.

The US has declared a policy of rebalancing and pivoting to Asia. The policy is imprecise and created considerable confusion. Did the US ever leave Asia? If not, why is this talk of return to Asia? What will be the nature of the US defence postures? Will the 60:40 ratio in military deployments between Asia and the rest of the world be sufficient to strengthen the US defence in Asia Pacific?

In recent times the rebalancing strategy has been further elaborated by officials in Obama 2 administration. Economic and cultural dimensions of the strategy have been elaborated. The aim of rebalancing strategy has been defined to be the strengthening of the existing alliances, searching for new partners (India, Indonesia), forging economic partnerships (TPP) and achieving a constructive relationship with China.

But, Beijing has taken rebalancing as an attempt to contain China. It clearly is suspicious of the US partnerships especially the one with India. The Chinese are developing their own A2D strategies to prevent the US from coming too close to the Chinese shores. The Chinese assertiveness in South China Sea, East China Sea and other areas are part of its strategy to keep the US away and to signal Chinese area of influence.

The US is concerned about China but it has to avoid open confrontation. The US statements on China indicate the US' desire to engage with China as deeply as practical. The strategic and economic dialogue between the two countries has been institutionalised. Yet, the relationship between the two countries is far from smooth. Elements of competition and confrontation are manifest in the US-China relations. The rest of the world is also unsure about the direction in which the US-China relationship is proceeding.

How other countries are readjusting?

It is in this shifting background that other countries are adjusting their policies.

The ASEAN Region, traditionally a region divided by numerous internal fault lines, has sought to put its act together particularly since the 1997 Asian financial crisis. ASEAN countries have sought to resolve their disputes through consensus and dialogue. They have engaged with the outside world while emphasising the ASEAN centrality in so far as their region is concerned. With a combined GDP of over $ 2 trillion (2011) and total trade of $ 2.4 trillion (2011), ASEAN has emerged as a formidable economic force. Yet stability in ASEAN is crucially dependent upon internal as well as external factors. China and the US factors have brought ASEAN to a crossroads. ASEAN unity is under strain. Vietnam and the Philippines are directly affected by China's rise. The South China Sea is a hotspot of tension and is likely to remain so. The mistrust between China and ASEAN is increasing because of South China Sea issues.

The ASEAN is trying to forge an economic union by 2015. ASEAN+6 have Regional Comprehensive Economic Partnership (RCEP) even as the US is pushing for a Trans-Pacific Partnership (TPP) which excludes China. Some countries like Myanmar, Laos, Cambodia and Indonesia have doubts about joining the TPP negotiations.

Japan is getting revitalised. Prime Minister Abe is determined to restore Japan's primacy. Japan's New Defence Policy guidelines indicate that Japan is likely to devote increasing attention to recrafting its military strategy and enhancing its defence postures. China's assertiveness and North Korea's nuclear programme are serious security concerns for Japan. In the altered scenarios, Japan is focusing on India as a security partner. Prime Minister Manmohan Singh's visit to Japan got worldwide headlines as it signalled deepening of India-Japan strategic and security partnership. Prime Minister Abe is reported to have proposed "a strategy whereby Australia, India, Japan and the US state of Hawaii form a diamond to safeguard the maritime commons stretching from the Indian Ocean region to the Western Pacific... I am prepared to invest to the greater possible extent, Japan's capabilities in this security diamond." The Indian Prime Minister spoke of India and Japan as "natural and indispensable partners for...a peaceful, stable, cooperative and prosperous future for the Asia Pacific and Indian Ocean regions." Clearly, India-Japan relations are important in the context of peace and stability in Asia Pacific.

Australia

It would be useful to see how Australia is adjusting to the rise of China. Australia sees opportunities for itself in the so-called "Asian Century". It welcomes the rise of China and accepts its military growth as "natural". Australia is pulling out all stops to deepen its relations with China at every level. At the same time, Australia is also hedging against China by building its own defence capabilities and supporting US rebalancing & pivoting to the Asia Pacific. It is seeking partnerships with India, Japan and South Korea. In particular, Australia takes note of India's growing strategic weight in the region and assigns special importance to India in the context of "Indo-Pacific". It regards Indian and pacific oceans as "one strategic arch". India needs to deepen its relations with Australia, particularly in the context of Australia's emergence as a major supplier of coal and possibly uranium in the future. Australia is also helping India in education and skill developments.

South Korea

South Korea faces a volatile security environment, particularly in the context of North Korea's nuclear and missile programme and its unpredictable behaviour. South Koreans pay major emphasis on the protection of the sea lanes of communication in the East Asian region and seek cooperation with India in this regard. They also take note of Chinese hegemonic outlook in the region. While maintaining close ties with India, the Cheonan incident and Yeon Pyieng Island shelling in 2010 have highlighted the increasing military trend in that area. The RoKs realise heavily on international maritime lanes and shipping. In recent track-2 level discussions, South Koreans have underscored desirability of a cooperative mechanism and dialogue between RoK and the Indian navy; institutionalising an official bilateral mechanism for planning and coordination of maritime issues on the lines of an annual maritime dialogue. The South Koreans also want maritime cooperation with India such as joint naval exercises.

OPPORTUNITIES FOR INDIA

The PM's visit to Japan in May 2013 has been commented upon widely. Strong strategic relationship with Japan is in India's favour. India has strategic partnerships with the US, Japan, South Korea and Australia. These countries want to have closer security cooperation particularly in the maritime sector. India-Japan-US trilateral dialogue should focus on Asia-Pacific issues including security cooperation. These partnerships would promote stability in the region. China should realise that India has legitimate interests in the region.

What should be India's long term strategy in Asia-Pacific? With the shift of centre of gravity to the Asia-Pacific region, India must seek a role in the shaping of political, economic, social and security process in the region. Not doing so could adversely affect India's interests. India's strategy should be to seek deeper engagement & economic integration with the Asia-Pacific region. India should be particularly engaged in the security dialogues and processes in the region.

India enjoys high credibility in ASEAN and East Asia. India and ASEAN have raised their partnership to strategic level. The challenge is to deepen it further.

The ASEAN-India Commemorate Summit Vision Statement has identified a number of projects for cooperation in the fields of political and security, economic, socio-cultural and developmental, connectivity in regional architecture. Earlier, the

ASEAN-India Eminent Persons Report (2013) had identified even a larger spread of projects for cooperation. Thus, there is no dearth of ideas. However, what is required is the identification of resources, establishment of institutional framework, monitoring mechanisms, coordination etc. to ensure a timely implementation of these projects.

The next big trend in ASEAN region will be ASEAN economic union & RCEP. This will open up opportunities for India. The success of ASEAN-India cooperation will depend upon how rapidly the two sides move towards economic integration through FTA in services and in future through RCEP. India has yet to weigh the costs & benefits of joining the RCEP. The connectivity between ASEAN and India has been talked about for a long time but the progress has been slow. Similarly, the regional cooperation, particularly within the framework of BIMSTEC and Ganga-Mekong Cooperation, the Trilateral Highway etc. has also been slow. The two sides need to focus on implementation issues.

One of the weaknesses of India's Look East Policy has been the relatively less involvement of India's North East in it. This lacuna must be addressed urgently. The benefits of the Look East Policy, particularly, the increased trade, better connectivity, greater socio-cultural links, cooperation in the area of capacity building, education, youth etc. must be felt by the people of North East, who are otherwise sceptical of the LEP. Therefore, it is essential that the governments in the North East and the social and cultural institutions in the region should be involved in the formulation and implementation of India-ASEAN policies. Of the numerous activities outlined in the Vision Statement, some should be based in the North Eastern states. For instance, an India-ASEAN cultural centre could be set up in Guwahati. Similarly, Imphal could host an India-ASEAN sports academy. A study of local cultures can be undertaken through an NE university. A special programme can be designed for capacity building targeting the youth of the North-East. Trade facilitation centres encouraging trade between the North-East and the South-East Asia could be set up in the North-East. The government could also consider setting up the branches of these institutions in the North-East.

The Vision Statement talks about security cooperation between India and ASEAN. An institutional framework needs to be set up for this purpose. For instance, the India-Japan security statement of 2008 could be adopted for India-ASEAN security dialogue and cooperation. This will help set up a broad-based security dialogue between the Indian and ASEAN institutions. India-ASEAN counter-terrorism dialogue should be stepped up & information sharing should be facilitated. Mutual legal assistance treaties and extradition treaties should be set up. Maritime security dialogue should be initiated

Andaman and Nicobar Islands should be brought into the framework of India-ASEAN relations. Giving due consideration to the concerns of the tribes, it is possible to develop some of the islands, particularly, in Nicobar, for tourism. Nicobari youth are keen to take to modernism. Scholarships for A&N youth could be provided to make them a stakeholder.

In terms of trade linkages the Dawei port offers numerous opportunities. During the Thai Prime Minister India and Thailand agreed to develop Chennai-Dawei corridor project. Dawei is a city in southeastern Myanmar and is capital of Tanintharyi Region. Myanmar government has already approved plans to develop a large port and industrial estate in Dawei with the Italian-Thai Development Public Company Limited (ITD) as a major contractor. The entire project estimated to be at least US$58 billion. In November 2010, ITD signed a 60-year framework agreement with the Myanmar Port Authority to build a port and industrial estate on 250 square kilometres of land in Dawei. This is likely to transform Thailand into a major transit hub within the East-West Economic Corridor. Japan is also keen to invest in the Dawei project. India must invest in Dawei project as also work on the Chennai-Dawei corridor.

People-to-people connectivity needs to be improved. But this will require liberations of the visa regime between India & ASEAN countries. India needs to pay special attention to Myanmar, Thailand, Vietnam, Indonesia and Singapore on bilateral level. These countries can help India in raising Indian regional profile. Additionally, India needs to focus on Indian Ocean issues and those of Ocean governance. India needs to take active role in the shaping of the agenda of IOR-ARC. In recent times the Australians and the Japanese have talked about the concept of Indo-Pacific.

INDIA'S NEW APPROACH IN THE ASIA-PACIFIC AND THE INDIAN OCEAN REGION

Developments in the South China Sea (SCS) have significant implications for India's strategic interests and its role in the Indo-Pacific. Yet New Delhi has traditionally maintained a safe distance from direct commentary on issues like SCS maritime disputes, instead emphasising the need for freedom of navigation.

However, India now appears to be picking up the pace. Under the Modi government, New Delhi has turned the 'Look East Policy' into the 'Act East Policy', made direct comments on the need to resolve the SCS dispute, signed a joint strategic vision with the US for the Asia–Pacific and the Indian Ocean region and is in talks with key regional countries to increase security collaboration, especially in the maritime domain.

The Modi Government recognises the SCS as an important elementof New Delhi's relationship with the East, for both trade and strategic reasons. In order to strengthen its relationship with Southeast Asian nations, India has to portray itself as a credible security actor in the region. In making comments on the SCS disputes, India took a step in directly voicing its concerns rather than tip-toeing around the matter. New Delhi was clear to state the potential of the disputes in destabilising regional security through Joint Statement with the US, with Vietnam and at the East Asia Summit and the India–ASEAN summit 2014.

India's new posture on maritime security in the Asia–Pacific is perhaps a reflection of India's willingness to set aside its rigid non-alignment policy when required. With the rise of China and its push into the Indian Ocean, India now may be realising the need to align with other key players in the region in moulding the evolving security architecture of the Indo-Pacific. Yet as another rising Asian giant India will always walk a thin line with China in as far as its engagement with Asian strategic affairs goes. Modi's pragmatic understanding of the challenges and benefits of India's relationship with China mean that a cautious approach to China will likely continue.

Such caution is evident in New Delhi's approach to increasing its security profile in the Asia–Pacific and Indian Ocean region. Soon after making some noise on the SCS affair, India softened its demeanour. New Delhi refrained from commenting on the dispute when the US flew a surveillance aircraft over China's artificial islands and the international community joined Washington in condemning Chinese actions in the region.

In the background, India has experienced some fresh troubles along its border with China and watched with concern as China has ventured into the Indian Ocean. In fact, Beijing recently warned India about cooperating with Vietnam on oil and gas exploration projects in the SCS, all the while China defends its own economic corridor with Pakistan. One of the crucial developments that could affect the future maritime security architecturein the Indian Ocean region was the docking of Chinese submarines in Pakistan following the docking in Sri Lanka late last year. China has also warned India about its reference to the Indian Ocean as its backyard.

Chinese presence in the Indian Ocean is no longer a possibility, it is a reality. For India the challenge is in managing this development while securing its strategic interests in the region. The Indian Ocean has always been an area of primary interest for New Delhi and an increasing Chinese presence is bound to challenge the existing security order in the Indian Ocean region. India and China have always had troubles along their land boundaries but their strategic interests are now converging into the maritime domain as well. There will be serious ramifications for maritime security in the Indian Ocean if relations between the two rising Asian powers can't be managed.

The message from China is loud and clear. It wants to be a great power and will therefore take to the seas to establish its presence in the Asia–Pacific and beyond. India's been relatively quiet as China has done so and made a strategic miscalculation by not sending its defence minister to the Shangri-La Dialogue 2015—it's crucial to show up and shape the discourse at any opportunity. The dialogue is a critical platform to voice concerns about regional security challenges. The Indian Defence Minister's presence and his interactions with the other key players in the region would have been instrumental in putting across the message that India's willing to take on its responsibilities and is preparing to play its part.

India is now stepping forward by focusing on building and strengthening bilateral ties with the key regional actors like ASEAN. New Delhi has realised the need for multilateral engagement to balance the emerging security architecture and is focusing on building such models in the Indo–Pacific. Modi has reportedly talked about reviving the Quad, Japan will be again participating in Exercise MALABAR after eight years, India and Australia will be starting their first naval exercise in October and New Delhi appears to be interested in forming a stronger naval relationship with Indonesia. India also held the first Foreign Secretary-level trilateral meeting with Japan and Australia in June this year.

Shared responsibility is the best way forward in the Indo–Pacific and India appears keen to play a more active security role in this environment. And there's certainly scope for New Delhi to do more—being too cautious may harm the 'credible security actor' image that New Delhi desires. For now, New Delhi should continue to engage with other key players in the region and contribute more actively to the region's security architecture and fora. But if New Delhi is to be taken seriously in the security space, it needs to more regularly and more publicly take action, both symbolically and substantively.

FROM 'LOOK EAST' TO 'ACT EAST'–INDIA SHIFTS FOCUS

India's "Look East policy" has long shaped the nation's ties with the Asia-Pacific. But PM Modi now pursues a more ambitious agenda based on stronger ties to Japan, Vietnam, Australia and ASEAN, says Danielle Rajendram.

For over two decades India's "Look East" policy has shaped the way the country deals with its neighbors in the Asia-Pacific region, leading to substantially deeper economic, institutional, and security relations. Driven in part by India's strategy of counter-balancing China's influence, the policy was initially aimed at diplomatic and economic engagement with Southeast Asia.

But over the years, the policy has evolved to include broader security and defense ties across the whole Asia-Pacific, with India signalling its willingness to play a greater strategic role in the region. Given the swiftly changing security dynamics in the region, Indian PM Narendra Modi - who swept to power in a landslide victory in the April-May election - rechristened the approach as the "Act East" policy, stating the importance of also seeking deeper ties with partners such as Japan, Vietnam, South Korea and Australia.

Danielle Rajendram, India expert at the Sydney-based Lowy Institute, explains in a DW interview what lies at the core of the "Act East" policy and why she believes the Modi-led government will pursue a greater and more ambitious role in the Asia-Pacific in line with the country's growing economic and strategic interests.

Danielle Rajendram: India's Look East Policy was initiated in the early 1990s with the aim of increasing its economic relations with Southeast Asia. Since then, the focus and objectives of Look East has broadened to include the entire Asia-Pacific, and building economic, institutional and defence links with the region. India's interest in the Asia-Pacific is being driven by both an understanding of the economic benefits of closer engagement with East and Southeast Asia, a convergence of strategic objectives, and a desire for a larger global role for India.

PM Narendra Modi's new approach towards the Asia-Pacific differ

In many respects, Prime Minister Modi's approach to the Asia-Pacific builds upon the policies of previous governments. However, his government has intensified its outreach to India's key partners, such as Japan, Vietnam, Australia and ASEAN. His key goals are to deepen economic ties with the Asia-Pacific in order to boost India's own economic growth, to balance externally against Chinese influence in the Indian Ocean, and to expand India's global role. While the Modi government must work quickly to ensure that 'Act East' goes beyond a rebranding of an existing policy, the upgraded policy signals India's intention to assume a greater role in the region.

India's relationships with major Asian players such as China, Japan and ASEAN

China's President Xi Jinping is set to visit India as the two nations seek to sign deals in railway development, boost trade and resolve a border dispute analyst Liu Zongyi views as the biggest obstacle bilateral ties. (15.09.2014)

India's relations with China have long proceeded upon two distinct economic and security tracks. Although Beijing is New Delhi's top two-way trading partner, tensions along their disputed border and China's increasing presence in the Indian Ocean, continues to make India uneasy. The Modi government will take a pragmatic approach to the relationship, and will attempt to maintain positive economic ties. However, it can be expected that Modi will take a stronger approach to incidents such as incursions across the Line of Actual Control.

India is certainly wary of China's growing presence in the Indian Ocean and its relationships with India's South Asian neighbours. In light of this, India's Look East Policy can be conceived as part of an external balancing strategy against China. At the same time, Beijing is also displaying wariness towards India's growing relationships with key partners in East and Southeast Asia, particularly with Vietnam and Japan. While it is not in India's interests to engage in direct rivalry with China, it can be expected that an element of competition will continue to characterize the China-India bilateral relationship.

These tensions will also serve to reinforce the relevance of investing in India's relationships with partners such as ASEAN and Japan. ASEAN will remain a critical component of India's Look East Policy. Chinese assertiveness on territorial disputes has given India the opportunity to enhance its strategic presence in Southeast Asia, and ASEAN states are increasingly looking to India to play a balancing role in the region. Bilateral partnerships within individual ASEAN states, such as Vietnam and Indonesia, hold particular promise.

New Delhi's relations with Tokyo are likely to undergo the most change under the Modi government, particularly in light of his personal connection with Japanese Prime Minister Shinzo Abe. Japan's tense relationship with China has prompted it to reach out to India as a potential strategic partner. As the most advanced Asian naval power, and as a potential source of considerable investment and technological assistance, Japan offers India significant partnership opportunities as it shifts its focus eastwards.

Although the Australia-India relationship has in the past suffered from inattention, there is currently recognition in both Delhi and Canberra of the economic opportunities of closer ties, and a growing convergence of strategic interests between the two. This year has already brought about an unprecedented level of engagement between Australia and India, and the upgraded 'Act East' policy will continue to have a positive impact on bilateral ties. There is much potential for greater cooperation between the two Indian Ocean democracies on security, particularly in the maritime domain. In recognition of this, the two countries recently concluded a Framework for Security Cooperation in order to consolidate and provide direction for their expanding defence and security ties.

The Modi government will need to proceed carefully with its engagement with the Asia-Pacific, particularly with regards to Chinese sensitivities. But should it be able to do so, successfully enhancing its role in East and Southeast Asia could signal the beginning of the pursuit of a more serious approach for India across the entire Indo-Pacific region.

"INDIA'S LOOK EAST POLICY, ACT EAST AND SOUTH CHINA SEA: POLITICO-STRATEGIC DYNAMICS

Politico-strategic and economic imperatives impelled India to launch its 'Look East Policy' in 1992. From the initial political and economic underpinnings, two decades later, India's 'Look East Policy' has matured into a comprehensive political, economic, and strategic and defence relationships between India and ASEAN and India and East Asia. In the two decades of India's 'Look East Policy' existence, the politico- strategic dynamics stand significantly transformed. The first decade marked India's concerted efforts to integrate itself with ASEAN and East Asia economically and politically. India was adapting to the post-Cold War era and its economy badly needed repair and resuscitation. Politico-strategic dynamics in play in the Asia Pacific in the second decade hastened the process of the strategic discovery of each other between ASEAN and India and between East Asia and India.

In the second decade of India's 'Look East Policy' the politico-strategic dynamics in play need to be briefly stated. In the opening years of this Century, India stood tall as an economic power and a military power. India's nuclear weaponisation had taken place. The United States made a political and strategic reach-out to India and forged the US-India Strategic Partnership.

Contextually, the Asia Pacific by middle of the last decade witnessed the phenomenal rise of Chinese military power and naval build-up. The use of this power for conflict escalation and military brinkmanship by China created strategic distrust in East Asia and ASEAN about the not too benign strategic intentions of China. Both in East Asia and in ASEAN there were growing expectations that India should emerge as the strategic regional balancer and hence the moves for strategic engagement by both sides. On the verge of the third decade of India's 'Look east Policy' , ASEAN accepted India as a full-fledged "Strategic Partner" at the 11th India –ASEAN Summit held in New Delhi in December 2012. The validity of India's 'Look East Policy' and its record of 'Act East' stood validated.

India's 'Look East Policy' initiated in the early 1990s was a well-crafted and visionary foreign policy strategy initiated by then Indian Prime Minister P V Narasimha Rao. To him and him alone goes the credit of reversing India's economic and foreign policy directions which put India on the path of economic liberalisation and divesting India of its erstwhile idealistic foreign policy mind-sets. India's 'Look East Policy' fortunately enjoyed consistent political support of all political dispensations that followed the Late Prime Minister P V Narasimha Rao.

Ordinarily, a presentation on India's 'Look East Policy' and 'Act East' initiatives would have sufficed with enumeration of statistical data and listing the political and economic achievements of the last twenty years. Thee in any case stand well documented in writings by policy analysts. But now that the strategic component in India's 'Look East Policy' is gaining salience, as this policy enters the third decade, it would be appropriate to dwell more on this aspect.

In politico-strategic terms, in the pursuance of its 'Look East Policy', India without much diplomatic flamboyance, has established substantial and comprehensive politico-strategic linkages in East Asia with Japan and South Korea and in South East Asia with the entire group of countries comprising the ASEAN Region. That now provides the bedrock of more substantial strategic openings as ASEAN and East Asia nations seem to be investing in India's reputation as a benign emerging power not only in the Asia Pacific but also the Indo Pacific.

The broad template having been laid of the main theme, a closer examination is merited of India's Look East Policy, India's record in terms of "Act East' and India's policy approaches to the South China Sea disputes. A look is also being given to the global and regional acceptability of this Policy.

India's 'Look East Policy': The Politico-Strategic Dynamics of the 1990s

India's Look East Policy crafted and given impetus by India's Prime Minister Narasimha Rao in the early 1990s merits to be qualified as one of the masterstrokes of Indian diplomacy. The persistent pursuance of this Policy by subsequent political dispensations in power in New Delhi highlights India's long term interest and commitments to South East Asia and East Asia. Politico-strategic dynamics in play in the 1990s, the first decade of India's 'Look East Policy' need to be viewed in two separate time frames, namely the early 1990s and the closing years of that decade.

India's 'Look East Policy' needs to be viewed as a logical reawakening of India to the strategic reality in the post-Cold War era that India had 'Other Neighbours' too, besides South Asia. The ASEAN neighbourhood had gained both political and economic salience in regional and global affairs. While India shared land borders with only Myanmar, India shared maritime boundaries with many ASEAN countries like Myanmar, Singapore, Thailand and Indonesia.

ASEAN Region therefore offered an attractive proposition for an Indian political and economic reach-out. Politically it offered India wider openings to ASEAN countries and East Asia as a whole. Economically, India could benefit with this economically dynamic and vibrant region for its own economic ascendancy with economic liberalisation having already being initiated.

India's initial thrusts in its Look East Policy were primarily political and economic, and one could say that the emphasis was on the latter. The point that needs to be emphasised initially itself is that India had maintained good relationships with South East Asian countries and also in East Asia with Japan even before it initiated its 'Look East Policy'.

India's 'Look East Policy' progress in the initial years may seem slow to many policy analysts but then it needs to be remembered that this was the time of India and ASEAN and East Asia politically discovering each other and sizing-up each other. This was also the period when ASEAN was focussing more on integrating China into various ASEAN mechanisms. India's 'Look East Policy' gained more traction as the decade of the 1990s was coming to a close due to a combination of prevailing politico-strategic dynamics. By 2000 India had emerged as a rising power both economically and militarily. Economically, India had registered strong economic growth rates and India now presented an attractive destination for economic investments. With its nuclear weaponisation in 1998 and its advanced missiles programmes India's military strengths were on display.

At the turn of the Millennium, India's power potential and attributes of power stood recognised by the United States which prompted it to forge the US-India Strategic Partnership. India's 1.2 billion domestic markets in a liberalised economy and India's growing defence purchases programme provided the stimulus to United States recognition of India after shunning it in the Cold War era.

The unstated factor in United States recognition of India's power potential and its courting India were the balance of power considerations in Asia Pacific in relation to China's disturbing military rise. Politico-strategic dynamics had propelled India on an upward strategic trajectory in the Asia Pacific. This had a two way effect on the maturing of India's 'Look East Policy'.

East Asian countries like Japan and South Korea tied in security relationships to the United States found it easier to move closer to India in terms of openness to strategic partnerships and economic cooperation. Similarly, ASEAN Region nations were moved to make strategic openings to India in view of India's rising international profile. ASEAN Region's creeping disappointment with China not delivering on their security expectations of a conflict- free South East Asia despite ASEAN integrating China in ASEAN dialogue mechanisms prompted them to look for alternatives,

India with its benign image of a responsible stakeholder in South East Asian stability and security provided that alternative. India's initiation of its 'Look East Policy was therefore not only in effect a 're-return' of India to a far more active and integrative role in South East Asia and East Asia affairs, but in terms of the Global Shift of Power to Asia provided an alternative to China in the region.

India's 'Act East' Profile in the Political and Economic Domains

Politically and economically, India's 'Act East' record in relation to South East Asia seems to have followed a two-strand inter-twined strategy. The two noticeable strands were one getting integrated at the regional level maintaining the centrality of ASEAN as the long-standing regional organisation of South East Asian countries. India's approaches in East Asia to Japan and South Korea followed a similar pattern. The second level was focussed on the forging of close political and economic linkages with each of the South East Asian countries in the bilateral format but within the overall framework of ASEAN centrality.

India's political and economic overall record in pursuance of its 'Act East' record is exhaustive and therefore this presentation would focus on the more salient achievements to highlight India's

'Act East 'record. Politically, India pursuing its 'Act East' strategy reached a creditable high point when the India-ASEAN Summit was held in New Delhi in December 2012 attended by Heads of ten ASEAN countries. It marked the coming of age of India's 'Act East' drive.

The ASEAN-India Commemorative Summit was held in New Delhi in December 2012 to mark the 20th Anniversary of India-ASEAN relations and the 10th Anniversary of India becoming a Dialogue Partner of ASEAN. The most notable achievement of this Summit was the issue of a Vision Statement which significantly declared that "We declare that the ASEAN –India Partnership stands elevated to a strategic partnership." The Vision Statement lays down in great detail the blueprint of ASEAN and India to surge ahead in in all fields in a comprehensive manner.

Complementing this 'Act East' political achievement of India is also its record of establishing substantial political relationships with individual ASEAN countries on a bilateral basis. India has forged strong political linkages with Vietnam, Indonesia, Thailand, Malaysia, Singapore and Myanmar. High level exchanges of political dignitaries take place regularly. Dialogue mechanisms exist for regular exchange of strategic views and advancing economic relations to higher levels.

Bibliography

Ahmad, Imtiaz: *State and Foreign Policy: India's Role in South Asia,* New Delhi, Vikas, 1993.

Amitabh Sikdar: *India and China : Strategic Energy Management and Security,* Manas, Delhi, 2009.

Babbage, Ross and Sam Bateman: *Maritime Change: Issues for Asia.* St. Leonards: Allen & Unwin, 1993.

Basu, Prahlad K.: *Governance and Public Administration for Poverty Reduction,* Salvador, Brazil, 1997.

Bateman, Sam & Stephen Bates : *Calming the Waters. Initiatives for Asia Pacific Maritime Cooperation.* Canberra Papers on Strategy and Defence, 1996.

Blake, Gerald H.: *The Peaceful Management of Transboundary Resources.* London: Graham & Trotman, 1995.

Churchill, R.R. and A.V. Lowe: *The Law of the Sea.* Manchester: Manchester University Press, 1983.

Damrosch, L.F.: *Law and Force in the New International Order,* Boulder, Westview Press, 1991.

Dan Nabudere: *The Political Economy of Imperialism,* London, 1977.

Dhagamwar, Vasudha : *Law, Power and Justice : Protection of Personal Rights under Islam,* Popular Prakashan, Bombay, 2001.

Downs, Anthony: *An Economic Theory of Democracy,* New York, Harper and Row, 1957.

Evelyn Goh, *Meeting the China Challenge: The U.S. in Southeast Asian Regional Security Strategies,* DC: East-West Center, 2005.

Friedman, G.: *The Future of War of Cyber Crimes,* N.Y., Random House, 1996.

Galdorise, George V. and Kevin R. Vienna: *Beyond the Law of the Sea.* New York: Praeger, 1997.

Garver, John W.: *Face Off: China, the United States, and Taiwan's Democratization.* Seattle: University of Washington Press, 1997.

Greenfield, Jeanette: *China's Practice in the Law of the Sea.* Oxford: Clarendon Press, 1992.

Harrison, Selig: *China, Oil and Asia: Conflict Ahead.* New York: Columbia University Press, 1992.

Hasan-Askari Rizvi, *Nuclear Terrorism and South Asia,* Albuquerque, NM: Sandia National Laboratories, February 2003.

Jagannath P. Panda: *China's Path to Power : Party, Military and the Politics of State Transition,* Pentagon, Delhi, 2010.

Kelly, John B.: *Britain and the Persian Gulf 1795-1880,* Oxford, Clarendon Press, 1968.

Kittichaisaree, Kriangsak: *The Law of the Sea and Maritime Boundary Delimitation in Southeast Asia.* New York: Oxford University Press, 1987.

Loomes, G.: *Current Issues in Microeconomics,* New York: St. Martin's Press, 1989.

Mahajan, C P : *Commerce and Business Management in Modern World,* ABD Pub, Delhi, 2008.

Maheshwari, Shriram: *Rural Development in India: A Public Policy Approach,* New Delhi, Sage, 1995.

Moseley, Philip E.: *Russian Diplomacy and the Opening of the Eastern Question,* Cambridge, Harvard University Press, 1934.

Peter Lambron Wilson : *Traditional Modes of Contemplation and Action,* University Press, Tehran, 1977.

Roth, A. E.: *The Handbook of Experimental Economics,* Princeton, Princeton University Press, 1995.

Schroeer, Dietrich, *Science, Technology, and the Nuclear Arms Race,* Ontario: John Wiley & Sons, 1984.

Sinha, R.K.: *Economic Development since Independence,* New Delhi, Deep and Deep, 1988.

Thomas J.: *Dynamic Macroeconomic Theory,* Harvard University Press, 1987.

Valencia, Mark J.: *Malaysia and the Law of the Sea.* Kuala Lumpur: Institute of Strategic and International Studies Malaysia (ISIS), 1991.

Walker, Benjamin : *Foundation of Islam : the Making of World Faith,* Rupa & Co., New Delhi, 2001.

Index

❑❑❑